Rudow's Guide To
Fishing The Mid Atlantic

By Lenny Rudow

GEARED UP PUBLICATIONS, LLC
EDGEWATER, MD
WWW.GEAREDUPPUBLICATIONS.COM

To Mollie, Max, and David—there's no one on Earth I'd rather fish with.

Contents

INTRODUCTION

Are you ready to catch more fish? If you like to go fishing inshore or offshore in the Mid Atlantic region, then this book is for you. In it we'll look at inlets and coastal bays, inshore and offshore hotspots, and the canyons. Each area is detailed with custom-marked charts, showing you over 300 hotspots—some well known, and some secret favorites. We'll also take an in-depth look at each of the Mid Atlantic sportfish targeted by recreational anglers, and describe where, how and when you'll catch them. Whether you're a bay angler drifting for fluke or a canyon commando on the hunt for yellowfin tuna, you'll find the how-to/where-to for your favorite fish meticulously covered. Standard rigging is included in the third section of this book, so you'll know how to cover all the bases even when trying a new type of fishing.

No longer will you have to try dragging fishing information out of the captains you compete against, and no other book on the market today will give away the golden nuggets of information that you'll find on these pages. I fished with or interviewed more than 20 charterboat captains and fishing guides before writing this book, amassed the past decade's worth of fishing reports from up and down the coast, and reviewed my own offshore and inshore catch logs. No stone was left unturned so that this book would prove to be the most useful fishing tool available to Mid Atlantic anglers, period.

It's not always easy to get professional captains to give away their secrets, but through the years all of those listed here were willing to share, to some degree, their tactics or hotspots with me. So we all owe a special thanks to: Capts. Ted Ohler, *Volcania*; Rob Skillman, *Endeavor*; Bill Verbanas, *Reelistic* (in memorial); John Raguso, *Mar Cee Jay*; Jose Millan, Bertram Yachts; Cliff Parker, *The Big Easy*; John Bayliss, Bayliss Boatworks; Terry Stansel, *Hatterascal*; David Fields, *Hatterascal*; John Unkart, *Strike III*; Burch Perry, Albemarle Boats; the Roberts brothers, *Welder's Arc*; Rom Whitaker, *Release*; Andy Eget and the Integrity Marine Fishing Team; professional mate Jon Meade; and inveterate anglers Kevin Falvey, Pete McDonald, Dan Long, David Glenn, Walt Jennings, Matt Boomer, Jack Saum, and Rocky Calia. Additional thanks go out to John Beall of Victor Graphics.

PART I
Mid Atlantic Regional Guide

How To Use the Regional Guide

Each particular hotspot shown on a chart corresponds to an explanation of that hotspot in the text. Hotspot designations are made with the state's initials, followed by the area's initials ("O" for ocean, "I" for inlet, or "B" for bay, or in the case of Delmarva simply DMV) then the hotspot number. The tenth New York ocean hotspot, for example, will appear as NYO10, both on the charts and in the text. You'll notice that in certain areas, the hotspots don't always seem to be organized in an orderly fashion. Great care has been taken to organize them as best as possible, but due to the uneven coastline, contours, and winding channels, it's simply impossible to arrange them in a perfectly logical manner. Also note that in many areas spots identified as off the coast of one particular state may also be regular fishing grounds for anglers from a different state. Many New Jersey and New York ocean hotspots, for example, overlap. In these cases, the spots are identified with the state they first appear charted on.

In order to cover the entire Mid Atlantic region in this book the charts had to be shrunken quite a bit. At times it may be tough to see a particular contour, wreck, or other item mentioned as a hotspot. For this reason, the best way to use this regional guide is to have a full-sized chart open and at-hand at the same time. This will allow you to go back and forth between the book's charts and larger, easier to see charts. For computer-savvy anglers, I strongly suggest getting Maptech's Chart Navigator Pro (800/839-5551, www.maptech.com). It covers the entire coastline, including 3-D Bathymetric views.

A word about the GPS coordinates included for hotspots in this book: Different GPS units use different chart cards, and none of them are exactly alike. At times, the exact spot located by one unit will differ slightly from another. It may look on your chartplotter like you're directly on the spot, when you're not. Or, it may look like you're off the mark, when you're actually on it. On top of that, although GPS is extremely accurate it does not have repeatability as consistent as LORAN. Bottom line: Plugging the numbers into my machine may take me to an ever so slightly different place than plugging the numbers into your machine will. Yet in the ocean, being a few feet off can be a world away when you don't know where a specific wreck or feature is. This can be incredibly frustrating and disappointing, and for these reasons I almost didn't include GPS coordinates in this book. You can have confidence that plugging in the numbers given in this book will put you in the right area, but don't plan on hitting the nail on the head on your first attempt each and every time you venture off to a new hotspot. Instead, realize that when you arrive at the coordinates, as often as not you'll have to start a search pattern to locate a specific wreck, reef, or drop. The quickest way to go from being in the right neigh-borhood to being dead-on at a spot is to activate the "track" feature on your unit, so you can see exactly where you've been and where you're going. Start off at the coordinates then circle around in an ever-widening spiral. Within a few minutes, you should see the feature you're looking for pop up on the fishfinder screen.

CHAPTER 1
New York and New Jersey

The northernmost areas of the Mid Atlantic region hold world-class fishing for several species. The most popular is the striped bass, which shows up in New York and New Jersey waters in the spring and remains through the fall. Here, you'll encounter some of the largest specimens in the ocean. While 30- or 40-pound stripers count as true trophies in other parts of the Atlantic, in this area at certain times of year they're commonplace. Flounder also thrive in northern waters, and New York and New Jersey offer some of the finest flattie fishing in the entire region. Ground fish such as cod and haddock, which won't be found on a regular basis to the south, are a staple here. And although the season is shorter than it is in areas to the south, offshore pelagics can be hunted with great success from ports such as Montauk and Cape May. Ready to venture into the Mid Atlantic's northern reaches? Let's go.

New York Ocean Hotspots

Hotspot NYO1 (a large area that extends from Montauk Point out to the green #1 marker at 41'06.045 x 71'46.244) is a famed area commonly called "the Rips," or "Montauk Rips." One trip here, and you'll know how it got its name—colliding currents and uneven bottom conspire to create standing waves and visible rips on the water's surface. The chaotic conditions confuse baitfish and make them easy prey, and much of the season big stripers prowl the Rips looking for an easy meal. Action will start in late April or early May depending on the weather conditions but the peak activity hits the area in the fall. Best fishing is with live baits—porgy, bunker, and the like—live-lined or drifted along the bottom. Trolling (bunker spoons and umbrella rigs with hose eels are standard fare) is also effective and at times sight-casting to breaking fish is in the game plan. Much of the time, however, the fish you see at the surface will be blues. Many anglers after stripers, and stripers only, will ignore surface-feeding fish until late in the season, usually November or even December, when the blues are gone but stripers are still in eating mode.

Flounder can also be found in the Rips, usually from May on. The biggest ones tend to arrive first; they're following migrating squid and they like big baits, so fishing whole squid is an expensive but effective method of taking doormats up to the 10-pound class. Smallish sea bass will also be caught on hard and live bottom areas in the Rips, starting later in the spring. They'll grow larger as the season progresses, but better bass fishing usually takes place elsewhere.

Cox's Ledge, NYO2 (41'02.927 x 71'12.053) is a little out of the range of our geographical boarders, but it's a must-know spot for bottom fishermen who like hooking up with cod. Hit Cox's Ledge in the summer, and use clams or diamond jigs

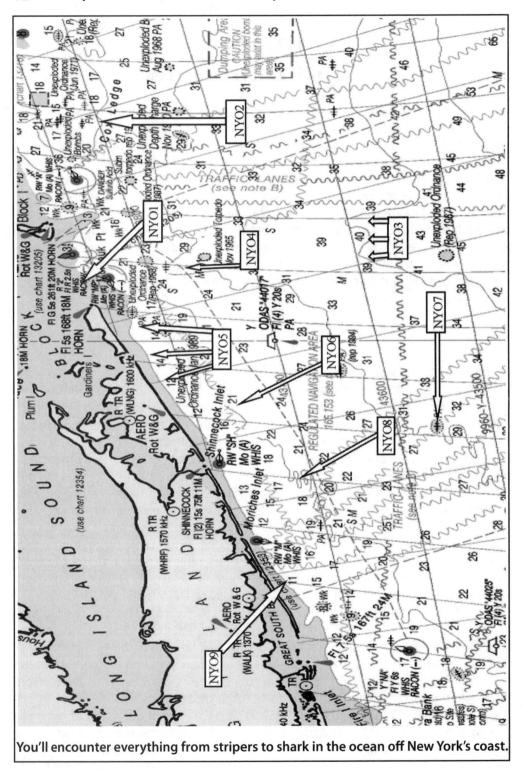

You'll encounter everything from stripers to shark in the ocean off New York's coast.

to get the fish on a hook. Note that dogfish often thrive here as well, and at times you'll have to weed through them to catch the cod. When this happens you're best off concentrating your efforts on jigging, since the dogfish don't usually chase metal. By October, the action usually slows here.

Anglers on the hunt for mahi-mahi will be more interested in NYO3. There are trap floats in this area, which, during seasons when mahi move inshore from the deeper waters in good numbers, they often gather under during the warm summer months. Troll around them with small skirted baits or pull up to the floats and try bailing for these fish. Even though it's significantly inshore of NYO3, NYO4 (40'53.379 x 71'42.279) is often a better place to hunt pelagics. Known as the Butterfish Hole, this spot is close to port and will be crowded at times. The west bank is a traditional tuna chunking spot, and sharking can be good throughout the area. The action here usually starts in mid to late June, with bluefish and shark arriving first, followed by the tuna. As with many traditional, close-to-home hotspots, in decades past the fishing here was much better than it has been lately. But remember that during any given season, the fish could show up here in relatively strong numbers.

Anglers who want to stay closer to land and search for stripers should check out the stretch of beach along NYO5. This is a good place to intercept big striped bass as they migrate south from the Rips and other points to the north in November and December. Many anglers will troll for these fish, but for a light tackle challenge try fan-casting bucktails through areas where you see gannets.

The area around NYO6, just outside of Shinnecock Inlet, is of note because some seasons you'll have success chumming for shark here in June. It's certainly not your best bet, but it's the closest spot to port you can hope to find them. So tuck away this spot for a windy day when runs farther offshore are impossible. When conditions allow, however, make the run to NYO7 (40'22.249 x 71'12.053). Anchor up or drift over the wreck while chumming, and you've got an excellent shot at mako and blue shark from June through October. Same goes for the 20 Fathom Fingers, found at NYO8 (40'38.980 x 72'32.155), but note that since the structure here is a bit more spread out, you'll usually want to stick with drifting.

NYO9 does not mark a specific spot, but a starting point. From here up to Montauk you'll find fluke along the drop off the beach, during the summer months. Drift these edges with small live snapper blues, spearing, or big killi fish, or bounce bucktails tipped with live minnow along the bottom. During the month of September pay special attention to the stretch from Montauk south, about half way to Shinnecock. In this area you can intercept the biggest of the flatfish as they start to migrate south from the point and the Rips.

Fishermen who have boats and gear that are capable of handling blue water will often want to make the longer runs and reap the greater rewards of fishing offshore. NYO10, known as the Chicken Canyon, is one of the closer spots you might locate yellowfin tunas and mahi-mahi during the summer months. Bluefin are also a possibility here, and if a warm water eddy spins in from the Gulf Stream, all bets are off. Plan on trolling around in this general area during the summer months, with your usual offshore spread. Push out a little farther to NYO11, which New York and New Jersey anglers call the "Texas Tower" (39'47.663 x 72'40.082), late in the summer and early in the fall. There's lots of structure in this area, as there used to be an offshore radar platform which fell apart during a severe storm. Chunk here for bluefin tuna, and you have a good shot at sticking the hook into a large fish.

Keep on cruising and soon you'll be at The Bombs, NYO12 (39'36.851 x 72'25.241.) This is a great place to try trolling for yellowfin and big eye tuna, and you also have a shot at longfin here. Mahi-mahi, wahoo, and billfish could make an appearance in this spot as well. Chunking at night here late in the season is considered a good bet by knowledgeable area anglers.

From The Bombs it's a short run to the edge of Hudson Canyon. The spot marked by NYO13 is known as the East Elbow (39'33.392 x 72'23.125) and NYO14 is the West Elbow (39'32.609 x 72'25.991). These are prime spots to try trolling for the usual blue water suspects including billfish during the day, or chunking for tuna at night. This is also an area where swordfish may appear while night fishing. A little farther offshore NYO15, the Tongue (39'28.952 x 72'15.592) is the beginning of extremely deep water and all of the pelagics including blue and white marlin can be trolled up here. Note that some extremely big fish will come from this area—in the 80's a 364-pound big eye tuna, a 1,046-pound blue marlin, and a 137-pound white marlin were all caught in the Hudson.

If you want to make a serious effort to catch big eye tuna, push out to the area around NYO16 where the 600-fathom curve takes a 90-degree bend. Drift and chunk along the edges here at night or troll at dusk and/or dawn, during August and into September. And if you spot a pod of whales in the area, remember that they often indicate there are big eye below.

There's a similar edge with a slightly less extreme drop located at NYO17 (39'43.237 x 71'39.035.) This spot will prove just as productive at times, especially when a good temperature break is located in area. NYO18 (39'43.237 x 71'39.035) is much shallower but again forms a nice drop-off which pelagics will gather around some seasons. It's also shallow enough here that you may find bluefin mixed in with schools of yellowfin tuna. Remember—in most of the deep water offshore spots bluefin will not be present.

Atlantis Canyon (NYO19) will produce similar results as Hudson. If you're targeting albacore tuna in either of these canyons, remember: green, green, green is the way to go. One interesting note: many seasons Atlantis seems to be the best bet for finding big blue marlin during the summer and early fall months. It could be that this canyon gets less fishing pressure than the Hudson, it could be because of geography, or it could be a function of current patterns we've seen in the past few years. In any case, pull large surface teasers (bowling pin styles are good) and bait up large blue/white llanders with horse ballyhoo to target the big blue guys.

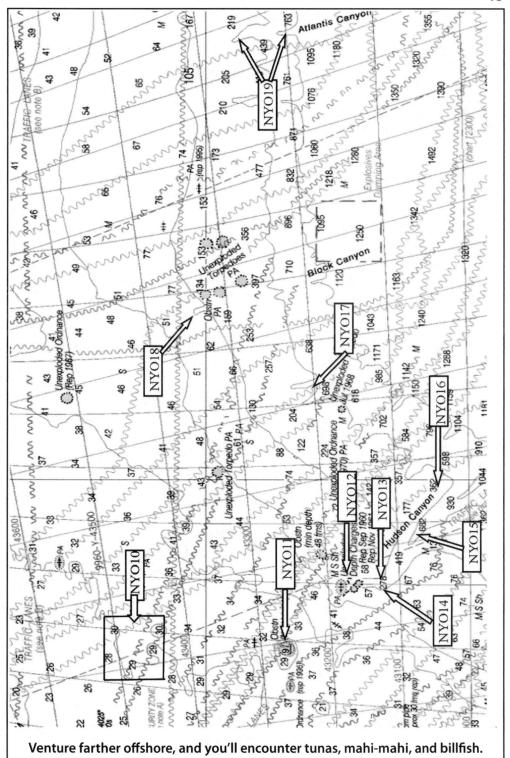

Venture farther offshore, and you'll encounter tunas, mahi-mahi, and billfish.

New York Inlet & Coastal Bay Hotspots

The flats just inside Shinnecock Inlet, marked by NYI1 on the inlet enlargement chart, provide light-tackle and even fly fishing enthusiasts with a shot at stripers in skinny water. From May through December you can find them here, feeding in the shallows during incoming and high tides. Toss plugs to see exciting topwater explosions, or bounce 4" twister tail jigs, bucktails, or Bass Assassin style soft plastics along the bottom. On falling and low tides fish the deeper waters of the channel at NYI2. You'll also find flatfish in the channel here, from June through September. Most anglers will drift minnow/squid combinations to catch the fluke, but bouncing jigs and bucktails tipped with live bull minnow also does the trick and allows the use of lighter gear with less weight.

The edge just outside the inlet at NYI3 is a great drop-off to drift for fluke during the summer months. Remember to try for the flatfish when the sun is high and the water is clear; the last hour of incoming tides usually provides the best conditions just outside the inlet. The deeper water in the inlet channel, at NYI4, is a good spot to target large stripers, especially relatively early in the summer (usually June). Live-bait them here with bunker, and fish the last hour of each tide into the first half-hour of the next tide.

Inside the bay, bluefish will often be found at or near NYB1. From the early summer through late fall, as long as blues are in town, they'll pop up and churn the surface in this zone. Don't expect to find the huge choppers here, but remember that smaller blues are better eating, anyway. Shift down to the edge of the bar at NYB2, and you have another drop-off that will produce both flounder and stripers.

When you want to target stripers in the heat of the summer, night fishing is often the most effective way to do so. Anchor up around the bridge pilings at NYB3, and fish clam baits while chumming clam bits.

The spot at NYB4 is notable because the muddy bottom here is good for locating winter flounder. Early in the spring and late in the fall try anchoring in the muck and chum clam and worm bits. Bloodworm usually makes the best bait, and remember to scale down hook-size to match the winter flounder's small mouth. The edges of the point at NYB5 are more good areas to shoot for summer flounder, while drifting live or cut bait.

Some years you can experience a nice change of pace in the spring, by drifting jigs tipped with squid strips in the channel at NYB6. Weakfish will sometimes migrate in, starting in late May or early June.

Moriches Inlet is another area you can target stripers, fluke and blues. In fact, bluefish will often become so prolific they are a nuisance during the summer months to those targeting other species. You'll find them in the deep water at NYI5, but you'll also find stripers here holding along the edges of the drop. Cast jigs or bucktails along the edges, or live-line bunker or herring down deep at the

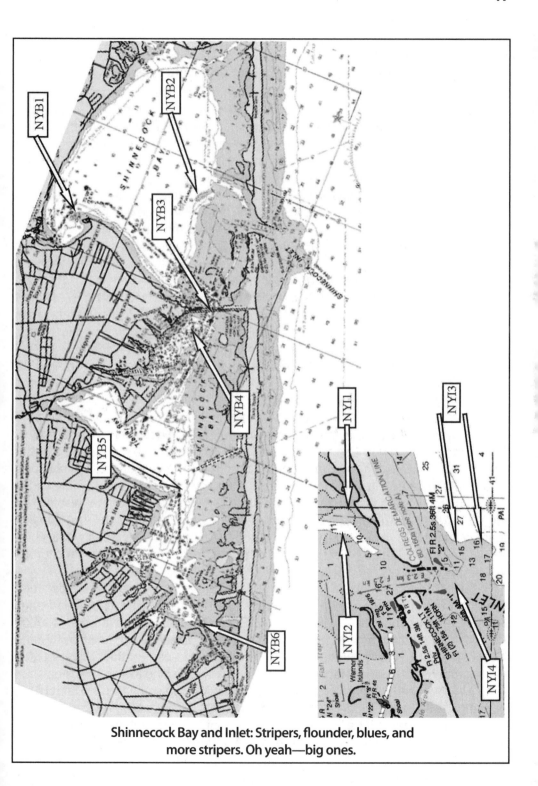

Shinnecock Bay and Inlet: Stripers, flounder, blues, and
more stripers. Oh yeah—big ones.

very end of an outgoing tide. NYI6 is another area you may encounter weakfish, if they move this far north in the spring. In the spring and fall, fluke will also gather in the deep water here during a dead-low tide, and in the shallower water to either side of the channel on an incoming tide. When flatfish are the target and an out-going current of turbid bay water creates a plume of dirty water here, shift over to the edge at NYI7. If you arrive to find a flood tide, try up inside the inlet at NYI8. Position your boat at the edge of the channel, and bounce 4" chartreuse or white paddle tails from the shallows to the drop; you'll be surprised at how many of the flatties you hook come from the shallowest water here.

Anglers fishing in this area should also be aware of a couple of artificial reef sites just outside of the inlets. Moriches Reef is 2.4 miles south of the inlet, in 70' to 75' of water, and consists of several boats, barges, and concrete pipes. It's located at 40'43.500 x 72'46.500. Shinnecock Reef is two miles south of the inlet in slightly deeper water, and consists of multiple tire units, boats and barges, and rubble. You'll find this one at 40'48.130 x 72'28.500.

When you're after large stripers in Moriches Bay, head for NYB7. It's not shown on the charts but there's a deep hole here—and big fish will sometimes stack up in it. Your best bet is to snag a bunker or herring, lip-hook it on a live-lining rig weighted down with an egg sinker on your main line, and let it soak.

Once summer hits, the channels marked by NYB8 are all a good bet for fluke. Drift minnow, squid, or a combination of the two on Fluke Killer rigs, or bounce bucktails tipped with minnow or spearing.

NYB9 in Great South Bay is another channel that offers up flatfish during the summer months. As usual in this type of area, drift up and down the channel edges. When the tide's high you'll be better served by NYB10, where a shoal comes all the way up to 2' or 3'. As long as the water's clear, fluke will move up into the shallows here to feed, presenting you with another opportunity to cast jigs.

In the late spring and again in the early fall, you may encounter weakfish in this zone. This is by no means a sure thing—it will vary each season—but if you've heard weakfish are in the bay try drifting bloodworms or squid strips on white, char-treuse, and yellow Fluke Killer rigs. When the wind kicks up and the water's turbid, give purple and dark blue a shot.

You'll find more fluke in the channels and cuts running around and between Fire and Sexton Islands, at the points marked by NYB13. This spot also brings stripers back into the picture, in a big way. From May through November you'll of-ten find them feeding in channels in good numbers. These won't, however, be the 40-pound and 50-pound fish targeted in the inlets and rips. For the most part plan on encountering schoolies here. Casting, trolling, and fishing live or chunk bait can all be effective, and even though the sizes will usually be smaller the numbers will be higher. If you want to target the stripers at night, head for the bridge pilings at NYB14. This is a tall bridge but it throws off a great lightline, and it's a favored area of the locals. Fish it with the usual methods, but don't try chumming menhaden at

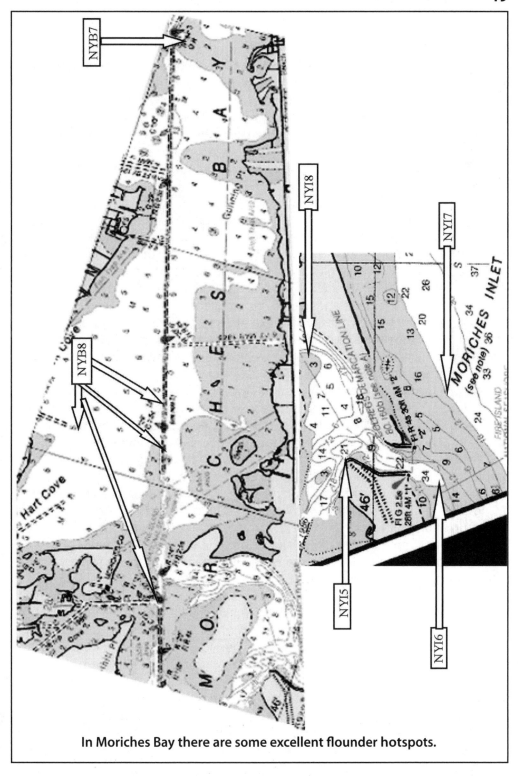

In Moriches Bay there are some excellent flounder hotspots.

night or there's a good chance you'll get swarmed by snapper blues once summer has set in. Slide over to the channel junctions and fish the deeper water, and during the summer months you also have a decent shot at finding sea trout here. Again, night fishing will be the most productive method. Live-line peanut bunker at the light line, or fish chunks of squid on drop-off edges.

NYB15 is an artificial reef site in relatively deep bay water (20' or so in most areas) made up of tires, concrete blocks, rubble, and barges. When you want to go wreck fishing and the wind's blowing too hard to go outside the inlet, this could be your next best bet for sea bass and the like.

NYI11 in Fire Island Inlet and NYB17 inside of Jones Inlet mark two more bridges you'll want to check out. Stripers can be found near each from May through November, and blues will be all too common in these areas. Note that the currents at both of these bridges will be ripping and relatively inexperienced boaters may (and should) be nervous about fishing in this area after the sun has gone down. That said, stripers will be found hugging the lightlines. The area encompassed by NYI10, farther out in Fire Island Inlet, is all excellent territory for eeling during the summer and into the fall. Trolling for stripers is also good from the mouth of the inlet down to the edge marked by NYI12, at Jones Inlet. Wire-lining is the traditional method in this area, with bunker spoons, umbrella rigs, and surgical hose.

Work the area marked by NYI9, just west of the Fire Island inlet, particularly hard in the fall. Note the jetty marked by NYI13; as of the time of this writing it was possible to approach and cast to the jetty but shoaling in this area is constant and unpredictable. You'll find big stripers feeding here, but I wouldn't recommend fishing in close unless someone who has current local knowledge is onboard and the weather conditions are good. Inside of Jones, at NYB16, you'll find a stretch of the shore lined with piers and pilings. During the summer months cast plugs, swimbaits, and jigs up to these piers and you'll discover schoolie-sized stripers hiding around and under them. Note that for whatever reason, stripers seem to like one pier or another out of every dozen, and which specific ones they orient to will change over time. Accordingly, take no more than a couple of casts at each. If there are no hits don't hesitate to move on, but when you do get a strike work the pier over thoroughly before leaving.

NYB18 is another zone that's productive for both stripers and fluke. Drift squid, spearing or minnow on Fluke Killers along the channel edges for the flatfish. To catch good numbers of school-sized stripers cast plugs and jigs up against the marsh banks, particularly on a high tide. As the tide comes in look for points with small standing rips, indicating a spot where the current slaps into the marsh or an underwater point. When the tide starts dropping focus your effort on small creek mouths that drain the marshes—as the water rushes out predators will wait in these areas to pick off small fish and crabs flushed out by the tide.

As you head into Hempstead Bay, the territory becomes more and more marshes and cuts, with less and less open water. Stripers and fluke are still the

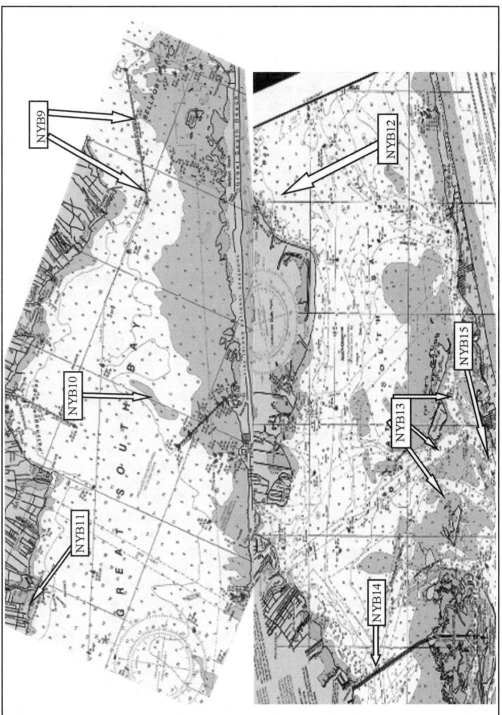

The areas around Great South Bay are more populated and competition rises, but the fishing is still red-hot.

two main sport fish in this zone, although you'll do more and more cast and retrieve fishing along marsh banks, cuts, and pier pilings, and less and less bait fishing and trolling. Flounder fishing becomes more a game of finding the right depth the fish want to feed at during any given time frame, and sticking to that depth as you drift along the channel edges. Many of the drop-offs are sheer, and at times, the biggest challenge to catching fish will controlling the boat's position while on the drift. During flood tides when the fish move shallower, casting jigs and bucktails dressed with minnow becomes more effective than dragging baited rigs. Regardless of conditions, you'll find fishing for fluke good here from June through September, most seasons.

East Channel, at NYB19, is smaller and shallower than many in this area but the channel is squeezed right between the marsh grasses, so there's usually a good current in it. During a low or outgoing tide, try drifting live killiefish through here—you'll like the results. Garrett Lead, marked by NYB20, is significantly larger. The edges shoal up and provide the opportunity to cast surface plugs and jigs for school-sized stripers, from late spring until winter. Hog Island Channel (NYB21) and Shell Creek (NYB22) are both great areas to cast light tackle for stripers during the same time frame. Although the flounder fishing won't be quite as active in these channels, they're deep and lined with piers. That gives you the opportunity to target both species at the same time. Drop a Fluke Killer (for flounder) to the bottom, and sit the rod in a holder. Then cast 4" to 6" twister tails, plugs such as Rat-L-Traps and Mir-O-Lures, and stinky plastics like Berkley Gulp swim baits, up to the pilings (for stripers) as you drift. Broad Channel (NYB23) doesn't have all the pilings, but it does have fish. This cut is large and deep, but shoals along the edges in many areas. Drift through it on the low tides for fluke, and on the flood tide cast to the marsh banks for stripers. Treat the cut at NYB24 similarly, especially on a strong moving tide.

Many folks will wonder why, at this point, there isn't a chart detailing some of the excellent fishing grounds in Jamaica Bay. Much as I'd like to get into this one—wonderful territory for light-tackle casting to stripers along the marsh banks and cuts—it will not be covered in this book. It lies in close proximity to JFK airport, and since the disaster of 911, boating in this area has been severely restricted. I believe there are some areas you can still get into, but between the Department of Homeland Security, the USCG, and state authorities, it's anyone's guess as to how and when the exact areas you're allowed to be in will change at any given time. If you wish to fish here your best bet is to hire a local guide, who has current knowledge of the regulations on any given day.

The waters of New York Harbor's entrance and Lower Bay are surprisingly productive, considering how close they are to the biggest mega-city in this region. Stripers, bluefish, and fluke are present in good numbers in this area, and weakfish start becoming a more common target as well. The drop-offs marked by NYB25 are both excellent flounder spots from late spring through the fall. Try the usual tactics,

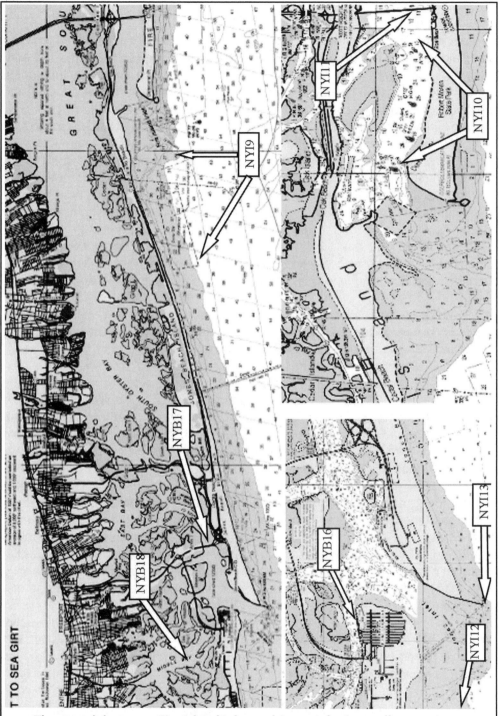

The stretch between Fire Island Inlet and Jones Inlet is excellent territory for wire-lining big bass.

but note that flounder sometimes go deep in these holes during the ebb tide and getting to them with jigs will be nearly impossible; heavier rigs baited with squid, minnow or spearing are usually required. During the flood tide, slide over to the humps marked by NYB26. The shallower water at both of these knolls will produce flatfish, and if you jig for them, you'll also catch stripers along the edges of the drops.

Both NYB27 and NYB31 mark major channels—Chapel Hill North and Ambrose. From June through October during years when weakfish migrate this far up the coast in good numbers, huge schools of fish will often stage in the deep water of these channels. Their exact location will change from time to time, but their general locations are usually marked by the party boats drifting over them. In any case, they're fairly easy to spot on your fishfinder. Just look for caterpillar-like masses holding very close to the bottom. Many people will drift with those very same Fluke Killer rigs used for flatfish and these are effective on trout, when baited with squid, silversides, or peeler crab chunks. In these deep-water situations, however, the most effective way to take trout is often by jigging heavy spoons. Three- or four-ounce Braid, Hopkins, or Yo-Zuri spoons in blue/silver, green/silver, plain silver, and pink/silver patterns are all good bets.

In the entire area outlined at NYB28, bluefish abound. Often, from June through October or even early November, you'll see birds working in this zone. Snapper blues in the 1 to 5 pound range will be under them, and under the blues, you'll find school sized stripers and sometimes trout as well. To catch the blues fish topwater lures or crank any lure across the surface at high speed. To catch the stripers drop jigging spoons or tandem rigs 20' to 30' down, directly underneath the blues. (Spoons are a good bet, as they won't be shredded by the inevitable accidental bluefish.) To target the trout drop all the way to the bottom, and jig your offering as deep as possible.

NYB29 marks the edge of Coney Island, which is lined with small jetties. There's good water approaching most of them up to the tip of the arrow, but north of that point there are some submerged rocks and accessing them gets sketchy. In any case, approaching any of these jetties should be considered with caution and should only be attempted when the seas are calm. That said, if you putt within casting range of the tips of them and throw bucktails, 6" twister tail jigs, or heavy plugs, you'll find stripers (often large ones) feeding on disoriented baitfish and dislodged shellfish.

The channel at NYB30 is a good area to try trolling for stripers. The heavy current and deep water makes wire line more or less necessary (braid will do the trick, too, paired up with plenty of lead) and bunker spoons or umbrella rigs are your best bets. After dark, try drifting the edges of the channel with live eels.

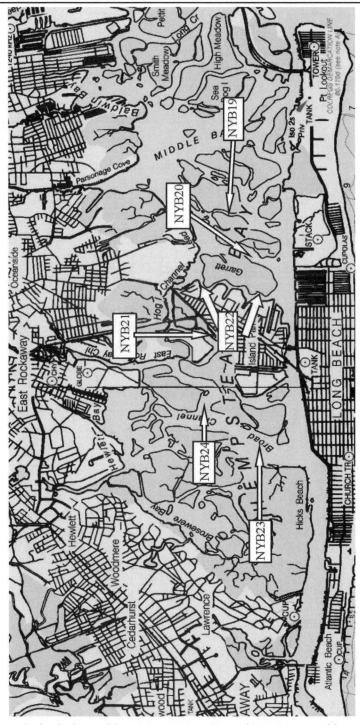

Ready for light-tackle casting? Hempstead Bay is a good bet.

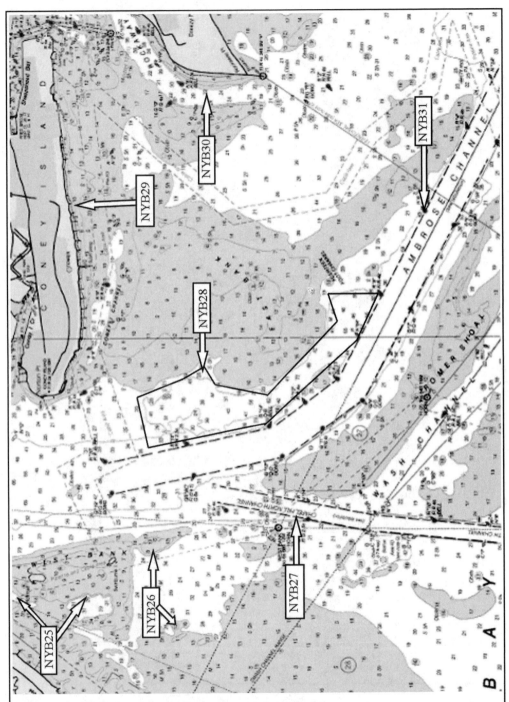

Despite it's proximity to the Mid Atlantic's largest population center, the waters just outside New York City are excellent fishing grounds.

New Jersey Ocean Hotspots

Many of New Jersey's blue-water offshore hotspots overlap with those of New York and Delmarva. But there are also some awesome opportunities that are best accessed from Jersey's own ports. One such spot is at NJO1, the Sandy Hook reef site. This spot is just a couple miles offshore, off of Sea Bright, in 45' to 55' of water. Reef materials planted here attract sea bass, tautog, flounder and stripers. Jigging or drifting baits across the bottom will produce fish, as will trolling bucktails for stripers in the spring and fall. 40'22.135 x 73'56.225 will put you right in the middle of the zone. NJO2 is another bottom fishing site close to shore, called Shrewsbury Rock. There's good hard bottom here which comes up to 15' from 40', at 40'20.742 x 73'57.198.

NJO3, called the Mud Hole, is an entirely different kind of hotspot. Here, farther off the beach, you'll find pelagics such as bluefin and yellowfin tuna. But it's still a relatively short run from home, and on a seasonal basis is the closest reliable tuna spot for many anglers. The entire area here is a popular for trolling early in the season, and chunking through the summer months into the fall. The northern edge of the Mud Hole is commonly known as the "Monster Ledge," (NJO4, 40'10.255 x 73'40.800) and laying on the bottom in this spot is the *Arundo,* a freighter sunk during World War II. It sits in 140' and comes up to 110' while the surrounding areas of the Mud Hole and the Monster Ledge vary between just over 100' and just over 200'. During July try trolling cedar plugs, Green Machines, and ballyhoo through this zone. Once the chunk bite starts up most anglers will toss butterfish over the side, and chunking squid will be quite effective here, too.

NJO5, slightly to the north-west of the Mud Hole, marks the Oil Wreck. This area is popular for a multitude of reasons: trolling for tunas and bluefish, and also for sharking, usually during the month of June. The wreckage is scattered here and drifting across the bottom with squid strips on top and bottom rigs will produce sea bass and tog.

Inshore at NJO6 lies the Sea Girt Reef site, which is a huge artificial reef. It includes several wrecks as well as reef balls, rubble and concrete, and will produce lots of sea bass along with tautog and flounder. Try starting inside the site at 40'07.710 x 73'55.600 and drift squid for the bass, crab or sand fleas for the tog, and minnow/squid combos for the flounder. NJO7 is another artificial reef site, Shark River Reef (40'06.550 x 73'41.350), but this one's much farther offshore and sits in water well over 100'. Right next to the reef is another significant wreck, the *Algol.* This 460' freighter comes all the way up to 80' from the surrounding 135' to 140' of water. Since NJO7 is farther offshore than most of the other area artificial reefs, you stand a better chance of finding lager fish here—especially when it comes to the slow-growing tautog. Of course, wind and weather will conspire to keep many boats closer to home on many fishing trips. On days like this anglers running from points south like Barnegat Inlet will want to head for the Barnegat

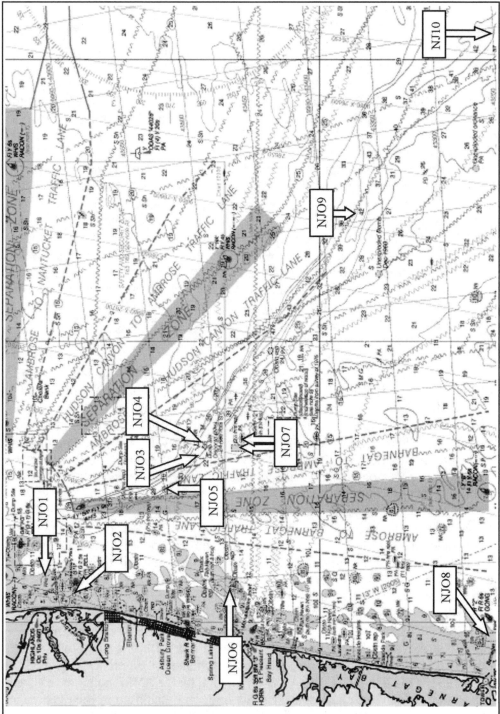

Faux-canyons, holes, and underwater ridges were scoured out of what is now the ocean floor during the ice age—providing us with plenty of Jersey coast hotspots.

Reef, NJO8 (39'45.00 x 74'01.500.) This site is a mere three miles off the beach, and will produce the usual bottom fish. During the summer months, you can also expect to find plenty of snapper bluefish in the area.

NJO9, the Glory Hole, is another spot for pelagic anglers to file away. Start off at 39'56.300 x 73'16.500 and troll across the drops from 200' to 250' for tuna from early July through the season. A few weeks after the tuna arrive, so long as the inshore waters warm up a bit you can also expect to find mahi-mahi and sometimes wahoo here, as well. In the mid-summer or fall many anglers will switch over to chunking along these edges, both with butterfish and squid. Farther offshore at NJO10 is the Chicken Canyon. Now wait a sec—wasn't NYO10, a spot well to the north, called the Chicken Canyon? (Note—it's pure coincidence they both turned out to be tagged with the number 10.) Yes. While doing research for this book I found that New Yorkers and New Jersey anglers each lay claim to the same name but in differing spots. Call it what you will, this stretch of deep water drops down to over 250' and attracts the same species as the Glory Hole. It's not a true canyon, of course, but another chunk gouged out of the bottom by glaciers during the ice age. Just beyond the southernmost extremity of this feature (39'44.039 x 72'53.928) the bottom comes up on a nice hill which reaches all the way up to 125'. Whenever you're trolling in the Chicken Canyon, be sure to include this feature in your flight-plan.

South Jersey has a nice selection of artificial reefs, both close to home and farther from shore. The first in this zone, at NJO11, is the Ocean City reef site at 39'10.500 x 74'33.500. It's four miles from the beach, so anglers after sea bass, flounder, and spring or fall tautog should have good luck here. NJO12, the Wild-wood reef site, is also about four miles from shore and will have the same species in attendance. It's built at 38'57.697 x 74'41.362, right next to the wreck of the *Gibson*. This reef is particularly easy to find, since there's a green "3FB" channel marker just off the south west corner.

The artificial reef site marked by NJO13 at 38'58.500 x 74'11.000 is significantly farther offshore, over 23 miles from Ocean City, New Jersey. Depths here range between 90' and 120' and the reef carries the appropriate name "Deepwater Reef." Since it's a farther ride from the inlet, anglers who want to specifically target larger fish, particularly tautog, should head this way. Note that during the late spring, summer and fall months, you'll often find plenty of bluefish here as well.

Farther to the south NJO14, the Cape May reef, sits at 38'52.025 x 74'41.450. There's a wreck on the northern edge of the reef, and since this site is long and stretched out, it covers quite a bit of territory. Depths range all the way from 35' to 65' and drift fishing throughout the reef site will be productive.

Just to the left of NJO14 on this chart, look for the "24M" right next to Cape May. Unfortunately, this chart doesn't show enough detail here to really zoom in, but Cape May Channel—you can find it easily in any close-up chart of Cape May, exactly where the 24M is—has rips both to the north and south. Work these rips

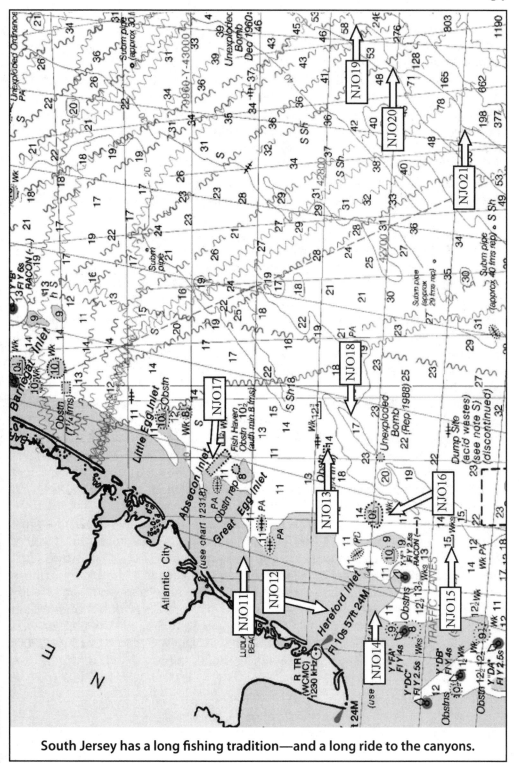

South Jersey has a long fishing tradition—and a long ride to the canyons.

in both the spring and the fall, for stripers. Eeling, live-baiting and fishing bunker chunks are all effective tactics.

NJO15 marks a section of a wreck that broke apart into several segments, the *Jacob Jones.* The two large sections sit at 38'40.362 x 74'24.414 and there's wreckage between them, as well as a significant third section to the south east. These will be toughies to find and get right on top of, but if you can locate them and drop your rigs over the wreckage, you'll hook into nicer fish than most of the area wrecks and reefs.

The East lump, at NJO16 (38'48.110 x 74.24.414) should really be called the east hole. Yes, the bottom rises here and there, but there's a section that drops down to 139' and is surrounded by 110' on all sides. This is the most significant bottom contour at the lump, and it certainly isn't what you'd call extreme. The early season bluefin migrating up the coast may pass through and stage here for a bit, bluefish will certainly make their presence known, and shark fishing is productive here some seasons. Usually, however, all of these fisheries will be better at the Cigar (NJO18, 38'54.115 x 74'08.412) lump. This spot is still iffy; most seasons it sees some shark, often there's an early pass by the first bluefin, and bluefish are present. But for mid-summer bluefin and yellowfin tuna, the spot is very hit or miss. Some years these fish will move in and feed aggressively, others the water will seem barren. So keep an ear to the ground and your eye on the local fishing reports, before planning a trip to this hotspot. NJO19 (38'54.405 x 72'54.355), a mere 105 miles (call it 91 nautical miles, if that makes you feel any better) from Cape May, is far more reliable for pelagics. Both white and blue marlin, tunas of all types, mahi-mahi and wahoo will all show up in Carteret Canyon. This isn't nearly as abrupt a feature as some of the other well-defined canyons, like Hudson or Wilmington. But once you cross over the 100-fathom line, all bets are off. It's a spot particularly popular for night-time chunkers, fall chunking for albacore tunas, and trolling for other pelagic species during daylight.

Lindenkohl Canyon (38'48.210 x 73'02.275, marked by NJO20) has just slightly more significant structure than Carteret, and is a 98 mile run. If you're headed out here be sure to keep an eye open for scallopers, which provide just about the only significant shot at reliably catching tuna between the Cigar (39 miles out) and the edge of the shelf (excepting the appearance of a warm-water eddy or other mobile structural break.) The commercial boats do work this area during most summers, and often have fish tagging along behind them. The third canyon notch in the shelf in this area, Spencer Canyon, at NJO21 (38'38.014 x 73'12.800) shares similar characteristics but is five miles closer to port.

New Jersey Inshore Hotspots

The waters of Lower Bay and Sandy hook hold a lot more fishing opportunities than one might think, when glancing at a map of New Jersey. Sure, the New York/New Jersey metropolitan conglomerate are just a stone's throw away. But the Hudson has always supported a large spawning stock of striped bass, and flounder, blues, and weakfish make good showings in these waters, too. Throughout this entire zone, you can find big stripers in random areas by cruising around and looking for gannets early in the spring. Usually mid-April is the best time to employ this method. Trolling big spoons or swimming plugs is the favored method of taking fish from under the gannets, but when they're staying in a specific area you can often drop jigging spoons with lighter tackle. Once May hits, chunking and chumming with menhaden will become the more effective method of attracting the stripers.

NJB1 is the first specific New Jersey bay area to note. The stretch of bottom between the arrows and much of the surrounding mud flat is good territory to try for winter flounder. Chumming with grass shrimp and/or corn while fishing bloodworm or shrimp bits for bait in the late fall, winter, and early spring will prove effective throughout this area. In the summer, check out the channels at NJB2. This is one of the northern areas that weakfish regularly make a significant summer run in very large numbers. Some seasons massive schools of these fish will inhabit the deep water areas here and stick around until chilly October nights send them scurrying south for the winter. You can usually tell when they are present in good numbers because you'll see several head boats drifting across the channel edges. Don't worry about getting close to them, as it isn't necessary—when the schools of weakfish are in town, groups of them can be found throughout the area. Putt along the channels, while zig-zagging back and forth across the edges and looking for caterpillar-like marks on your depth finder, right above bottom. Then drop jigging spoons like Yo-Zuris or Braids (start with green and blues, then try pinks) or tandem rigs.

The deep water around the channel edge at NJB3 will also hold trout many seasons, and should be addressed with the same tactics. You'll also find a lot of bluefish in this area. Usually they'll be snappers in the 1 to 5 pound range, although larger ones do pop up. Often the location of the fish will be obvious thanks to working birds, and when the blues are churning the surface remember that there's a good chance of locating both schoolie stripers and weakfish hanging deep below. Chumming with ground menhaden will also produce plenty of blues in this zone. You caught a small snapper blue? Don't throw it away so fast. Drift small snappers or spot across the strip of water at NJB3 and you'll have a good shot at hooking into a doormat flounder.

At NJB4, fishing in the rips, the hot ticket is often trolling with bunker spoons and/or big plugs like Stretch 25's. Concentrate your efforts here in the spring for fewer but larger fish, and in fall during the change of the tide, for larger numbers but usually smaller fish. Late in the fall, you will catch some real cows as the bigger fish move back down the coast on their annual migration. Move slightly away from the channel and chunking or chumming menhaden on any of the drop-offs and shoal edges will produce stripers from May through June, and again in September or early October. Drifting live bunker or eels in the rips will also produce good numbers of fish, and when there are a lot of sand eels around, try trolling with umbrella eel rigs.

NJB5 marks a strip of deep (20') water, right at the mouth of the Shrewsbury River. It's surrounded on all sides by very shallow flats, and the edges will produce fluke from mid to late April through the fall. Some years, weakfish will also move into the area. During seasons of good trout runs, come here in the middle of the summer armed with night lights. Set up along the edge of the deep water and fish crab chunks or live peanut bunker at the edges of your light lines, to score big numbers of weakfish. You'll also take plenty of schoolie stripers, fishing this way.

Most of the good fishing in the vicinity of Shark River Inlet takes place outside the inlet, at least partially because at low tides, there's not much water left. There are, however, a couple of opportunities here. The first is in the surf, as marked by NJI1. Casting into the suds along the beach here is good for stripers—sometimes very large ones during the spring and fall—and bluefish. At NJI2 and on the other side of Shark River Island there are some winter flounder to be caught, but many recreational anglers feel the netting that takes place inside the inlet takes a serious toll, and flounder fishing is a shadow of what is once was. Since much of the area is more or less dry during low tides, your choices will be pretty limited a lot of the time. You'll also find some fluke inside Shark River, but again, the better fishing is outside the inlet.

NJI3, the surf outside of Manasquan, is also a good area to cast for stripers in the spring and fall. Big bunker chunks and at times shucked clams will do the trick. Before attempting to use clams in the surf, it's always a good idea to salt them for a few hours to toughen them up so they stay on the hook. The channel at NJI4 will produce summer flounder through most of the season. There's a strong current running through here, so you'll need to plan on keeping your motor running and bumping the boat in and out of gear. The shoreline along NJI5 is covered in piers and pilings. You'll catch fluke along here, too, but the main interest will be for light-tackle anglers going after schoolie stripers. From late spring through the fall casting plugs, twister-tail jigs, or Fin-S type lures will produce fish, particularly right at sunrise and sunset.

NJI6 marks a nice shelf just outside Barnegat Inlet. Drifting squid strips or small live spot will produce big flounder here, particularly in the fall. Trollers working up and down the beach will catch stripers on umbrella rigs, bunker spoons and big swimming plugs, as well as lots of bluefish.

Surf fishermen will be interested in the area of the north jetty. The area where it meets the beach, marked by the lower arrow at NJI7, (commonly called "the pock-

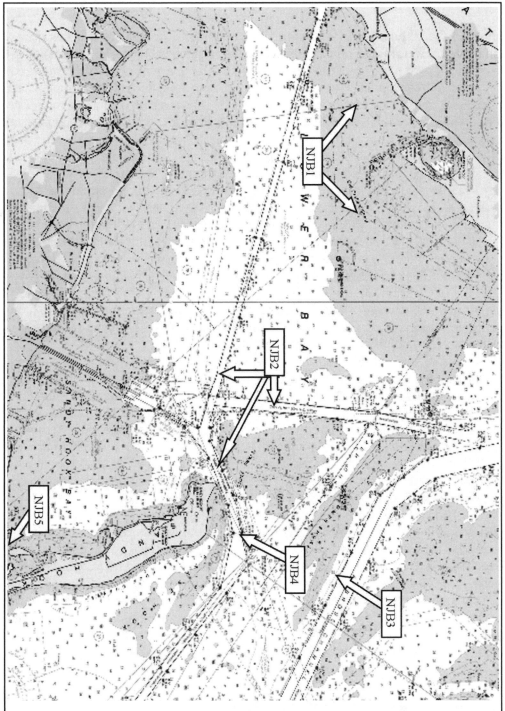

Lower Bay and Sandy Hook have some surprisingly good fishing areas, when you consider the close proximity to densely populated areas.

et" or "the north hole") is a good area to cast both lures and bait for stripers, blues, sea mullet, and some seasons, weakfish. In the fall, false albacore will also be taken here. Just beyond the tip of the jetty, marked by the upper arrow of NJI7, there are some deep holes that often hold large weakfish from June through September. Cast bucktails trimmed with crab chunks or squid, or swimming plugs, for these fish. Note that there are plenty of rocks that are under the surface closer in to the jetty, which makes for a lot of snags—bring along plenty of tackle, and plan on losing a good deal of it. If you're feeling bold enough to drop crab baits right in amongst the rocks, you'll also have a shot at picking up tog, early in the spring.

Just inside the inlet at NJI8 there's some excellent flounder fishing. It will start up in mid to late April, and run through the season. Weakfish will also take up residence in this deep water some seasons and can be caught by vertical jigging. And eelers will have success on striped bass in the spring and late fall, in this same area. Right where the channel dog-legs here, the deep water is commonly known as "Meyers Hole" and should be specifically mentioned for one other reason: some seasons black drum will show up here in early May. Often they'll be discovered by striper anglers fishing with whole clams, which drum just happen to love. So early in the year if you're heading to this area to fish for stripers, dropping a line or two with clams does offer some potential for a big surprise.

NJB6, the mouth of Tom's River, is important to note for a couple of reasons. During the summer months you'll find schools of snapper blues roaming the area, attacking shoals of baitfish. As usual, you can catch them on just about any lure and the fish will often be apparent thanks to flocks of diving gulls. Cast heavier lures and get under the blues, and you'll sometimes run into schoolie striped bass. This area is also good to keep in mind for winter flounder. Although the runs here are not what they used to be, you will catch some of these flatfish by anchoring up and chumming with corn and clam bits while fishing bloodworm or grass shrimp baits; focus your effort on the last hour of the tide and the first hour of the next tide.

The bridge at NJB7 will hold schoolie stripers, especially around the sunken pilings on the north side. Cast bucktails and plugs, or live-line peanut bunker under the bridge to catch them. If you want to target mid-summer weakfish, slide over to the deep water pockets on the north side of Pelican Island marked by NJB8. Weakfish will move in here as early as May some seasons, and often remain through the end of September or the beginning of October. Catch them by night fishing or by vertical jigging with small Braid or Yo-Zuri spoons. Grass shrimp also put the weakfish into feeding mode, at times. During low tides, you may also want to try dragging minnow or minnow/squid combinations across the edges of these holes, for fluke. The same goes for the deep water marked by NJB9. It gets even deeper here (down to 25', while other nearby holes reach 20') and again, weakfish will move into the hole and stage here during the warm months of the year.

NJB10 is, unfortunately, off the charts. In order to fit Barnegat into the page size it was necessary to lose the northernmost section of the bay, which has two

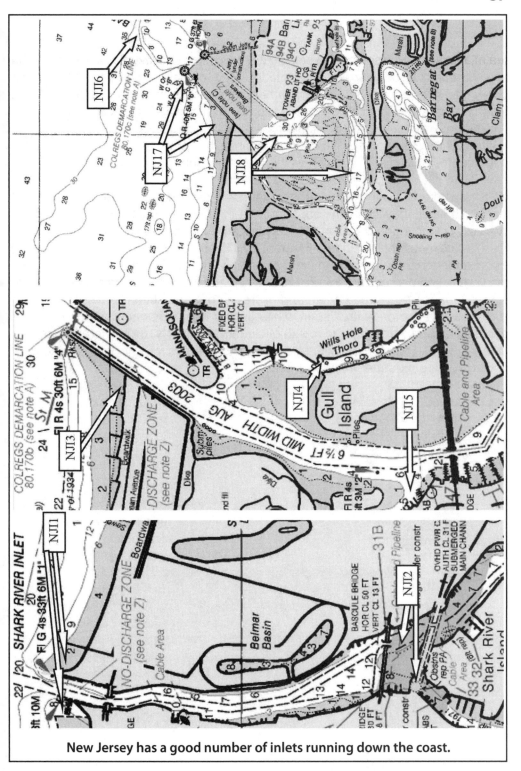

New Jersey has a good number of inlets running down the coast.

spots which must be noted: the deep water around Herring Island, and the channels under Matolokin Bridge (don't worry—you'll be able to easily spot these places in any chart book or on your GPS/chartplotter.) Both of these areas will hold weakfish during the summer months, which are best attacked at night around the lightlines. Fish chunks of peeler crab or live peanut bunker. You'll also catch stripers using this method, and during the daylight hours, you'll catch schoolie stripers around the bridge. While you shouldn't expect to encounter big cows here on a regular basis, good numbers of smaller bass prowl the area from June through October.

NJB11 points out Oyster Creek Channel, coming in from the inlet. This is an area where you will find the larger stripers—most seasons, during the month of April. In the fall, they'll usually reappear here for a while. Local anglers favor either live eels or whole shucked surf clam, when targeting these fish.

The mouth of the Forked River, at NJB12, is a spot you'll want to visit during the change of tide late in the fall and extremely early in the spring. Most seasons the creeks and canals here freeze hard; soon after ice-out is a prime time to locate winter flounder. Again, chumming a mixture of corn and clam bits while at anchor is the best way to draw the fish in, while baiting up the hooks with bloodworm or shrimp bits. Same goes for the mouth of Cedar Creek, at NJB13. There is a deeper channel here, however, and during the warmer months you have a good shot at finding summer flounder along its edges.

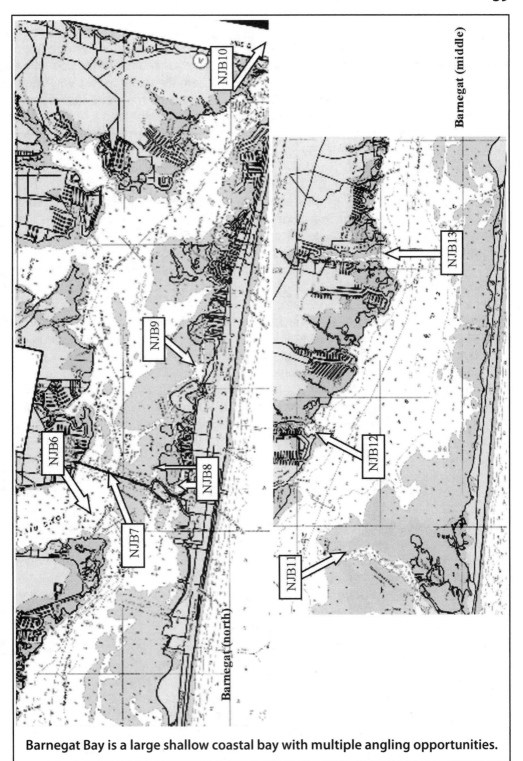

Barnegat Bay is a large shallow coastal bay with multiple angling opportunities.

Just inside Barnegat Inlet, at NJB14 in Double Creek Channel, there's more deep water, high-current area that creates good conditions for finding spring cow stripers during the months of April and May. About the time these fish arrive you'll also encounter good numbers of fluke here, which will remain throughout the season. Just across the bay at NJB15, winter flounder will be the main quarry. Try this spot when the tide's falling and the canals are draining, using the usual winter flounder chumming techniques. In the relatively deep water at NJB16 you'll also find winter flounder. Look for 12' to 16' depths in this area, and again, set up with corn and clam chum. NJB17 marks an area where the current has scoured a channel up close to the marsh. Hit this spot when the tide's running strong, creating nervous water. Cast bucktails, swimming plugs and plastic jigs up close to the shore and retrieve them at a lively pace, to attract schoolie stripers during the late spring, summer, and fall months, with larger fish mixed in in the spring and fall.

At NJB18, you'll want to drift the channel edges with Fluke Killers. Flounder will move in here in the middle of the spring and may be found in the area until the winter winds blow. You'll also find a few at NJB19 along the edges of the drops, but this spot is better remembered as a weakfish hole. There's a deep water stretch here that drops down over 25' and if weakfish move in during the late spring or early summer, they'll usually hang out for the season. Jigging spoons or bucktails tipped with crab chunks will catch these fish, but as is often the case, you'll rack up higher numbers by fishing here after dark, with night lights and baits such as peeler crab and peanut bunker. The water at NJB20 isn't nearly as deep; the channel under the bridge is fairly small and most of the weakfish caught in this area will come at night along the lightlines—during daylight, they'll usually disappear. School-sized stripers, however, will make their presence known once the sun's up.

The channel running behind Thoroughfare Island, at NJB21, is a great spot to hit for all of the above: drift the edges of the drops for fluke, cast jigs and light tackle up to the edges of the marsh for stripers (commonly called fishing the "sod banks" by most Jersey anglers), and set up over the muddy bottom areas for winter flounder. On a dropping tide, shift just a hair to the west and catch the water flowing out of the creeks and canals here, for the best results.

The mouth of Westecunk Creek joins with the channel running through Little Egg Harbor at NJB22, creating a hole that drops down to over 15' for a long stretch and over 25' in one spot. During the summer months this is another area where weakfish may ball up and hold through the season. When the tide's running you'll also catch stripers here, particularly during the spring when the sun-warmed creek water flows out into the bay. At NJB23 behind Haven Beach there's another deep hole, though it's not quite as deep. Look for the spot that's 18' and search for trout along the bottom, or move over to the edges of the drop-off and drag baited rigs for fluke from late spring through fall.

The entire stretch between the arrows of NJB24 is important to note, be-

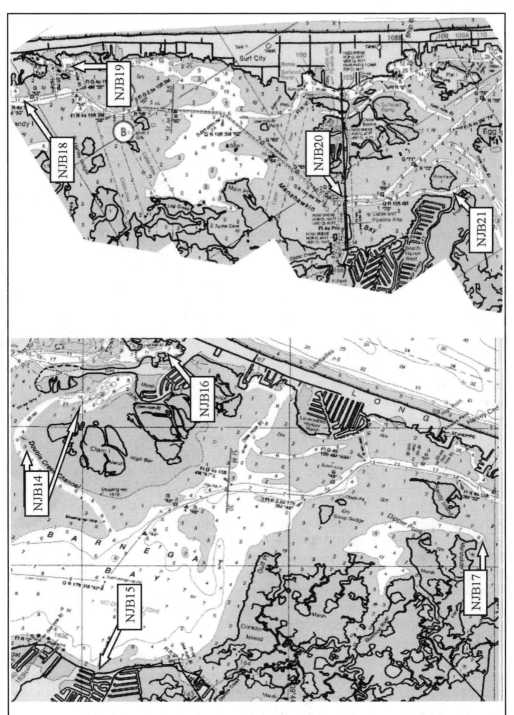

The southern end of Barnegat and Manahawkin Bay: some of the best
winter flounder fishing along the coast.

cause the channel here runs from 25' to 35'. Trout can show up in this area any time from May through October, and larger stripers will run through early in the spring. During the summer and fall months, look for lots and lots of snapper blues to cruise around here, with their exact location marked by working birds. Schoolie stripers, fluke, and many ocean panfish will also come into this channel. At NJB25 the cuts running between Hither and Story Islands will also see some stripers, but the main catch coming from these cuts will be fluke. Drift through on an incoming tide and bounce jigs up near the shore line for both species, and when the tide drops or dies, drift the deeper sections to catch the flounder.

NJB26 marks more deep water channels like NJB24. Again, there's plenty of water reaching down to the 30's and the larger stripers moving through in spring time will take advantage of it. This will be a good area to drift live eels or spot, and if it were legal, small founder. Stripers in these channels close to the inlets feed on large numbers of palm-sized flounder, which of course are illegal to bait with. There are flounder-imitations, however, such as the Petri-Fish lure.

At NJB27, the channel cuts are similar to those at NJB24: deep with lots of current, attractive to large stripers, fluke, snapper blues, and ocean panfish. These channels are best remembered, however, as flounder spots. From spring through fall, they'll usually be rich with flatties.

NJB28, Gravelling Point, is an area well known for its early striper runs. Although most of the fish are "shorts" and large numbers are not common at this time of year, stripers will be caught here as early as the month of March. As the spring progresses, the area usually gets hotter and hotter. Many anglers will fish whole bloodworms threaded onto a hook, while others try clam baits in this area. In either case, the deep Mullica River meets the shallow Great Bay at Gravelling point, creating some great currents and drops. Come here in April, and you do have a good shot at locating fish in the 20-pound class.

NJI9, in the mouth of Little Egg Harbor Inlet, drops down below 40' in a couple of spots yet has knee-deep shoals in close proximity. Again, this area will be frequented by both stripers and fluke. Target the flatfish on the top of the shoals during high tide, and on the edges of the drops during low and falling tides. Shoot for the stripers with live eels or spot, fished in deeper water. Sea trout will also make a showing in this area, and although the numbers won't be huge, the fish will. The largest specimens are often taken from the deep water just inside the inlet, by anglers throwing bucktails trimmed with crab or squid, red/white Mir-O-Lure plugs, and chartreuse twister tails.

Outside of the inlet, there's a nice hole at NJI10 which is another good trout spot—but most years this will be a fall run spot with less action during the spring influx of fish. The drop that goes down to 35' and is surrounded by 25' is a stop-over point for the fish as they migrate out of the bay or come down the coast. Look to find them here in September or possibly October, particularly during an outgoing tide. If there's a mud line formed by the water coming out of the inlet, search along it.

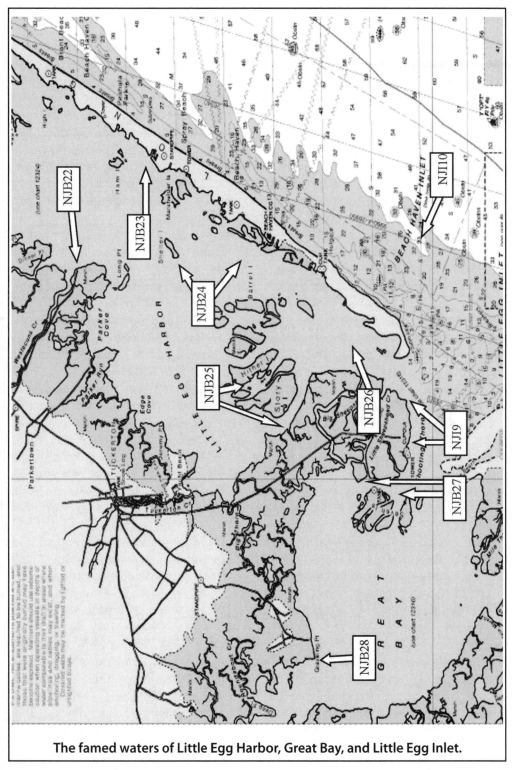

43

The famed waters of Little Egg Harbor, Great Bay, and Little Egg Inlet.

Brigantine Inlet has a nice, wide channel with plenty of depth and strong currents. It also feeds a huge matrix of cuts and channels running in and around marsh islands. The sheer amount of territory is huge, and it provides lots of opportunities. The first comes in Brigantine channel itself. Summer flounder will stage a nice spring run through here, usually beginning in April (even though the season may or may not have "officially" opened). You can hope to find some big doormats by drifting your baits along the edges of the entire channel, and specifically at the drop-off marked by NJI11. Drifting live baits during the same spring time frame will produce large stripers, usually a couple of weeks after the fluke arrive. Once May hits, fishing big bunker chunks, herring, and whole clams will also take the stripers. Some seasons, black drum will also make a showing here.

The myriad of cuts and channels running through the islands, as marked by NJB29, is all good fluke territory. From late spring through the summer plenty of flatfish can be caught here, with the usual techniques. Note that the water running from the back-bay areas sometimes has a dark color, and when it does, root-beer, red, and purple colors are often more effective than brighter choices.

Another great fishery provided by the cuts and deep channels is light-tackle casting for medium-sized stripers. From mid May through October, drifting through these channels while casting jigs or swimming plugs up to the banks will produce good numbers of fish in the 16" to 26" class. Larger fish, usually in the 32" to 36" range, can often be caught in good numbers early in the season. Many times these fish will come from a mere foot or two of water, up close to the shore. While access to deep water is key when hunting for these fish, actually being in deep water (particularly during flood tides) is not—don't be afraid to cast your jigs right up to the edges of the shorelines, even when there are shallow flats between the channel and the bank. When the tide is dropping or low, look for cuts and creeks that drain into the main channel, like the cut just above the northernmost arrow on NJB29. Anywhere a rip or nervous water forms around a point or edge is also a good area to cast to.

The bridge over the inlet in Atlantic City, at NJI12, as one might expect is in an area of deep water and high current. As such, this is another good area to drift live baits for large stripers in the spring—especially at night, around the lightlines. Fish with clams and there's an outside shot at black drum, usually during May.

During the late spring and summer months you'll also see plenty of bluefish moving through this area. Up along the edges of the channel flounder can be caught, and sea trout will stage in the holes. There's a 20' hole off the end of the northern jetty marked by NJI14, which is a good area to shoot for both big stripers and tide-runner sea trout from the spring right through the season. As is often the case with jetty holes, you're likely to find fewer but bigger fish here. Cast bucktails (whites and yellows) trimmed with peeler crab or twister tails for both species. On the south side of the inlet, marked by NJI13, there is a series of jetties which reach out to 12' to 18' of water. Fishing this area will take a lot of concentration on

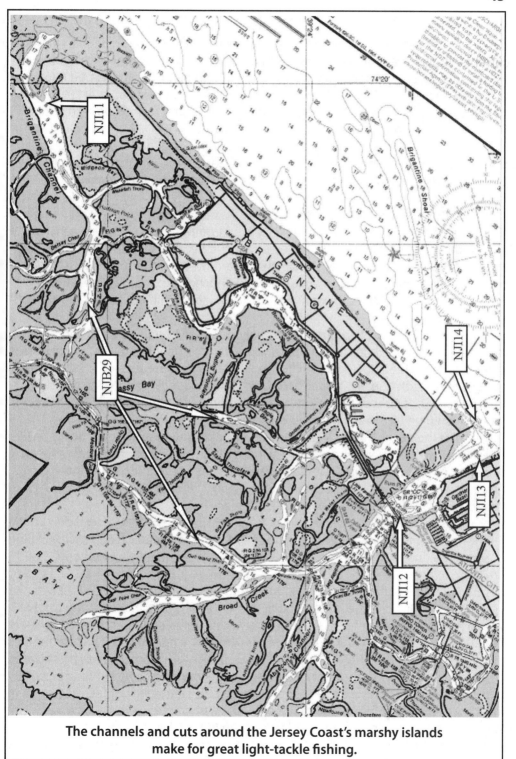

The channels and cuts around the Jersey Coast's marshy islands
make for great light-tackle fishing.

the captain's part, as he'll have to dedicate himself to constantly monitoring boat position. If, however, he can keep the boat within casting distance while the crew tosses bucktails or swimming plugs, lots of stripers and bluefish can be caught in this area. Fish here will usually feed strictly according to the tide; look for the bites to come during the last hour of one tide and the first half-hour of the next tide, with the end of the incoming usually being the best bet.

One should also remember that in the early spring tog may be caught along any of the rock jetties or bridge pilings in the area. Green crab makes the best bait, and you'll need to fish it in close to the structure. Remember to bring plenty of extra rigs!

NJB30, in Great Egg Harbor Bay, marks another good winter flounder area. It's not incredibly deep, and the currents aren't quite as strong as in many of the cuts and channels of the south Jersey bays, but the patchy mud bottom holds zillions of the tiny worms, shrimp, and other critters winter flounder like to eat. Chum them up with corn and clams, while baiting with bloodworm bits. Note—Fish Bites artificial bloodworms seem to work just as well as the real thing for this type of fishing.

At NJB31 you'll find some extremely deep water behind Drag Island. Look for weakfish to ball up in here through the season, and jig on bottom with jigging spoons to catch them. If you're a night angler, once the sun goes down shift over to the bridges and set up your lights on the channel edges. Bait up with crab chunks, bloodworms, peanut bunker or grass shrimp, and fish the edges of the lightlines. You'll catch plenty of medium-sized stripers, too.

The holes at NJB32 are more deep spots (several go well beyond 30'). Trout may move in here and croaker will also some seasons. Light-tackle trolling with feather jigs, Rat-L-Traps and bucktails will also prove effective in these areas, and since they are well-protected from the wind, should definitely play a role in your plan "B" when the weather doesn't cooperate.

Just off of our charts and outside of Great Egg Inlet, bars—commonly called the north bar and the south bar—protrude out into the ocean on either side. In the fall trolling along the edges and/or drifting clam baits or live eels will produce stripers here.

NJB33, just north of Corson, doesn't mark a particular spot so much as the general area. All of the creeks and mud flats in this area have good potential when you're looking for winter flounder. Extremely early in the spring and again very late in the fall, concentrate your efforts in these creeks where one or more channels meet. The spot marked by NJB34 indicates a different kind of junction between channels—one with deep water and close inlet access. Both tide-runner weakfish and good sized stripers will be found where these channels join, starting early in the spring. By late spring bluefish will also move up into this area. And if you want to drift for fluke, this spot should certainly be on the list. Up in the mouth of the inlet, at NJI15, there's more opportunity for the same species. Since there are a couple

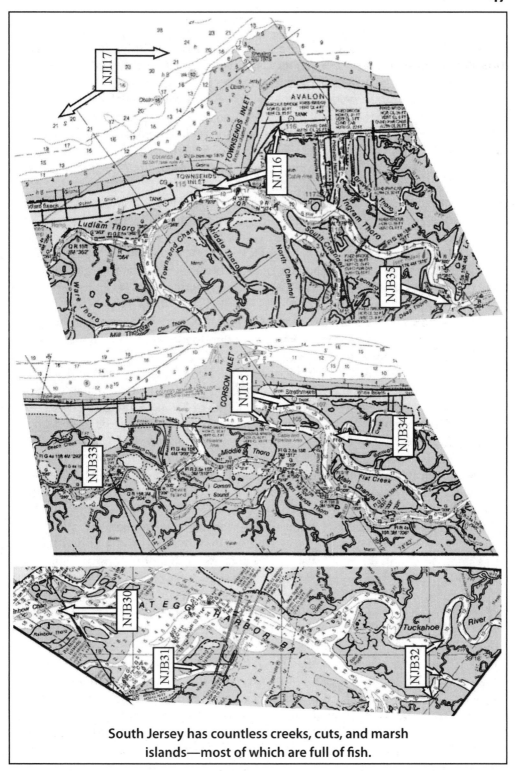

South Jersey has countless creeks, cuts, and marsh
islands—most of which are full of fish.

of bridges in this vicinity, however, there are more options. Both stripers and a few weakfish will be found along the lightlines at night, and during daylight hours, fishing around the bridges with bucktails, swimming plugs and jigs will produce plenty of stripers. Working big poppers and fishing live eels will take fish right outside of the inlet mouth. The beach on either side of the inlet is productive surf, and can be fished either from the sand or from a boat during the fall months for stripers. Same goes for the stretch from Corson down to Townsend, where many boat anglers will simply look for working birds and cast bucktails, jigs, or surface chuggers for stripers from September on through the fall.

Townsend Inlet has good light-tackle opportunities for striper anglers. The inside northern edge of the inlet and the canal running between the marsh and Avalon, marked by NJI16, are covered with piers and pilings. Particularly during the summer and early fall months, try casting jigs up to the pilings. Most of the fish may be on the small side at this time of year, but the potential for catching large numbers is great. From here to NJB35, running down Ingram Thoroughfare, fluke fishing should kick in during late April and remain decent until the fall. But the point marked by NJB35 is where the channel opens up, and produces another good area to shoot for winter flounder. Try this spot during the last couple hours of a falling tide, while chumming at anchor.

Jenkins channel, just inside Hereford Inlet, is marked by NJB36. Like most of the channels running through the area stripers can be caught casting up along the banks, but this channel should be noted for fluke fishing. During a low or falling tide try drifting through the deep area at NJB36, and when the tide's in or high, try at the edges of the flat where the channels meet, just down-creek from the marked hotspot. Regard NJI18, 19, and 22 as good places to try during either tide; cast around the bridges for schoolie stripers or drift live baits through the channels running under them for larger fish. Weakfish may be found at any of these bridges, with NJI22 probably being the best bet for that species (it will vary somewhat, from season to season.) Of course, night fishing and working the light-lines is almost always the top method of taking trout in these areas. Early in the spring tog can sometimes be caught here, as well. If you stick in the deeper areas and fish clam baits, particularly during the end of April or the beginning of May, you may discover black drum as well. NJI21 marks deep channels which support decent runs of fluke most seasons, as well as schoolie stripers from late spring on.

NJI20 and NJI23 (left arrow) mark more sections of the inlets which have jetties that run out into fairly deep water. These will attract most of the species found in these waters, and provide a great opportunity particularly when the wind's blowing out of the north. While the other side of the inlet may be washing machine-conditions, these spots will often be like lakes. (Note that when an outgoing tide opposes the wind, the opposite is true in some areas of the inlets.) The south jetty at Cape May, marked by NJI23, has good fishing along the rocks with a hole off the end; the north jetty also has deep water where the rocks end, though the drop is

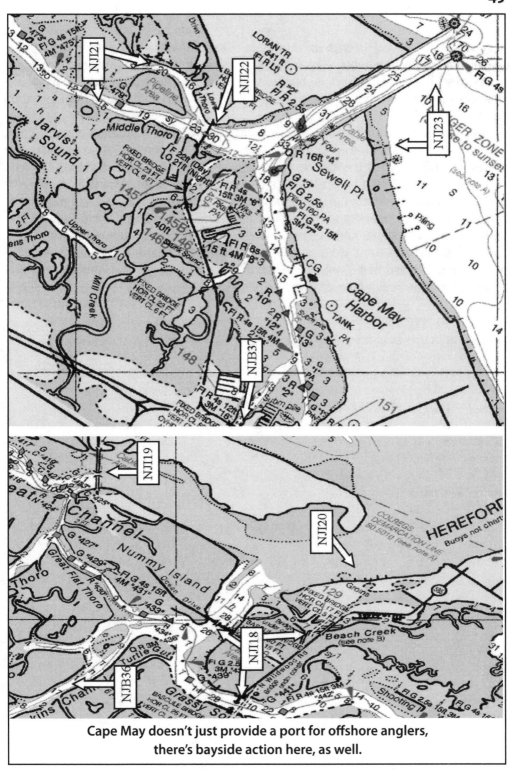

Cape May doesn't just provide a port for offshore anglers,
there's bayside action here, as well.

not quite as extreme. Put crab baits on bottom for tog but cast and retrieve for both stripers and weakfish in this area. In the wash on both the north and south sides of both Cape May and Hereford Inlets, sea mullet usually make a decent showing, as well. Fish for them with bloodworm-baited top and bottom rigs, cast right into the suds.

One final note about the south Jersey inlets: In the early fall, usually after the first serious temperature-changing cold front in September or early October, mullet will move out of the back-bays and into the ocean. As one might expect, both the stripers and the bluefish take an interest in this development. Surf casters and jetty anglers can get in on the action by fishing live finger mullet, cut mullet, or by casting surface poppers and/or swimming plugs. Expect the fishing to peak after a nice north-east or south-east wind which pushes the bait up near the surf, and cast tackle that can stand up to relatively big fish—10-pound to 30-pound stripers and 10-pound class blues are not out of the question in the surf and around the jetties, at this particular time of year.

CHAPTER 2
Delmarva

The coastline of Delmarva offers some of the most under-rated fishing on the Atlantic seaboard. Places like Montauk and Hatteras get far more attention, but during certain parts of the season the waters of Delaware, Maryland, and Virginia, will have hotter action than either.

In bays and inlets, the hot northern species such as flounder and stripers are present in good numbers. But species more commonly sought to the south, such as drum and cobia, are also viable options. Inshore ocean waters may not have the cod found in New York nor the grouper found in North Carolina, but there's a strong mix of northern and southern species such as tautog and spadefish. And the offshore action for pelagics can get hot—very hot—for a season that lasts longer than the northern reaches of this region but is notably shorter than in southern climates. In essence, the Delmarva area enjoys the best of both worlds on a seasonal basis.

Delmarva North Ocean Hotspots

The first Delmarva hotspot, DMVO1, is an artificial reef just north of Indian River. Head for 38'40.398 x 75'00.272 and drop bottom rigs baited with squid strips for sea bass, or use green crab for tautog. Flounder will also be caught from among the wreckage, from May through October. DMVO2, known as the Twin Wrecks, is about the closest to shore that one can ever hope to hook a bluefin tuna or mako shark when fishing from these ports. In mid to late June or early July, when bluefin first move through the area, a few will sometimes be found this close in and can be caught on traditional spring gear: cedar plugs, spoons, and Green Machines. The bottom in this area has scattered wreckage, and it will also be of interest to bottom fishermen in search of sea bass and tautog. Cobia are also spotted near the Twin Wrecks some summers, too, usually during mid to late July or August. The wreck itself is located at 38'13.350 x 74'43.950, but the wreckage at 38'12.505 x 74'43.954 is easier to locate because it's been built up as an artificial reef. During the summer months bottom fishing is often excellent here for sea bass and smallish tog, and along the edges of the reef, you're likely to encounter good sized summer flounder.

A little farther from shore, the 20 fathom fingers (marked by DMVO3) is known as a good spot to try sharking during June and into early July. Some seasons bluefin will be found here as well, as they migrate up the cost. There are also fish traps in this area, which are marked with small floats. Jacks, bluefish, and sometimes small mahi-mahi can be caught from around them, depending on the conditions any given season brings.

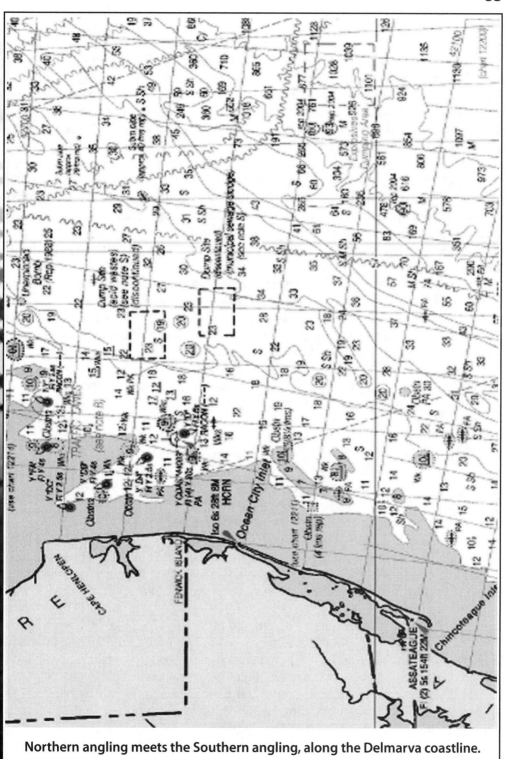

Northern angling meets the Southern angling, along the Delmarva coastline.

The *African Queen* wreck site, at DMVO4 (38'09.115 x 74'57.251), is one of the best bets for bottom fishing reefs near Ocean City, MD. Laying in 65' or so of water this area often swarms with sea bass, flounder along the edges, and spade-fish during the month of August. Cobia also will be found meandering through the area during the heat of summer. Tog are present but usually not really big ones, since this area is well known and gets a lot of recreational fishing pressure. The original wreck site has been expanded with several barges, old armored personnel carriers, and M-1 tanks, so it covers quite a bit of territory and fortunately, even on sunny Saturdays it's possible to find fishing space for many boats.

DMVO5 (38'04.700 x 74'47.235) marks the Jack Spot, one of the most famous fishing spots in the Mid Atlantic. It was the Jack Spot that first inspired Ocean City to lay claim to the title White Marline Capital of the World. Decades ago whites were taken in good numbers at this spot, a mere 24 miles from the inlet. Today you're less likely to hook a marlin here but they do still make an appearance from time to time. The Jack Spot comes up to 45' and is surrounded by 90' to 110'. Chunking and trolling along the south-east edges produces bluefin virtually every season, and some years, yellowfin tuna as well. Mahi-mahi will pop up frequently once the water has warmed and wahoo also pop up here, though a lot less fre-quently. Big bluefish in the 15- to 20-pound class often stack up at the Jack Spot, and many seasons it's possible to catch 50 or more in an afternoon. Sometimes this will make chunking for tuna all but impossible (when this happens, try mov-ing off the edge to slightly deeper water). During the summer king mackerel also make an appearance but most are on the small side, just 5 to 10 pounds. For some reason the schools of kings here rarely stay still for long and won't stick to a chum slick; you'll have to troll spoons (usually on planers) to catch them.

DMVO6, the wreck of the *Marine Electric* (37'52.818 x 74'46.445), is an-other good early season bluefin tuna spot, and is also good sharking grounds. Cobia will hang around this wreck too; try sight-casting to them when you spot the cobe on the surface, or chum for them with ground menhaden.

Up off of Delaware, the Elephant Trunk, at DMVO7 (38'32.905 x 74'03.950) is a traditional tuna chunking area for boats running out of both Indian River and also Cape May. It sees decent runs of small to medium bluefin in the early summer many seasons, but usually few yellowfin or very large bluefin turn up in the area. Mahi-mahi will also appear in chunk slicks here. Massey's Canyon, at DMVO8, is not a canyon at all, but it does feature a nice drop-off at 38'20.447 x 74'25.904, which goes from 95' to 125' in a very short distance. It's a good chunking area for bluefin many seasons, and often sees some fish from June right on through the fall. Yellowfin tuna will also arrive here some seasons, although their presence is highly variable.

DMVO9, the Hot Dog, is one of the best known spots in this region. The anglers leaving port in Maryland make this 45-mile run regularly, but boats also run here from as far off as Cape May on a regular basis (nearly a 60-mile cruise.) Some seasons "the dog" is red hot for bluefin tuna ranging up to 150 pounds and

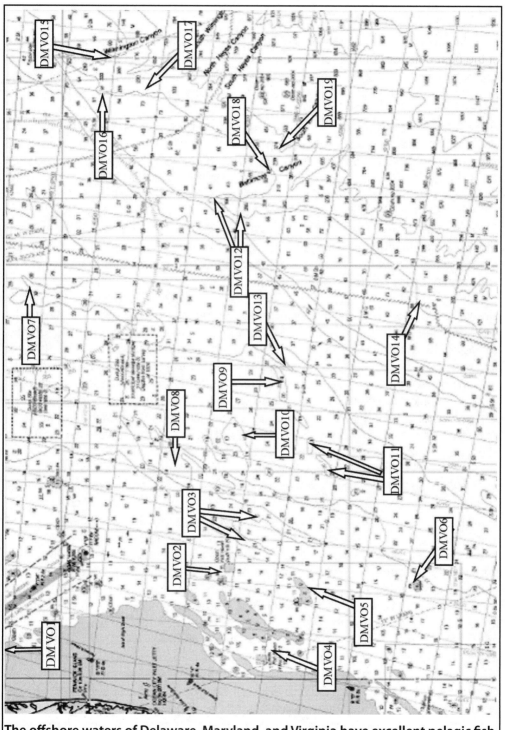

The offshore waters of Delaware, Maryland, and Virginia have excellent pelagic fisheries during the summer and fall months.

yellowfin tuna up to 80 or even 100 pounds, white marlin, and mahi-mahi, yet other seasons the fishing here is just so-so. As with all places it's impossible to predict fishing quality here from one year to the next, but most would agree that the Hot Dog is hot often enough that many people think of it as one of the best places to fish in the region.

In its shallowest areas the dog (38'07.012 x 74'16.512) is just a hair over 100' and off the outer edges, drops down to 145' or 150'. Chunking along this drop from Mid-July through September is particularly effective most seasons. The south/ east edge produces a good run of large bluefin in the 150-pound class many years (sometimes early, sometimes late—you never know), and you'll often find lots of rips and nervous water just east of the Hot Dog. One of the areas where you'll sometimes find these conditions is marked by DMVO13. This notch is favored by local professional captains and probably gets just as much pressure from them as the dog itself. It's a good area to troll ballyhoo from July through the season, for both bluefin and yellowfin.

The Hambone, at DMVO10 (38'11.837 x 74'25.169) is closer to the beach (about 35 miles from the Ocean City Inlet), and some years it also sees excellent fishing. More often than not once August hits you'll see boats chunking here for bluefin and yellowfin, with most of the fish in the 40- to 80-pound class. This is also an area which has seen a lot of action from scallop draggers in the past few years, and chunking behind the draggers has become quite popular. At times, it seems, a little too popular—during the '04 and '05 seasons there were times that 30 or 40 boats would be tagging behind a single scallop dragger on the Hambone, and mayhem ensued. Note that when the Hambone becomes crowded, you can often catch fish by sliding down to the southern tip, where there are usually fewer boats.

DMVO11 marks the Sausages, which are continuations of the feature that makes up the Hot Dog. There are several sausages and any can be as productive as any of the other "deli" spots (Hot Dog, Hambone, Chickenbone, Sausages—the deli) during any given season. Since, however, they are usually less crowded than the dog or the bone, they provide a good alternative when the water becomes crowded.

The waters along the south/western wall of Baltimore Canyon, at DMVO12, are incredibly productive. Yellowfin and albacore tuna, white and blue marlin, wahoo, and mahi-mahi are all potential catches in this zone. Try bailing under the polyball floats found in 300' to 600' along this edge, from mid-July through September, and you'll usually catch all the mahi-mahi you can stuff into the cooler. You'll also find golden tilefish here, in 600' to 800' in the tip of the canyon marked by the northern arrow, in the vicinity of 38'14.115 x 73'50.595.

Naturally, the center of the canyon and the north/eastern wall will also produce a great variety of fish. But the edge at DMVO18 (38'08.308 x 73'46.184) is exceptional. This is a good area to drift at night for big eye and yellowfin tuna, and during the day, some seasons albacore show up here as well. Push a little farther off the edge to DMVO19, where the depth drops down below 600 fathoms, into

South Vires Canyon, and you're in prime marlin territory. This is often the zone where you'll encounter the really big billfish, though their location can shift dramatically depending on the water temperature and quality at any given time.

DMVO14, well to the south but along the same 100-fathom curve, marks an area known as Poor Man's Canyon (37'52.190 x 74'06.497). While it's not a true canyon it is the shortest run from several ports to the "big drop," and on top of that, fishing here is quite good at times. For the past five years the polyballs found here have been smaller and haven't been rigged with radar reflectors, so they haven't attracted and held mahi-mahi in the same numbers as the canyons to the north. But trolling along the 100-fathom curve and just inside of it will produce yellowfin and albacore tuna, as well as marlin.

Farther north, at DMVO15, Wilmington Canyon is another overlapping spot that will be visited by boats running from several states. This spot marks another good white marlin zone at 38'25.258 x 73'29.492. When the water conditions are right, look for this area to turn on from mid-July through August. There are also polyball floats found here, and again, they're usually swarming with mahi-mahi during the summer months. At DMVO16 (38'25.658 x 73'34.641) the currents often collide and weedlines tend to gather (of course, depending on conditions) and when they do, there's a good chance of finding mixed yellowfin and albacore here. Troll with Green Machines and Green Machines rigged behind birds, and you have a shot at really loading the cooler. A little deeper at DMVO17, the small notch at 38'21.427 x 73'35.207 often has rips and disturbed water near-by, and has proven a good white marlin area during the summer months, when water conditions were correct.

One more item that will be of interest to anglers fishing in these waters: The Ocean City Reef Foundation (www.ocreeffoundation.com) publishes a listing of several dozen artificial reef sites they have built, including GPS coordinates. Many of these sites are great places to fish for sea bass, tautog, flounder, blues, and at times spadefish and cobia. I have excluded the information in this book because it wouldn't be proper to re-print the information they provide to their members, only. You can become a member for a mere $50 per year, and you'll get all the numbers for all of these spots, as well as contributing to a worthy cause—they'll use that money to build more reefs, and improve the fishing for all of us.

Delaware Inlet & Coastal Bay Hotspots

The number one target for most anglers fishing in and around Indian River inlet is summer flounder, and they're found here in good supply from mid to late April through the fall. You'll find them along the deep edges of the northern shoal just outside the inlet, at DEI1. In the fall, this is also a good area to drift eels for ocean-run stripers. DEI2 is not accessible by boat, but is noted for the surf fishermen among us. Casting into the notch where the northern inlet jetty meets the beach is a good area to try for flounder during the summer months. The crabs can be fierce here, and minnow are usually beheaded in short order, so stick with tough baits like squid and use doodlebug rigs. You can also walk out onto the rocks and cast into this area from the jetty itself, if you're willing to brave the dangerous, slippery rocks (golf shoes work well for keeping your footing). Cast bucktails trimmed with twister tails or chunks of peeler crab (chartreuse, white, and yellow are winners) from those rocks to into the inlet itself, in the area marked by DEI3, and you have a good shot at stripers, blues and trout. Fishing from the rocks here will almost always be better for the trout and stripers at night, and blues usually hit better in daylight.

Bottom rigs baited with squid strips will also produce sea bass along the rocks, but usually they're on the small side. And for whatever reason, the north jetty in Indian River always seems to hold better fishing while the beach on the south side often has better surf fishing.

DEI4 marks the general area outside of the inlet, where you'll often find good numbers of oceanic panfish such as croaker, and at times, lots of sea trout. Look for color changes and mud lines during an outgoing tide, and putt along them with a close eye on the fishfinder. If fish are hanging along these edges you'll see them stacked up just above the bottom. Jigging spoons such as Braids and Yo-Zuris, or drifting Fluke Killers baited with squid or crab chunks, will both produce fish. DEI5 marks another nice edge where you'll find flounder during the summer months and stripers during the fall. During warm seasons you may also locate cobia on the surface, prowling this edge.

Indian River and Rehoboth bays are, for the most part, shallow and featureless. Once you move away from the inlet area it will be tough to find decent fishing other than for flounder in and around channel edges. Two such channels which can be extremely productive for flounder from spring through fall are the ones found at DEB1 and DEB2, below Bluff Point and at Massey's Ditch. Try bouncing jigs or drifting Fluke Killers with a minnow/squid combination, and at times, you'll load up on flatfish here.

DEB3, similarly, is a channel surrounded by shoal water. You can use the same tactics here for flatfish but also note that at times you'll encounter schools of pan fish in the channel and schools of snapper blues just about anywhere in this vicinity, usually marked by birds. The entire stretch of bay from DEB3 to DEB4 can produce flatties, and savvy anglers will slow-troll for flounder along the edges along this stretch with heavy bucktails tipped with minnow, or dropper rigs. Between the two arrows at DEB4 is probably the most popular area to flounder fish, and during the summer months on sunny weekends the boats here may number in the hundreds. It's crowded, but the flounder fishing is often quite good.

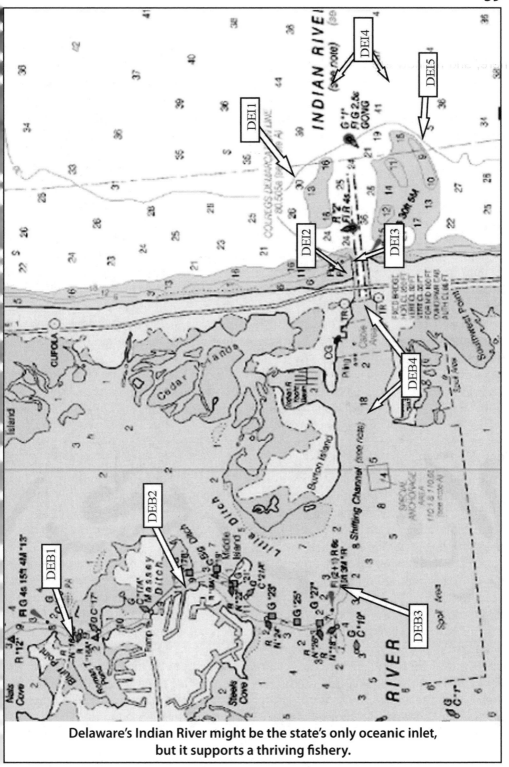

Delaware's Indian River might be the state's only oceanic inlet, but it supports a thriving fishery.

Maryland Inlet & Coastal Bay Hotspots

Although Maryland's one coastal inlet is great for anglers, it's also part of an east-coast vacationland Mecca. Ocean City swells with summertime visitors, and when fishing in this bay and inlet you'll be dealing with wind surfers, jet skiers, para-sailors, tour and eco-tour boats, dinner cruise boats, a Honda-powered pirate ship armed with water cannon (no kidding), two high-speed thrill boats, inshore and offshore fishing boats, and party boats. Yes, you'll also see multiple Marine Police and Coast Guard boats here. In short, the bay in Ocean City often resembles chaotic mayhem. The best precautions you can take are to try to fish here on weekdays or during the spring and fall, when the water is less crowded.

MDB1 marks an area generally known as the Thoroughfare and the Thoroughfare channel. Despite what the chart shows, there's deep water right up to many of the bulkheads on the western edge; in actuality the channels and shoals in this area of the bay change and shift from season to season. The Thoroughfare is a good place to catch summer flounder; most people fish here with the standard Fluke Killer baited with a minnow/squid combination, but bouncing jigs also works well. Small sea bass and assorted ocean panfish will also make their presence known in this section of deep water. Getting to the deep water at MDB2 is a little trickier than the chart would have you believe; the channel running along shore here is unmarked, and shoaling several years ago shifted the channel so it takes a big dog-leg to the left and runs up towards the Thoroughfare; people inexperienced with the area should follow the marked channel until passing Mallard Island.

Where a second channel splits off to the right (just off the boundaries of the chart showing these hotspots) you can follow it 100' before back-tracking, to enter the deep water at MDB2. This slice of water is not fished by many people, and supports good flounder fishing, particularly on an outgoing tide. On incoming and high tides, it's often swamped with so many juvenile sea bass and croaker, it's impossible to keep a bait out for flounder. (Note: The bar between the two deep areas here is great for digging clams!)

MDB3 marks the western channel running under the Rt. 50 bridge. This channel is unmarked on the north side of the bridge, but it is a good area to catch flounder during the daylight hours and stripers and weakfish at night. The current rips through here, and between the bridge pilings and shoals there's a ton of structure. (If you go under the bridge be sure to watch out for fishing lines hanging down from above, as lots of people fish from the catwalk here.) For the flounder follow the usual game-plan, and for the stripers and weakfish set up along the edges of the light line, and cast out live peanut bunker or spot. The main channel going under the bridge, at MDB4, is another area that's popular with flounder anglers. It would be suicidal, however, to drift right through the middle of the channel. Traffic here is often intense, and the current roars under the bridge. Still, you'll see people try it. Wiser anglers will move well away from the bridge and drift the channel edges.

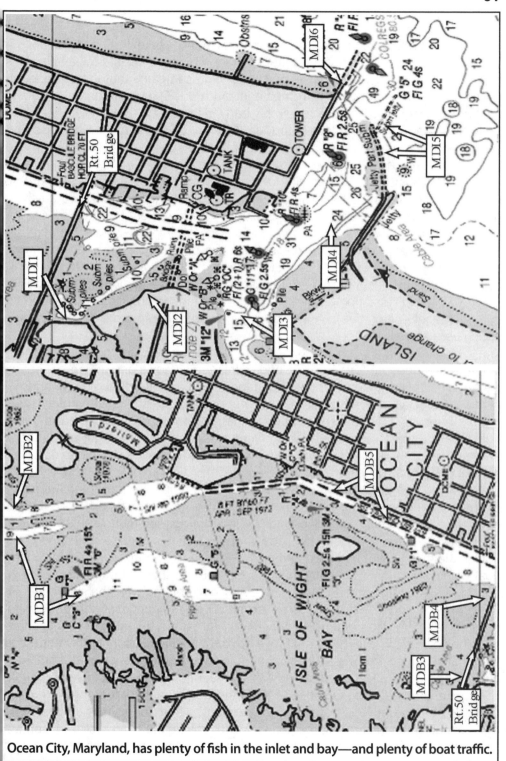

Ocean City, Maryland, has plenty of fish in the inlet and bay—and plenty of boat traffic.

Many anglers will also drift through the channel farther above the bridge, at MDB5, with some success. This spot is better to mark, however, for late fall angling. It's one of the few areas up inside the bay where you can catch tautog large enough to keep. You'll get them on green crabs and sand fleas fished on bottom and along the bulkhead here, sometimes extremely early in the spring (usually late March or early April) and commonly late in the fall (October or November.) Sea bass and croaker also frequent this area, with most of the bass being too small to keep and croaker catches varying wildly from season to season.

MDI1, just on the south side of the Rt. 50 bridge, is a small channel that runs along a bulkhead. This spot used to be called Shantytown and had a fishing pier which was quite popular. Today Shantytown is gone, but the good fishing remains. Set up on the channel edge at night and drop night fishing lights over the side, and you can experience excellent catches of sea trout during the summer and early fall months. Live-line peanut bunker or cast and retrieve bucktails and 4" twister tails (chartreuse, purple and black are all effective at night) along the light lines. Stripers will also pop up here in the dark. During the daylight hours flounder can be caught drifting this channel, and some years, horse croaker take up residence here as well.

MDI2 marks a point which has a small rock jetty sticking out into the channel. A tremendous rip forms on the end of this jetty, particularly during an incoming tide. You'll find decent numbers of stripers feeding here during the change of the tide, especially when it coincides with sunrise and sunset. Unfortunately, most will be undersized. Note also that during the summer months a number of large boats leaving the Ocean City Fishing Center use this channel right at daybreak and around four in the afternoon, and you'll need to exercise caution to fish here without causing a traffic jam.

MDI3, the junction of the channels running north-south to the marina and Sinepuxent and east-west to the inlet and into the commercial harbor, is another good area for catching flatties during the late spring, summer, and fall months. There's fairly deep water here and sometimes weakfish and horse croaker will also hold in the area. If you fish here, remember to give way to the commercial fishing boat coming through. You'll also have to look out for them at MDI4, the edge of the channel running out through the inlet. Fish here for flatfish in the summer (live-baiting with 4" to 6" spot takes some extremely large flounder in this zone most seasons) and drop eels or soft crab chunks for stripers in the fall. Schools of snapper blues also pop up in this area. Move up to the rocks adjacent to this edge and you'll catch stripers casting and retrieving bucktails, and sea bass on bottom—but come prepared with lots of extra rigs if this is your game plan, because break-offs will be numerous. During October and into the winter months, then again in early April, it's often possible to catch decent size tautog from the rocks here, too. The outer edges of the inlet rocks, marked by MDI5 provide the same action. Often the fishing is hotter on this side of the inlet, particularly at the start and end of incoming particularly at the start and end of incoming tides. But it also requires the captain to pay much more attention to boat position, since the waves will be pushing you in towards the rocks the majority of the time. The very end of the north rock jetty, at MDI6, is another area in which stripers, trout, sea bass and tog can all be targeted. During the summer months schools of bluefish will also rampage through the area, tearing up baitfish. Often it's hard to fish from a boat here, however, because people will walk out on the rocks and cast from them. Tangles become common, and tempers flare. Save this one for weekdays and the off season, and during the summertime leave the shore-bound guys their spot. If you're one of those shore-bound anglers, cast white bucktails trimmed with live bullhead minnow, peeler crab, or twister tails and retrieve them along the edges of the jetty for stripers and trout. Toss bottom rigs baited with squid for sea bass or sand fleas and green crab for tautog, while noting that you'll lose even more rigs fishing from the jetty than you will when fishing from a boat.

South of Ocean City, the Sinepuxent Bay does not hold a lot of attractive fishing. Flounder and juvenile sea bass can be caught in the channel, but good catches will be few and far between. On occasion, larger fish including some stripers and occasionally drum will move in under the bridge at Sandy Point, but most seasons you're better served by fishing elsewhere.

Delmarva South Ocean Hotspots

One of the closest spots where you might find bluefin tuna along the Delmarva Peninsula is the 21 mile hill, at DMVO20 (37'26.232 x 75'11.793.) The water here comes up to 60' from just over 100' and early in the season mako, blue and thresher shark pass through. Usually starting at some point in June, school bluefin can also be intercepted as they work their way northward. Later in the season larger bluefin may pop up here, and when they do they're usually caught by anglers chunking butterfish. DMVO21 will be of more interest to anglers looking for sea bass and tautog. All will gather around this wreck, the *Barnegat*, at 37'31.913 x 75'13.886. You'll also find plenty of bluefish in both of these areas, often all too many. DMVO22 marks a bottom fishing site that will be of even greater importance to most anglers. Commonly known as the Triangle Wrecks (36'58.550 x 75'24.850), it's a combination of many wrecks, artificially planted fish reefs, and sunken rubble. 36'59.168 x 75'23.675 will put you in the middle of the artificial reef area. There's also some serious stuff sitting on bottom here at 36'59.000 x 75'21.124, where Liberty ships and a Coast Guard cutter were sunk as additions to the reef. This is a well-known spot and will see plenty of pressure during all seasons, but there's so much rubble covering such a wide area, it can support many boats without feeling too crowded. You'll also encounter spadefish and cobia here, during the summer months. Usually the cobia will be spotted up near the surface and pursued by sight-casting. Chumming certainly will draw them in, but this is another area that often becomes

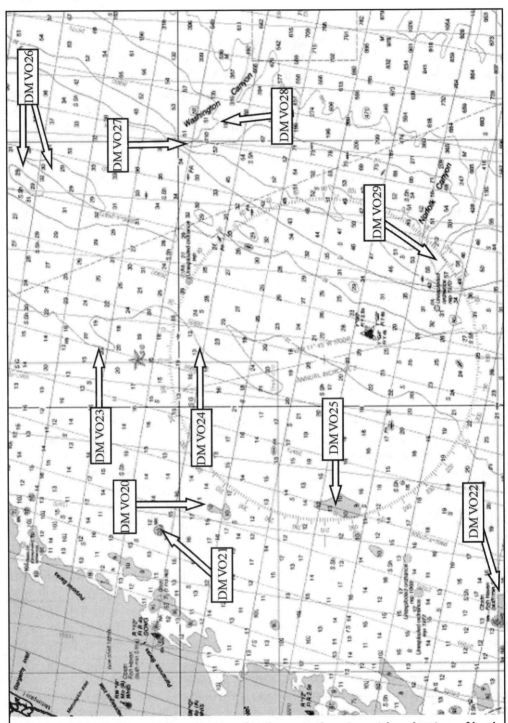

Off the beach of the southern section of Delmarva, there's a wide selection of both bottom fishing and offshore angling.

so inundated with blues that chumming for anything else is nearly impossible. Since spadefish are chummed up with clams, you won't have the same problem when going after these fish, and this is one of the more popular spots to hunt for spadefish in the Delmarva area with good reason: they're often present in big schools, from mid-July through August.

DMVO23, known locally as the Parking Lot, (37'37.723 x 74'53.177) is aptly named—when the big bluefin show up here, you'll encounter a city of anchored chunking boats, sometimes numbering in the hundreds. While this spot was extremely hot for bluefin in the 80- to 150-pound class around the turn of the century, it hasn't panned out as well for the last few seasons. Of course, that could change at any time. Slightly farther south at the Rocky Bottom (37'27.811 x 74'53.403) DMVO24, the bluefin bite has been better in later years. Although early in the season many anglers start off by trolling, again, chunking butterfish is the normal mode of attack when trying to catch bluefin here for most of the summer.

DMVO25 (37'14.847 x 75'11.340) is known as the 26 mile hill. Like the 21 mile hill, the Parking Lot, and the Rocky Bottom, it's an area that sees some shark in June then is most often chunked for bluefin tuna.

DMVO26, significantly farther off the coast, marks two large humps which lie just outside of the 30-fathom line. Going to 37'42.895 x 74'34.279 will put you right between them. For whatever reason, this seems to be a hit-or-miss area. Either you'll find tuna here (usually yellowfin but bluefin are a possibility) or you won't. Some years this area has also proved productive for white marlin. And unlike the areas farther inshore, these humps are usually attacked by trolling instead of chunking. Quite often, boats running for Washington Canyon (DMVO27, 37'28.983 x 74'30.261 at the tip) from points north will end their cruise just shy of the deep, at DMVO26, and troll across these hills on their way out. That gives them the option to find out if there are any fish around and stay if the action is good, of just continue trolling out for the deep water, if it isn't.

At the tip of the canyon, anything becomes possible. White and blue marlin, tunas of all sorts, you name it. DMVO27 also presents the opportunity to deep-drop for golden tilefish, if you have some heavy weights and fresh squid or clams aboard. Out at DMVO28 (37'26.367 x 74'27.715) you have a better shot at locating big eye, particularly if you spot whales in the area, and trolling along the edge here is an excellent game plan whether you're after billfish or tuna, during the summer months right through October.

Norfolk Canyon, DMVO29 (37'05.610 x 74'43.728), the next canyon heading south and the last truly well-defined canyon to cut into the 100-fathom line in the Mid Atlantic Region, offers the same potential. These two canyons will often see their first run of the spring weeks before those farther up the coast, and their fall run will continue longer as well. Some seasons the white marlin bite in this area is incredible, but it's also far enough south that when the water gets really warm and whites gather in large numbers, the yellowfin bite may fall off. With these conditions, however, an abundance of mahi-mahi and often wahoo also goes hand in hand.

Virginia Ocean Hotspots

Virginia Beach is a port that offers some excellent fishing, year-round. In the spring, usually starting during the month of April or May, big weakfish can be found at Rudee Inlet, VAO1. Inside of the inlet, speckled sea trout, redfish, flounder, and stripers can be caught by casting jigs, bucktails, and plugs during the same time frame. Once the water warms a bit more bluefish will also show up, and may dominate the action for much of the summer. As soon as September arrives, however, specs and reds come on strong again. During the winter months, the stretch marked by VAO2, just a couple of miles off the beach, is an excellent area to troll for big stripers. Umbrella rigs with shad-body teasers and Parachute hook baits, Mojos, and large Stretches are the usual lures, so this is heavy-tackle trolling. And considering the variability of the weather during the winter months, there may be weeks at a time that are un-fishable. But when the winds and waves cooperate, banner catches of fish in the 40" and above range are possible many seasons.

A little farther off the beach at VAO3 lies the freighter *Sanitore* (36'53.850 x 75'46.875), an old wreck which has broken apart and left a scattering of wreckage along the bottom. This is one of the better wrecks to try for big flounder, since the transition from wreck to open bottom (where the flounder often gather at oceanic sites) isn't as distinct as those found on many wrecks. Push farther out to VAO4, however, and you'll be at one of the more popular wreck and reef combinations, the Chesapeake Light Tower reef site. Even though this area sees a lot of pressure, it produces quality fish simply by virtue of the fact that there's so much stuff around, it doesn't all get fished-out. Here, everything from barges to tugs (36'54.000 x 75'43.300) to subway cars (50 of them, at 36'54.036 x 75'43.420) to missile launchers, pipes, and concrete rubble lies on the bottom. The bottom fishing can be great starting in April when tog show up and sea bass move in from the deeper haunts, and by the summer months spadefish usually take up residence in large numbers. Cobia are also present, and trollers pulling spoons or rigged baits will encounter good numbers of kingfish. This is about as close to shore as you can get and still expect to have decent king action or a regular basis, and unlike most of the spots where kings are found to the north, they'll often remain here in good numbers well into the fall—good catches even in late October are a possibility. They'll show up within two or three weeks of the arrival of bluefish, and often remain right on through the season. Note that dogfish also like this area, and their large numbers occasionally present a problem. VAO5, the next reef heading south (many people simply call it the "South Reef," and consider it more or less a part of the Light Tower Reef) is another good area for both bottom fishing and trolling for kings and blues. Head for 36'50.500 x 75'43.975, and plan on finding less rubble spread over a wider area. That essentially means you'll have to work harder but the prospect exists for larger fish, and when the northern Light Tower reef is overly crowded it provides a good back-up.

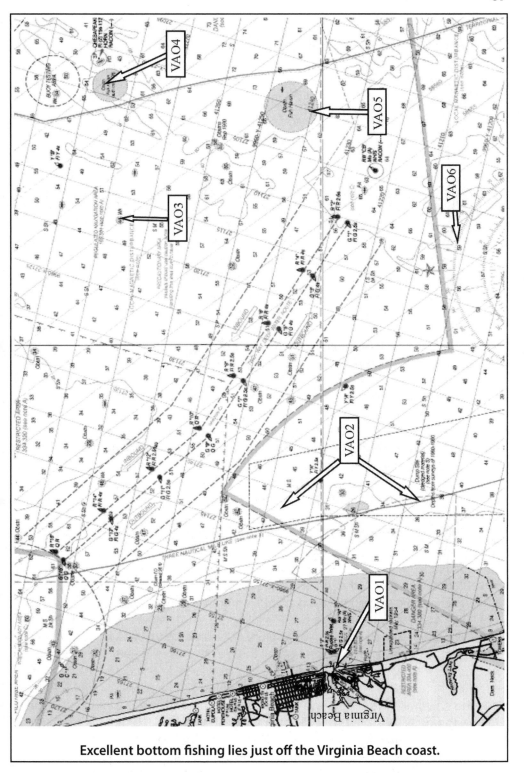

Excellent bottom fishing lies just off the Virginia Beach coast.

Head a little farther south and at 36'45.965 x 75'46.301 you'll find the Tiger Wreck at VAO6, a smaller but very productive wreck site. This is another spot that's close to home and can be reached by small boat anglers yet also holds the possibility of kingfish, big blues, and other large fish taken on the troll, as well as bottom fish.

Virginia Inlet & Coastal Bay Hotspots

The first inlet belonging to Virginia is Chincoteague. This is one of the Mid Atlantic's few under-fished areas, mostly because it's far from the major metropolitan zones of the east coast. And truth be told, there is not much bay fishing to be done here. Like much of the Delmarva coast, Chincoteague's fishing grounds are more or less limited to the waters in and around the inlet. VAI1, within sight of the inlet itself, is a good area to drift for flounder. In fact, all the edges between VAI1 and VAI2, right in the mouth of the inlet, are prime flatfish territory. They'll show up here a week or two after they make their first appearance in Wachapreague, one of the most famous flounder ports on the coast, and a week or two before they arrive in Ocean City's inlet. Usually, by the first week in April, they've come to town. This is the month during which the big "doormats" are caught, though large fish will pop up throughout the season.

VAI3, the 10' to 15' water which abuts shoals in the inlet, will also give up some flounder through the season. But these areas are more important to late summer and fall anglers searching for drum. Many seasons large black drum will root around just outside the inlet, and make up part of a mixed-bag which includes stripers and bluefish. Fish with peeler or soft crab, to catch all of the above. Focus your efforts at night to catch the drum, and on the last hour of one tide into the first half hour of the next tide, for the stripers. Although the sandy shoals don't appear as daunting as the rocky inlets to the north, they are every bit as dangerous; care must be used at all times, when fishing in the inlet.

VAI4, where three channels cutting through the marsh meet the main channel coming from the inlet, is another early season hotspot for catching flounder. The deep water at their junction will also hold some sea trout, which arrive in April but won't take a bait until the water warms, usually in early May. Then, they can be caught with jigs, jigging spoons, crab chunks, or live mullet.

Wachapreague Inlet, the next heading south, is even more isolated. It is, however, incredibly well known and anglers will trailer boats here by the hundreds in the last weeks of March and throughout the month of April, to catch the big spring flounder run. The spot at VAI5 looks like a bay but is really a huge flooded mud flat; get out of the channel and there's rarely more than a foot or two of water. Fishing along the channel edge at low tide and casting up onto the mud flats with bucktails tipped with twister tails or squid will catch flatfish here. VAI6, Hummock Channel, is another good area to target flatties early in the year. Try hitting this spot during a low or falling tide. When the tide is incoming or high, however, head over to VAI7. The shallow flat in front of the old Coast Guard station is a prime area to try for shallow-water flatfish; the channel running next to the flat will also be productive during low water, and often holds weakfish later in the season. Schools of marauding snapper blues will pop up here from time to time through the summer, and the holes in this area often fill up with croaker and spot.

VAI8, in Swash Bay, is another great area to fish the shallows for flounder. You'll see several PVC stakes coming out of the water here, which indicate oyster bars. Although casting up to the bars will produce some snags, it will also produce quality fishing. Try bouncing a 4" white or chartreuse/white grub along the bottom, and—particularly on calm, sunny days when the flats warm up a few degrees above the deeper adjacent waters—you should encounter some of the highest quality flounder fishing available in the Mid Atlantic region. Spot VAI9 marks the channel leading into Swash Bay. Early during the incoming tide this spot often becomes red-hot, and during a falling tide it's a good bet, too. But once the water's low shift over to VAI10, next to the marsh island which divides the channel from Swash bay. Flatfish will stack up in here, and later in the season this channel may hold just about anything—drum, trout, croaker, blues, and spot are all possible attendees.

Quinby inlet is the next heading south, and it's the last inlet that sees a serious amount of action from recreational anglers. As with Wachapreague, flounder is the big fish in these waters. VAI11marks the green #161 marker, and the junction of Sloop channel and the main channel; this is an excellent spot for early season fish, starting at the end of March or the beginning of April. The mouths of the creeks at VAI12 are both spots to try as the tide is falling. The northern creek, Revel, is shallower and will be hard to access during low tides, but fluke move up into it to feed during the flood tide. The Straits, to the south, has deep water and will be accessible at all times. The large flat at VAI14 is the spot to try during full flood tides. Drift over the 3'- and 4'-deep shallows while casting jigs, bucktails trimmed with squid strips, or squid/minnow combos, to take big flatfish. As the tide starts falling many anglers will shift their focus to VAI13, the main arm of the channel leading south into Hog Island Bay. Note the series of channel arms reaching into the flats on the southern side of this channel; when the tide begins flowing out on a warm, sunny day, cast up into the mouths of these channels to intercept fish that are enjoying the flow of sun-warmed water and baitfish. Later in the year, weakfish and at times schools of snapper blues will also move into the deep water of this channel. Fair warning: Once mid May hits, these areas may become inundated with croaker. There have been years in the past where it was literally impossible to fish for anything else, because so many croaker were flooding the area. If you find yourself in this predicament, try fishing a Fluke Killer with a huge bull minnow on the hook. Croaker will usually (though not always) leave the big minnow alone, while the flounder will still hit it.

The next inlet heading south is Great Machipongo, which doesn't see nearly the same level of action as the others mentioned in this book. It's included, however, because some summers either red or black drum will congregate just outside the inlet, in the deep water marked by VAI5. Try fishing for them with crab chunks or sea clams, and for the best action give it a shot right at dusk.

The CBBT (Chesapeake Bay Bridge Tunnel) at the mouth of Chesapeake Bay is the next major fishing zone. Since it's part of a major bay system (and is covered in detail in *Rudow's Guide to Fishing the Chesapeake*) it doesn't really belong here with these coastal bay and ocean waters. But the fishing is so incredibly good, I just couldn't resist including a few top CBBT hotspots.

CBBT1 and CBBT 3 mark the edges of the Middle Grounds, which is great territory for wire-lining flounder from late spring through the fall. Also starting in late spring, schools of stripers and blues will stage over the deeper areas here and often break water on alewives and bay anchovies. Fish (anything) on the surface for blues, let your bucktails or spoons sink 10' or 15' to target the stripers, and jig vertically along the bottom to catch weakfish. As the season progresses into the late fall, this style of fishing will just get better and better through November, most seasons.

CBBT2 is on the edge of Nine Foot Shoal. The eastern edge of this shoal is important to note because from June through September, cobia can be caught here. Try chumming at anchor, and fish large cut menhaden baits on the bottom and suspended at mid-depth. Savvy captains also use live spot to tempt the cobia.

Although for several years it hasn't matched up to past decades, it would be negligent to fail to mention the spring black drum run that also takes place in this area. Usually during May, gigantic blacks are tempted into biting with big shucked clams or whole peeler or soft crabs. Once upon a time this was a more reliable fishery, with blacks in the 50- to 80-pound class being taken in good numbers. Unfortunately, like the runs experienced up the Chesapeake, these days it's of a shorter duration with fewer fish. If you hear the bite is on, however, note that the hot areas generally run from CBBT2 all the way up into the Chesapeake, to the vicinity of the 36A marker off Cape Charles. These fish can move into and up the bay faster than one would think, and the bite could be in one end of that zone on day one, and the other on day two, so be prepared to hunt and move until you locate one of the tightly-packed pods of fish.

CBBT4 marks the fourth island, which can produce a plethora of fish. Stripers are present here year-round. Spring, summer, and fall mean trout, flounder, and blues. Summer produces spadefish (drift a chum slick of clam back to the rocks), cobia, and drum, and early and late in the year tautog can also be caught near these rocks. CBBT5, marking a shelf at "The Bend" in the CBBT, is another area where wire-lining for flounder accounts for a good number of large flatfish. Between the deep water and roaring currents it's nearly impossible to fish for flounder in any other way here, but if you can get that bait down to the bottom and keep it there, this is prime territory. Wire lining will also work around CBBT6, but the really exciting thing about this spot is the fall action on stripers, blues, and some years,

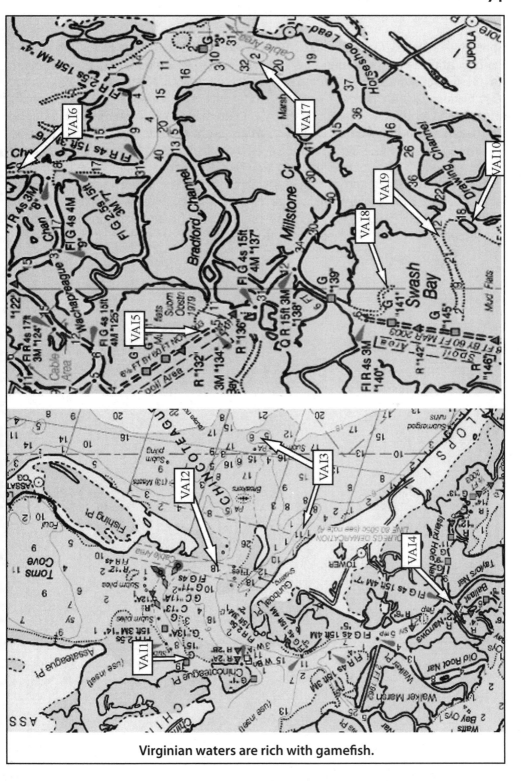

Virginian waters are rich with gamefish.

Spanish mackerel and/or sea trout. This is where the tunnel complex goes under the bay, and there are tremendous currents forced to suddenly change direction. As a result, this area has standing rips much of the time. Rockfish and blues may start breaking water here as early as June but most seasons, the action really heats up in September. Many seasons Spanish mackerel will be mixed in with the churning fish through August and September, but they usually disappear after the first few chilly evenings. Right next to CBBT6 on the south side you'll find the wreck of the *Yancy* (36'57.535 x 76'06.880) which comes up to 18' and is a good area for both bottom fishing and trolling. CBBT7 isn't right next to the bridge, but it is an important wreck for anglers in this area. Known as the Cape Henry wreck, it sits at 36'57.630 x 76'00.633. This is another popular spot for anglers hunting sea bass and tautog, and during the heat of summer, spadefish.

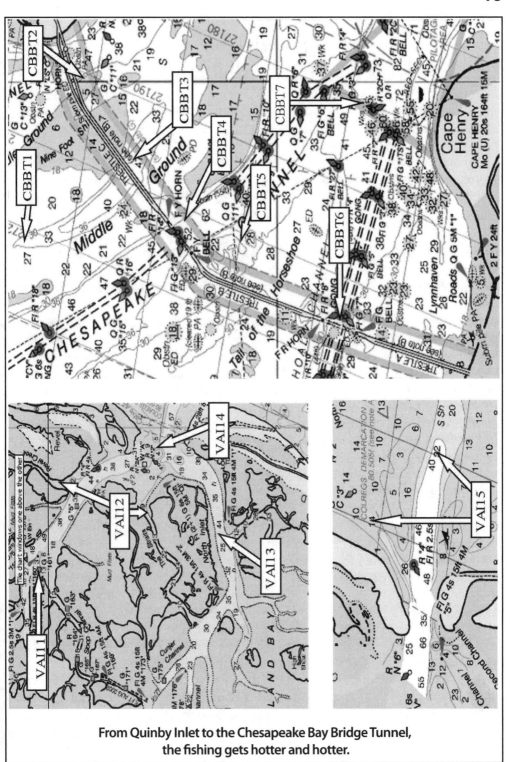

From Quinby Inlet to the Chesapeake Bay Bridge Tunnel,
the fishing gets hotter and hotter.

CHAPTER 3
North Carolina

Few areas of the Mid Atlantic region can lay claim to being true world-class fishing hotspots—North Carolina is unquestionably one of them. Between the winter blue-fin tuna and stripers, spring yellowfin tuna, summer mahi-mahi and billfish, and fall wahoo and yellowfin, coastal Carolina is visited by anglers of all types throughout the year. You should be one of them.

North Carolina Ocean Hotspots

Just northeast of Oregon Inlet, the first inlet along the North Carolina coast after a long stretch from Virginia's Rudee Inlet, there are several excellent inshore reefs. They're marked by NCO1 but are just above the chart boarder, a result of chart siz-ing that just couldn't be avoided. In any case, the first is AR-130, a reef made up of train cars (you'll often hear several reefs located along the Carolina coast referred to as "the boxcars," and this is one of them), concrete reef balls, and pipes. You'll find them about 12 miles northeast of the inlet, at 36'00.192 x 75'31.875. About three miles closer to the inlet lies the AR-140 reef site, which consists of more boxcars, two barges, and more concrete pipes. This one's at 35'56.745 x 75'31.880. AR-145, a half-mile closer, has a more interesting variety of reef fodder: an airplane, bridge rubble and pipes, a 115' decommissioned landing craft, and a 185' ship. This one can be found by plugging in 35'54.000 x 75'23.865. All of these artificial reefs will primarily produce sea bass, weakfish, and ocean panfish, along with some flounder and blues, during the warm months of the year. Some seasons, Spanish mackerel, cobia, and spadefish may also be found around these reefs. In the winter, trollers may locate some decent ocean-run stripers over-wintering in the area. Same goes for NCO2 (35'43.800 x 75'26.775), the Oregon Inlet Reef AR-160. This is a popular bottom fishing spot and a close to home chance at catching kings for small boat anglers, since it lies just four miles from the inlet. It's a pretty significant reef, too, including several large (400'-plus long) Liberty ships, a trawler, concrete rubble and pipes, and reef balls. One of the Liberty ships is the *Zane Gray,* and many people also call this the *Zane Gray* reef.

NCO3 marks a strip of water that's deeper than the surrounding area, gen-erally known as the First Slough. This water will produce winter-run stripers start-ing as early as November some years, and running through the winter months. If you locate flotsam in this area (including the red buoy #1 marking the end of the inlet) between May and October, there's a chance of finding cobia hiding below. NCO4, the Second Slough, is an even deeper trough which drops down to 100' in some areas. If baitfish ball up in this zone during the spring, summer or fall, it's a good bet that both bluefish and kingfish will be close by. In years past giant bluefin

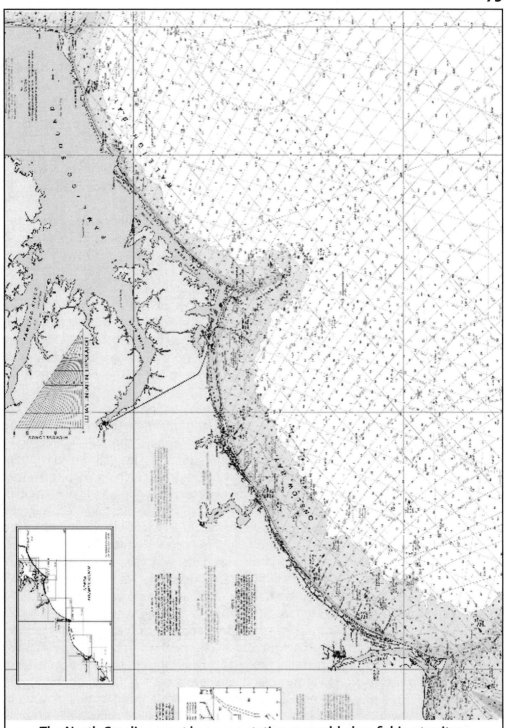

The North Carolina coast has a reputation as world-class fishing territory,
and it's well-deserved.

tuna have also made a winter appearance here, but that hasn't happened in a few years and never was as common (if such a word can be used when giant bluefin show up!) as it was slightly farther south.

NCO5 marks another wreck sea bass anglers will want to keep track of. It lies at 35'40.000 x 75'16.999, in about 100' of water. This is another old, scattered one, which is less significant than some newer planted reefs, but gets less pressure, too. NCO6, far out near the edge of the continental shelf, naturally gets a whole lot less pressure. It's hard to tell if this spot is a natural feature or a wreck, but it comes up a good 50' from the surrounding 275' of water. Here, sea bass will be joined by more exotic species like sand and blue-line tilefish.

NCO7 isn't a wreck but is an interesting dip in the 30 fathom line. When the pelagic bite is running hot just north of The Point (NCO10) on yellowfin, mahi-mahi or wahoo, and you know it will take some looking to find the fish, start off by trolling through this area. And if you head south, be sure to go over NCO8 at 35'37.782 x 74'53.635. This wreck comes up over 100', yet is surrounded by water over 180'. It's a good bet for king mackerel late in the year, which often run off the North Carolina coast into Christmastime and beyond. These kings are brutes, too, often so large that inexperienced anglers think they're wahoo at first.

NCO9, at 35'50.888 x 75'01.030, is another relatively deep wreck laying in 130' of water. Look to find big sea bass here early and late in the year, as they're migrating in and out of the deep water haunts.

NCO10 is the king of all hotspots in the Oregon Inlet area. Simply known as "The Point," it's the lone extreme feature along the edge of the Continental shelf in this area. The 30 fathom line shifts right up against the 100 fathom line, making for an incredible drop that confuses the currents. The Gulf Stream often pushes in close here, and creates awesome conditions for catching yellowfin tuna, mahi-mahi, wahoo, and white marlin. Blue marlin are usually pursued farther out in deeper water, but for most pelagics, this is the spot. The yellowfin can be caught all winter long (weather permitting) some years, if the Stream stays in close, and virtually every season they'll be taken in good numbers from March through June. Most of the early season yellowfin will be on the small side, averaging about 30 pounds, but 20-fish days will be commonplace at times. During the summer months they usually thin out, but are replaced by hordes of small to medium mahi-mahi. Often, these fish will be located under large mats of floating weeds. White marlin also move into the area in tremendous numbers some years, during the summer months. And in the fall the yellowfin tuna return, often with wahoo in the mix. Blackfin tunas also start showing up in this area, as do sailfish with more regularity. No longer do these fish make for a rare catch when you get this far south, although most seasons there won't be enough of either species around to dedicate your time solely to fishing for them. There's good reason for calling the waters around Hatteras and Diamond Shoals the Graveyard of the Atlantic. There are wrecks all over the place, some created during storms, some from hapless ships that ran

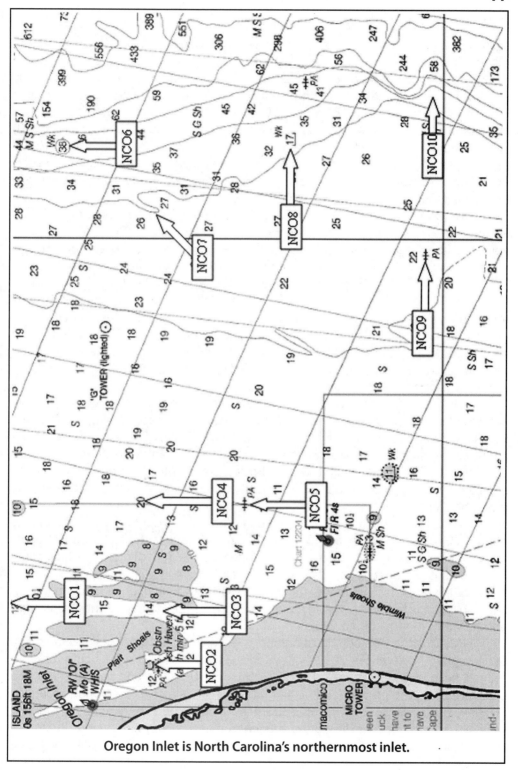

Oregon Inlet is North Carolina's northernmost inlet.

aground on the shoals, and many that were torpedoed by U-boats in World War II. All hold fish.

NCO11, known as AR-225, is one of the intentional wrecks. It's actually another boxcar reef, mixed in with chunks of concrete. You'll find it at 35'06.750 x 75'39.233. NCO12 (35'06.181 x 75'42.965, AR-230) is another artificial reef, this one made of a tug and a freighter, and NCO13 (35'08.100 x 75'40.755, AR-220) has more box cars as well as a scattering of concrete and reef balls. All three of these spots offer bottom fishing for sea bass, ocean panfish, and flounder, a short drive from the inlet. In rare years past, giant bluefin have made a winter cameo in the areas around these reefs, as well.

NCO14 is a little more interesting. You'll note it actually points to three different wrecks. The common name is the "Stink Wreck" or the "Stink Wrecks," and you may hear any of these three referred to in that manner, depending on who you're talking with. The original stinky one, however, is the farthest from the inlet, laying at 35'01.783 x 75'28.502, and its actual name is the *Empire Gem*. This was a 463' long tanker torpedoed in WWII, and got its name by virtue of the fact that you could smell the fuel leaking out decades later. Since it lies in fairly deep water (125' to 140') some of the more sought-after southern bottom species will be caught here: grouper and snapper are both distinct possibilities, as well as the usual sea bass. Amberjack also tend to frequent the wreck, and cobia may pop up during the spring, summer and fall months.

NCO15, off to the south of Ocracoke Inlet, marks AR-255. It's yet another combination of boxcars and other reef materials, in this case, rubble, bridge parts, and steel pyramids. You'll find it at 34'55.480 x 75'57.910. The usual inshore suspects will be caught here, and as you move farther and farther south, tropical species such as spadefish will be more and more prevalent. Same goes for NCO16, AR-250. This reef (at 34'56.680 x 75'55.100) also consists of boxcars, bridge parts, and rubble piles.

NCO17, however, was put in place purely by accident. This is the remains of the *Catherine Monohan,* a 185' wooden schooner lost in the distant past. Lucky for us, it was hauling bags of cement. The cement hardened into huge oval piles, as the ship itself rotted away. Laying in 100' at 34'56.900 x 75'42.879, you should head for this spot if you want to catch spadefish. For whatever reason, spadefish seem to love the cement pyramids, and will swarm over it in huge schools throughout the warm months of the year.

NCO18 marks a couple of hotspots that share the same basic vicinity. The 390' freighter *Proteus* lies in 120' of water at 34'45.918 x 75'47.010, and the area around here is generally called "The Rockpiles." On the bottom, you'll find sea bass, snapper, and grouper, and fishing higher in the water column often produces kingfish. There's also a chance of encountering tuna around here at any given time of year: yellowfin or blackfin during the warm months, and big bluefin during the cold months of the year. Of course, you'll also encounter fish like jacks and bar-

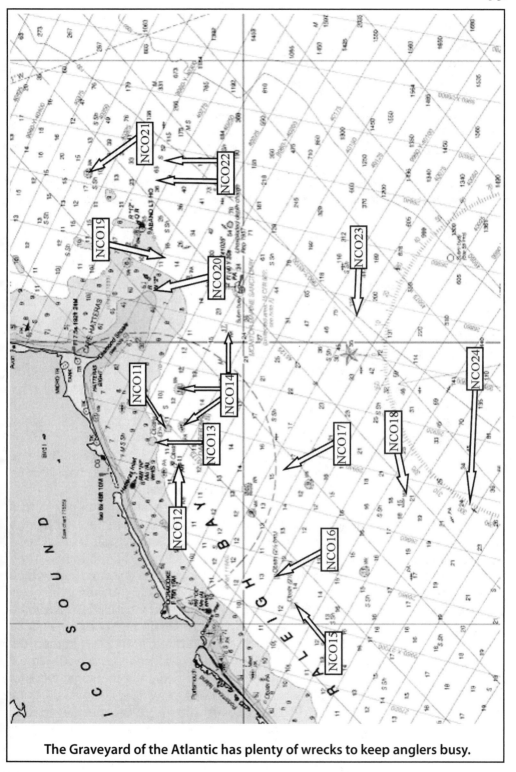

The Graveyard of the Atlantic has plenty of wrecks to keep anglers busy.

racuda fishing this far south in the Mid Atlantic.

NCO19, laying along the edges of Diamond Shoals, is the *Australia* wreck. This was a large 510' tanker which was torpedoed in WWII. After being sunk it was intentionally blown up and scattered, to prevent it from becoming a hazard to navigation. You'll find bits and pieces starting at 35'07.377 x 75'21.175. The wreckage is spread over a large area in depths varying from 85' to 110' so this is a good spot to drift fish, as opposed to anchoring. Trollers should also be interested in this area as it will produce king mackerel when they move inshore, and bluefish in large numbers. This also marks another spot where big bluefin have showed up during the winter months, but this is extremely hit or miss and it hasn't happened here for several years.

NCO20 marks the edges of Diamond Shoals. Don't think of this as a particular single spot, so much as a large area to be fished. All of the shoals edges and drops can produce good catches of fish: king and Spanish mackerel in the warm months and especially early in the fall; blues during spring, summer and fall; stripers in the winter (usually caught either trolling or drifting live eels or bunker); both black and red drum (usually on fresh cut bait fished on bottom) in the spring and again in the fall (September and October); and some summers even tarpon will make a showing here. It must be noted, however, that fishing the shoals is a dangerous proposition. They don't just shift from year to year, they shift from storm to storm and week to week. This is an area best approached with a healthy dose of caution, during good weather.

NCO21 (35'13.816 x 75'12.056) is another wreck that goes by several names, depending on who you ask. To some it's the Green Buoy Wreck, and to others, it's the *Empire Thrush.* In either case it comes up well off of the bottom, within 35' of the surface in water twice that deep, in some spots. Sea bass, ocean panfish, bluefish, and amberjack are the most common catches here.

NCO22 is another hotspot mark that indicates an area, as opposed to a specific wreck. There's an interesting feature in the ocean bottom here, where the depth drops from about 200' down to 350' then rises back up to 250' or so. This is a large area and any part of it can hold fish, but since it lies at the 50-fathom line and is close to the big drop, the mixing currents and confused waters in this area make it a prime zone to try trolling for pelagics. Yellowfin tuna and then marlin during the spring months, mahi-mahi and wahoo when the water heats up—even sailfish, many years—and then tunas again in the fall. This area also sees blue marlin some seasons, although the majority of blues taken in this area will come from deeper waters. NCO23 also marks a general area as opposed to a specific wreck, in this case, the 100-fathom line. Offshore trollers in search of the same types of gamefish as those found at NCO22 may find success anywhere off the coast, once reaching the general vicinity of this drop. Anglers targeting blue marlin in specific should mind it as their minimum run most seasons, and going well beyond the 100-fathom line is common when pursuing these billfish.

NCO24 marks the last wreck we'll visit in this zone. It's another with a name that changes depending on the source of your information. It's either the *Manuela* or the *Malcace.* (The charts show several other wrecks in close proximity, so it's easy to see how the names could get confused.) In either case, if you go to 34'40.615 x 75'47.135 you'll discover large debris fields in 140' to 160' of water. This is the wreck to head for if you intend to target grouper or big red snapper, and you'll pick up plenty of sea bass here as well.

The waters around Cape Lookout also have a number of artificial reef sites. The nearest to the inlet is NCO25, the Atlantic Beach Reef AR-315, at 34'40.330 x 76'44.665. This is quite a reef, and includes a huge amount of concrete rubble, reef balls, a tug, a sportfishing boat, a trawler, several airplanes, and a 440' Liberty ship. The spot is prime for drift fishing since the structure covers such a large area, and will produce sea bass, flounder, blues, and all sorts of oceanic panfish. NCO26 actually marks four separate reefs, including AR-330 (34'33.634 x 76'51.267), AR-340 (34'34.350 x 76'58.300), AR-342 (34'36.552 x 77'02.189), and AR-345 (34'32.300 x 76'58.467). These reefs are all a combination of tires, reef balls, concrete rubble, train cars, and a few other oddities, including a dozen boat molds from Hatteras Yachts (at AR-340). All of these reefs are close to home and present good opportunities for days when the weather prevents long runs. NCO27, the New River Reef at 34'21.183 x 77'20.000, is very similar in nature, with 20 train cars, bridge rubble and a ferro-cement boat. It's far enough down the coast, however, that it provides that close-to-home security to boats running through the New River inlet. NCO28, however, wasn't put in place on purpose—this is another wreck from the WWII era, a 450' tanker called the *WE Hutton* which was torpedoed at 34'29.990 x 76'53.879. The wreckage is scattered and the ship is broken up, so drifting the area is a good tactic.

NCO29, at 33'57.938 x 72'01.829, is a 400' cargo ship called the *Cassimer.* This wreck, laying in 115' of water, is a good one to try bottom fishing for snapper and grouper. This one's also far enough from shore that it doesn't get pressured like many of the other wrecks and reefs accessible from Morehead City and Beaufort, so the size of the fish you catch is likely to be pleasing.

The George Summerlin Reef at NCO30, AR-285, sits in 65' of water at 34'33.380 x 76'26.350. This site consists of reef balls, concrete, and the 130' fishing boat *Nancy Lee.* You might want to consider fishing here on a south-west wind, when it may be a bit more sheltered than other reefs off the beach.

Like Diamond Shoals, there's some great fishing to be done along the Cape Lookout shoals, marked by NCO31. And similarly, the sands and bars here are constantly shifting—the same element of danger exists. That said, you'll find blues, flounder, Spanish and king mackerel here through most of the warm months. Croaker also flourish near the shoals, and in the spring and fall, decent runs of redfish often develop. In the deeper waters surrounding the shoals, weakfish may also stage some seasons and can be caught on jigging spoons or squid baited top and bottom rigs.

NCO32 marks Hardie's Reef, AR-300 (34'18.500 x 76'24.545). This is a pretty popular spot, which lies in 90' of water and carries the possibility of grouper catches as well as large numbers of sea bass. If you'd rather focus on king and Spanish mackerel, shift over to the 10 fathom finger and 10 fathom lump at NCO33. Here, 55' water is surrounded by 70' to 80'. Look for this spot to produce best on a strong flowing current, and try trolling spoons on planers back and forth across the edges of the finger and hump.

The wreck of the *Papoose,* NCO34, another tanker torpedoed in WWII, lies at 34'08.633 x 76'39.155. The 410' long ship produces grouper, sea bass and snapper, as well as kingfish and often bluefish. If grouper is your main target, however, you may want to push even farther out to the *Naeco* (NCO35, at 34'01.520 x 76'38.878) a 430' trawler which also fell victim to a U-boat during the war. This wreck lies in 135' of water and is another that's far enough offshore that is doesn't get pounded by multiple anglers on a daily basis.

Up along the coast NCO36 lies just spitting distance from the beach and only two miles from Drum Inlet, at 34'50.095 x 76'16.880. It's an eclectic mix of concrete, boats and reef balls, set in 55' of water. Small boats running from Drum will want to utilize this one, when the weather makes longer runs tough going .

The *Tamaulipas,* NCO37, is a 450' freighter that was sunk in 150' of water. This is another good bet for grouper and snapper hunters. It lies at 34'32.800 x 76'00.830 and is off the chart shown in this book. Another ship to hit the bottom thanks to German U-boat torpedoes was at NCO38, the tanker *Atlas.* This 446' long ship holds unusually good numbers of sea bass, spadefish and cobia, and is fairly popular among area bottom fishermen. You'll find it at 34'31.689 x 76'14.500. The *Yancy,* a 459' transport ship that was sent to the bottom on purpose to enhance AR-302, the concrete pipe and rubble reef marked by NCO39, is another spot that's popular with local anglers. It lies at 34'10.265 x 76'13.703 in 160' of water and holds good numbers of grouper and sea bass, and I've even seen conger eels in the 6' range come up on the end of my line here.

NCO40 marks one of the best-known bluewater hotspots on the North Carolina coast, the Big Rock. There isn't one specific spot to be identified with GPS coordinates here; rather, this entire area is productive, right along the 100-fathom line. You'll certainly note some unusual returns on the fishfinder, but not one specific "rock." Plan on trolling this area in the spring for tuna, billfish, wahoo, and mahi-mahi. You'll catch both black and yellowfin tuna, but as you get this far south the yellowfin start to become more sparse and the blackfin more popular. Bottom fish off the edge here, and you'll encounter an interesting array of monster grouper, snappers, and tilefish. During the heat of summer the pelagics thin out a bit, with mostly mahi-mahi and wahoo sticking around under weed patties. Then in the fall, all of those pelagics will kick it into high gear again. Depending on the weather, the fall run here may last well into the winter with good fishing up until Christmas. If,

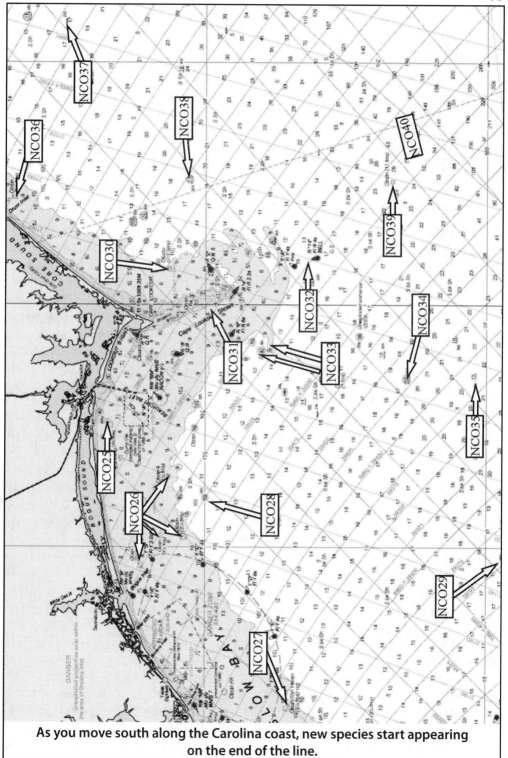

As you move south along the Carolina coast, new species start appearing
on the end of the line.

that is, the winter winds allow you to get out.

Just off the mouth of the Cape Fear River there's a pile of artificial reefs that are made up of everything from boats to barges to bridge parts to (seriously) a couple of old sewage tanks. These reefs are close to one another—they all could certainly be fished in a single day—and will hold the standard types of southern ground-fish. One interesting note: this far south, you'll start to see a lot more immature grouper on inshore reefs like these. Instead of addressing each on its own we'll consider AR-420, 425, 440, 445, 455 and 460 as a group. They are marked by NCO41, and lie at: 33'51.100 x 78'06.750; 33'53.010 x 76'06.600; 33'49.800 x 78'13.100; 33'44.785 x 78'14.125; 33'47.033 x 78'17.880; 33'50.215 x 78'22.033.

NCO42, on the far side of Frying Pan Shoal, marks AR-378, at 34'01.807 x 77'52.232. This is not any different from the other artificially planted reefs in the area but should be noted since it has some rather large fish-attracting objects sitting on the bottom: several barges up to nearly 200' as well as over 100,000 tires. Slightly deeper at 33'58.585 x 77'41.285, AR-382 (NCO43) lies in 60' of water, and will produce better fishing most of the time. Spadefish and small grouper are common here, but (as with many near-shore reefs) the larger grouper seem to be either smarter or even deeper offshore. So, you might want to head for AR-386 (NCO44), which is another seven or eight miles off the beach and lies in 80' of water. This is another "boxcar" site but it also has two huge dredges (215' and 320') plus a barge. The structure and the depth conspire to make this a good area to try live-baiting or trolling for king mackerel, as well as bottom fishing.

NCO45 marks the shoals, in general. As with Diamond and Cape Lookout shoals, these areas can be dangerous but are also incredibly productive. Redfish can be baited from around the edges of the shoals, and bluefish and Spanish mackerel will wander the drop-offs most of the season. Cast up into the shallower areas or drift along the edges with live minnow and/or squid and you'll locate plenty of flounder. And species most Mid Atlantic residents would call exotics—like tarpon and pompano—pop up seasonally. The warm water and relative proximity to deep water also mean that mahi-mahi wander this close in from time to time, and any time you see flotsam on the surface, check it out. There will also be a good chance of encountering triggerfish when you do so.

NCO46 marks the Frying Pan Shoal Light Tower, which most people would agree is one heck of a fish-attractor. Bottom fish, kings, you name it—the structure below the water's surface is incredible. Of course, as a well-known hotspot, it also receives a lot of pressure. If you're fishing for grouper, in particular, you may find numbers here but better sizes elsewhere.

NCO47 is a general area along the 100-fathom line known as the "2710 line." The specific coordinates for it really aren't important, as it denotes an area, not a particular spot, but 33'16.055 x 77'07.840 will put you in the correct territory. Like the Big Rock (some people call this the 2710 Rock) this is a good zone for offshore pelagic trolling. Billfish including sailfish, mahi-mahi, blackfin tuna, and

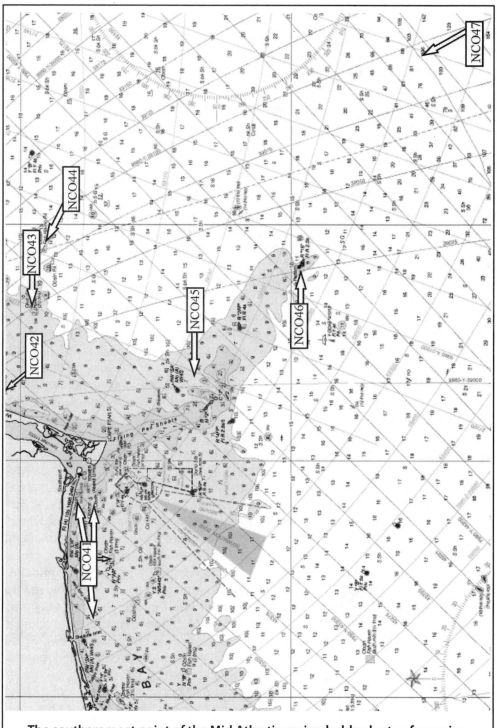

The southernmost point of the Mid Atlantic region holds plenty of promise, whether you're after bottom fish or pelagics.

wahoo will all come to the hook out here. Note that if you can find a nice edge or deep-water structure, deep-dropping in this area will produce much larger bottom fish than most of the inshore wrecks and reefs.

North Carolina Inlet & Coastal Bay Hotspots

Although NCB1 points to a hotspot just off the chart, this place is very easy to find: the Mann's Harbor bridge, which connects Roanoke Island to the mainland. The bridge is an important spot to note for winter angling, when stripers invade the Carolinas and offer hot cold-weather fishing. From late November through the winter, you can usually score on schoolie stripers with some larger fish mixed in by casting bucktails or jigs at the bridge pilings. Slow-trolling swimming plugs such as Rapalas and Rat-L-Traps along the pilings is another winning technique.

NCB2 marks the channel running from the inlet to the town of Wanchese. During the warm months of the year speckled trout can be taken all along the edges of this channel, by casting 4" or 5" plastic grubs, floating/diving plugs, or bucktails trimmed with shrimp or crab. Cast back over the shallows and grassbeds during high tides, and into the channel itself during ebbing or low tides. Bounce jigs or minnow along the bottom of the channel to catch flounder, as well. NCB3 marks a finger of deeper water which will produce specks during low tides and often redfish as well. Some years, however, fishing for these species in this area will be next to impossible because it will be choked with croaker. When this happens, stick with artificial lures and leave the bait at home.

NCB4, Duck Island, is an excellent area to try casting for speckled trout and redfish. Toss 4" soft plastic jigs, Mir-O-Lures (try the red head/white body combination) bucktails, and shrimp tail jigs. Note that there's a lot of very shallow water with grassbeds through here. Serious anglers will approach it in a similar fashion as Gulf Coast shallow water anglers after the same fish. Maneuver the boat with an electric motor once you're in the shallows, and cast to potholes in the weeds and flats. If you see puffs of mud cast to them—there's a fair chance the mud has been stirred up by drum rooting around on the bottom.

Old House Channel and the Oregon Inlet channel meet at NCB5, and create some unusually deep holes for the bayside in this area. Reds will move into these occasionally during low tides and flounder will regularly, but you may also run into weakfish here from the late spring through the fall. You'll also encounter sheepshead in some of the deep areas. The same is true of Davis Channel, which drops down to 20' and is marked by NCB6. You'll also have excellent flounder action along the southern edge, which has a very steep drop-off.

In Oregon Inlet itself, there is some astonishingly good fishing. We haven't scoped out many specific surf spots on prior charts, because, as mentioned earlier, they tend to change quite often as the beach shifts and bars or holes appear and disappear. But from year to year, the northern point of Oregon Inlet provides some

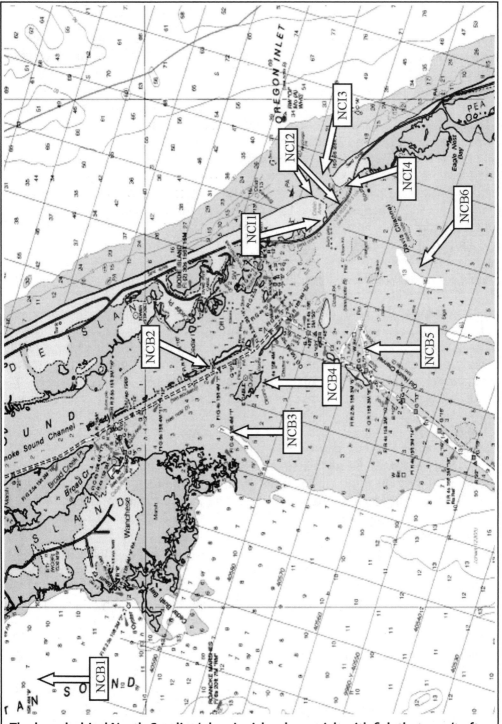

The bays behind North Carolina's barrier islands are rich with fish that aren't often seen in northern areas of the Mid Atlantic, like speckled trout and redfish.

of the best surf action on the entire Atlantic coast. Just about every month of the year, something will be biting here. The spot marked by NCI1 is commonly called "the pond," and it's a salt pond that is regularly formed, fills in, then is re-formed again. Sometimes when you visit the pond you can wade all the way across, other times it's much too deep. You can't count on it being there any given year, but after a big storm it can suddenly re-appear again at any moment. If you happen to be in this area and the pond is open, by all means, fish in it. Commonly it will swarm with horse croaker, spike trout (weakfish between 12" and 20") puppy drum of the same size, flounder, and snapper blues.

The bridge over Oregon Inlet and the outside of the point, the two spots marked by NCI2, support several fisheries depending on what season it is. In the winter months you're likely to catch stripers in both spots. Then in the spring, usually starting in April and running through May or early June, there's a run or redfish here. These aren't puppies—they're bulls and can range well over 40 or 50 pounds. Flounder can also be taken throughout the warm months here, and some seasons black drum also stage a run through the inlet. On rare occasions, cobia have even clustered around the point and/or the pilings in good numbers. You're more likely to find them just beyond the breakers around NCI3, where you'll also catch large winter-run stripers on eels and bunker chunks or by trolling. Note that the specific spots you'll catch the stripers on the outside of this inlet will change as the shoals shift, and remember to be extremely careful here. Grounding on the shoals can be deadly, as the waves will pound your boat to pieces.

NCI4 marks a notch between the south side of the inlet and the bridge. A small channel runs in here and this is another excellent place to try for flounder during the late spring, summer and fall.

Inside Cape Hatteras, there's some awesome fishing to be done. The deeper waters of the bay in the vicinity of NCB7 teem with snapper blues much of the summer. You'll also pick up good numbers of Spanish mackerel some seasons, though others they tend to remain outside the inlet. To catch both, troll spoons just below the surface or watch for flocks of diving gulls.

In closer to shore at NCB8, there's a finger of deep water with shallows around it. Jig in the deepest areas, which go just over 20', to catch weakfish and croaker from spring through fall. Some summers, tarpon will make a showing here in one of the northernmost areas they appear with any regularity. You'll also encounter flounder along the edges of the hole in times of high tide, and right in the middle during ebb tides. The near-by channel marked by NCB9 is a better bet for flounder anglers. Drift minnow, minnow/squid combos or bucktails tipped with minnow or cut fish, right on bottom. Casting out into the shallower water to either side may produce speckled trout or at times, puppy drum. You'll also catch drum by fishing the edges of the shoal water at NCB10.

For a change of pace, try fishing with a top and bottom rig baited with bits of shrimp at the artificial reefs marked by NCB11. It's hard to get a hook into them, but

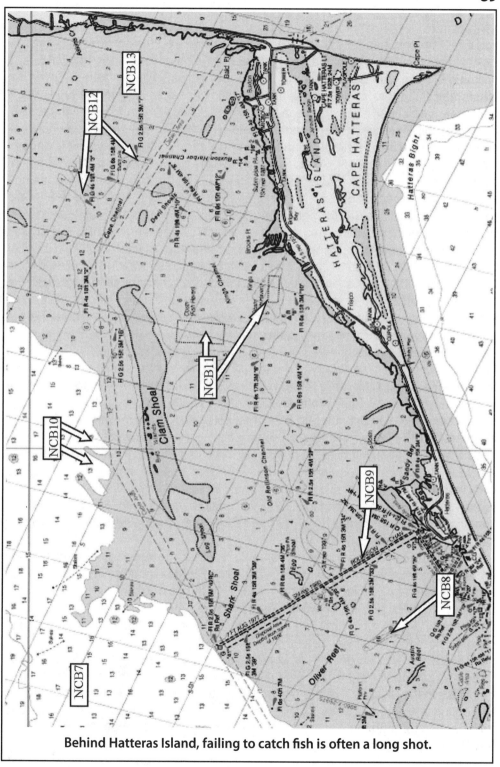

Behind Hatteras Island, failing to catch fish is often a long shot.

you'll find sheepshead here, if the croaker aren't so thick they eat your baits off.

The deep fingers of water at NCB12 are similar to the one at NCB8, and produce similar results: weakfish in the deeper holes, croaker often all over the place, and flounder on the edges. In the shallower water around the holes you'll catch both redfish and speckled sea trout. If you really want to focus on these fish, however, shift over to the weedbeds around NCB13. From here heading north all along the bayside of Hatteras Island, specs will feed in the weed. Savvy anglers will cast sub-surface plugs or light jigs with twister tails (a 4" chartreuse/pumpkin-seed combo is a killer) for these fish. Concentrate on the edges of the weeds and potholes. Old-timers know to employ a different tactic, of trolling light gear while rowing their boat. The erratic motion produced by rowing is often just what it takes to get the speckled trout to strike. Reds can also be taken from the weedbeds, through sometimes it's tougher to get them to hit lures. Cut fresh mullet, live finger mullet, or chunks of peeler crab fished on the bottom in potholes usually do the trick. Anglers stuck on casting artificials will find that scent-enhanced plastics, like Berkley Gulps (try the green shrimp in clear water, and rootbeer-colored shrimp when turbidity is up) and Mister Twister Exudes (the whites with a lime tail are a good choice), often produce the best results.

Surf anglers will want to fish out in front of the lighthouse. Although the beach doesn't look particularly spectacular here, for some reason speckled trout frequent the surf in this area. Sea mullet, pompano, and croaker are also commonly pulled from the suds in the shadow of the lighthouse.

Before moving south, one final note: There will be days when strong winds keep you off the water, or storms the day before have the water so riled up it's impossible to fish. If you need to pull a rabbit out of your hat, try wading the ponds on Cape Hatteras. The one on the left as you head into the state park has a good population of 2- to 5-pound largemouth bass, which willingly hit spinnerbaits most of the time. From the road, wade along the bank to your left and look for the deep spot right up against the shore, overhung by trees. Sometimes you can pull a dozen bucketmouths out of it.

Inside of Hatteras Inlet, at NCB14, a finger of deep water reaches from the inlet up into the bay. This is a great area to target weakfish, and as is often the case, the best way to go after them is by jigging along the bottom. The same is true at NCB15. NCB16, however, marks a spot where you'll want to try casting for speckled trout in the shallows. Particularly during April and May, then again in October or November most seasons, this will be a productive zone.

NCI5 marks an entirely different type of spot. This is an excellent place to target large stripers late in the year. From November through February you can catch fish in the 30" to 45" range by anchoring just inside the breakers, and tossing live eels into the rough water. The fish feeding here will be extremely sensitive to the tide, and through most of the cycle you'll catch nothing but spiny dogfish. Then, about an hour before the peak of the tide the stripers will turn on.

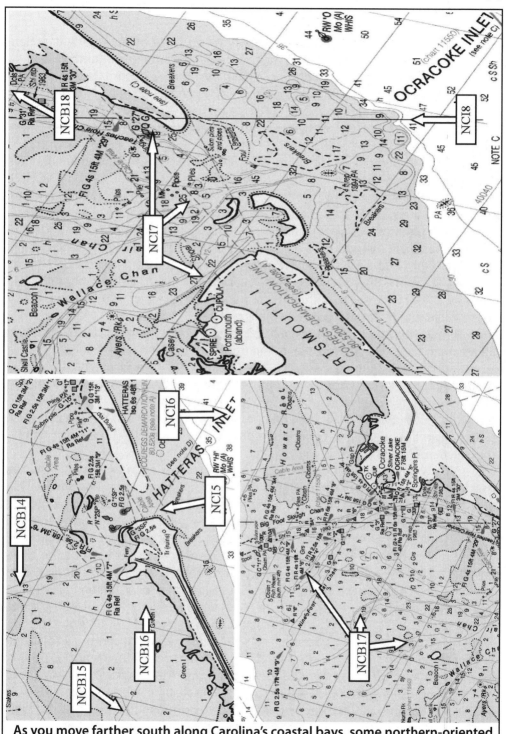

As you move farther south along Carolina's coastal bays, some northern-oriented fish begin to thin out, but exotics like tarpon become more and more common.

The area around NCl6 is also noteworthy because of its wintertime action. Some seasons giant bluefin tuna will move in here (occasionally within a mile or so of the beach) and rip through schools of bunker. When this occurs they can be targeted by either chunking bunker or by trolling horse ballyhoo. Usually it's an early bite, and during the seasons when they show up here the fish may be hot one day and gone the next—but it's worth some serious effort and travel time to feel one of these fish on the end of the line.

Inside of Ocracoke inlet, there is a series of much better defined channels which lead into the bay. Three of these are marked by NCB17, and by NCB18. Perhaps because of the deep channels, cobia will enter this inlet more readily than some of the others along the coast. Most often during June and July, they can be sighted on the surface or chummed with ground menhaden. If sighted up top you may be able to get them to take a jig or bucktail but more often, it will take a live bait to get them into eating mode. Tarpon will also occasionally make their way into these channels (try casting live shrimp or finger mullet with no weight or on jig heads, or toss D.O.A. artificial shrimp), and anywhere the water drops down below 15' you have a fair shot at locating weakfish.

Where the deep channels split off from the inlet itself, at NCl7, the best cobia fishing takes place. You'll also find good numbers of large flatfish at these spots, especially up along the edges of the channels. Early and late in the season, both red and black drum can be caught here as well. Well outside of the inlet at NCl8, however, the main catch will be Spanish mackerel and bluefish. This is also far enough south that kingfish may be encountered anywhere in the area. Trolling up and down the beach just beyond the drop to the 40' zone with spoons can be productive any time from April through late fall.

The waters inside Cape Lookout are quite confusing, and I wouldn't advise anyone to attempt to fish here without getting some local knowledge first. That said, there are several spots tucked behind the sand dunes that offer great potential. The first marked here, NCl9, marks the relatively deep water running into the bay. Cast bait and jigs along the edges of the drop-off for red drum in the spring or fall, and drift the edges for flounder through the season. Down towards the cape itself, the edges of the point at NCl10 have extremely deep drop-offs running right up to the beach. Drifting the edges here will produce flounder, red drum, and sometimes weakfish. Whenever you fish here, keep a close eye on the water's surface because you could spot a cobia at just about any time from May through October. Bluefish will often chew up baitfish in this area, too. If you're more interested in chasing speckled trout, move over to NCl11. If you have a shallow draft boat you can poke up into the creek mouths running through the small islands here, and intercept specs as they hunt for baitfish and critters being washed through the cuts at the very beginning of an outgoing tide. You'll find reds in these areas as well. NCl12, where the channel cuts through and runs into the bay, is another good bet for flounder anglers.

The areas around Morehead City and Beaufort are not only rich in history, they're rich in fish.

NCI13 marks a small rock jetty in Beaufort Inlet. It gets a lot of pressure since it's easily spotted and it's a good bet that if you hit it more than a few minutes after sunrise, it's already been fished by someone else. Even so, you'll often take Spanish mackerel and bluefish in the rip created as the current washes against the rocks. You'll also find Spanish Mackerel, blues, and the occasional small king-fish in the area of NCI14. In the fall when false albacore run through the area they usually stay a little farther out but sometimes will swarm in around NCI14 in tightly-packed hordes, to the delight of catch-and-release anglers looking for a good fight on light tackle.

The edges of the shoals at NCI15 are also rich in Spanish mackerel along with bluefish and a few kings. This is another spot you'll want to carry live baits to, in case of a cobia spotting. During the spring and fall when the cobia migrate through, spot-check each of the channel markers running out into the ocean. Of-ten, a fish or two will hide under the marks while waiting for a meal—hopefully, one with your hook in it.

NCB19 marks the sea wall at the port terminal, where you'll usually see barges or cargo ships tied up. The area is well lighted and during the warm months of the year, weakfish will move into the area at night to feed around the lightlines. During daylight, drifting baits along the bottom here sometimes produces flounder in the 5 pound and up range. And occasionally, black drum also stage in this area and can be caught on chunks of peeler or soft crab, or shucked clams. Of course, you have to be aware of the commercial traffic at all times, and stay out of its way.

All of the deep channels marked by NCB20 and NCB21 have good floun-der fishing most seasons, and when you find the holes you'll also find the weakfish. Take particular note of the bridge at NCB21, which is a great area to try for weak-fish at night. You'll also find speckled trout by moving out of the channels and into the shallows, throughout the area. If you really want to concentrate on these fish, however, shuffle over towards NCB22. This area, known as the Middle Marshes, has countless cuts and channels that specs will move up into on high tides. This is another fishery you'll need the shallow draft boat to access, but if you move up to the mouths of these cuts, particularly when the high peaks and just starts flowing out, you have an excellent shot at loading the cooler. Try casting (light) tandem bucktail rigs, 4" twister tails (white, chartreuse, and sometimes pinks are the kill-ers) and swimming plugs. Many seasons you'll pick up good numbers of puppy drum, in the same locations.

Heading south from Morehead, there are several different inlets, barrier islands and back-bays. They're changing constantly, and since the inlets in this stretch aren't as major as those to the north and those to the south they aren't maintained as well. People shouldn't dare to run these waters without some cur-rent local insight. The territory is all fairly similar, including Bogue, Bear, New River, and the Topsail inlets. Attack these areas with the same tactics: look for redfish,

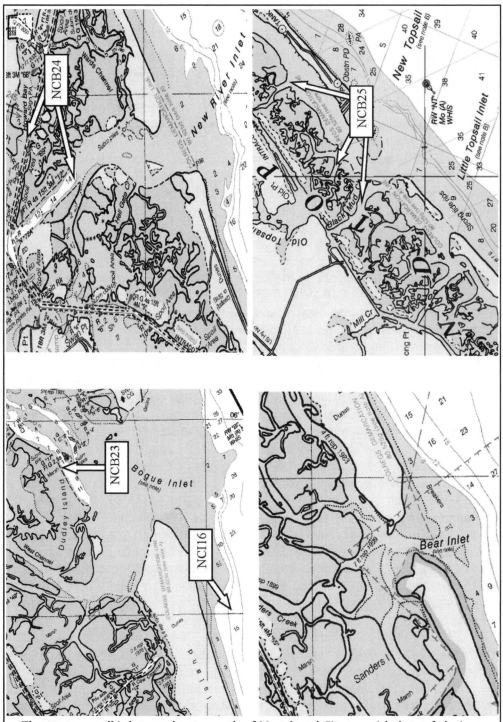

The many small inlets and cuts south of Morehead City provide lots of choices
to anglers of all stripes.

bluefish, flounder, and Spanish mackerel in and around the inlets waters. In the bays, look for flounder along the channel edges, specks and reds in the shallows and among the weedbeds, and weakfish and croaker in the holes.

NCB23 marks one such hole; try fishing cut bait or jigs on bottom. At NCI16, there's a nicer than usual drop just off the beach which forms an indentation in the contour lines. This is a good area to fish for blues and Spanish mackerel, and kings (usually small ones) will move in here following shoals of bait from time to time.

NCB24 points out some deep water channels inside of New River Inlet, which offers more opportunity to catch weakfish, croaker, flounder and snapper blues. Inside of both Topsail Inlets, the myriad of marsh creeks, cuts, and islands marked by NCB25 creates prime speckled trout and redfish waters. Fish here as you would to the north, by casting to cut mouths and current rips with jigs or buck-tails trimmed with minnow or squid strips.

Wrightsville Beach and the Masonboro Inlet have the same type of oppor-tunities as those found slightly to the north, but with an added twist: at this point along the coast, the speckled trout often seem to either begin to over-winter, or at least hesitate on their journey down the coast. The ecology of this may be in doubt, but the results are not—some seasons, you can catch specks both in the sound and from the beach right up to Christmas. Warm snaps may bring the fish back into feeding mode (or back into the area) and at any given point in the winter it's pos-sible to find specs here, when the conditions cooperate. The same goes for redfish although to a lesser degree; their presence in the colder months is more hit-or-miss from season to season. Black drum also stage a decent run at Wrightsville many seasons, usually in April and again in November or early December.

The Cape Fear River can lay claim to the southernmost striper run of any significance. In the river itself striper fishing is often good, and during the late fall and winter months into early spring you'll find them around the deep water at NCB26. Try jigging bucktails, or trolling plugs along the channel edges. You may also encounter them in the deep water fingers at NCB27, which (although they don't appear on the chart here) dip down below 20' in a couple of spots. This is also a good area to jig for weakfish. But it's best known as a black drum spot. Early in the spring, some seasons as soon as mid-March, blacks move through this area and can be caught on fishfinder rigs baited with crab chunks, finger mullet, or shrimp. Most seasons they disappear during the heat of summer, then reappear in the area during October or November for a fall run.

NCB28 marks a good area to try casting light tackle for specs and reds. Where the creeks converge there are often small rips. And the calmer, surrounding areas often support weeds which will also attract these species.

NCI17, at the mouth of the Cape Fear Inlet, denotes another good deep water area to sink cut baits for both types of drum, as well as flounder in the spring and fall. Trolling through the zone will produce Spanish mackerel during the warm months and stripers during the cold months. Tarpon will occasionally show up here

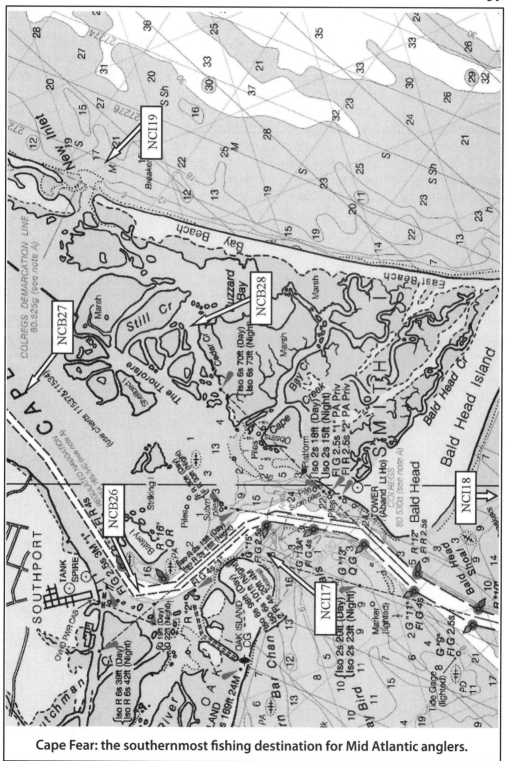

Cape Fear: the southernmost fishing destination for Mid Atlantic anglers.

as well. NCI18, however, marks an area where tarpon are more likely to stage. They may appear just off the beach here during mid to late summer, and remain through September. The shoals and drops outside of New Inlet at NCI19 may also see some tarpon, but are better thought of as another place to intercept black and red drum during the spring and fall runs. Although it's off the chart, two miles north of the inlet there's a shallow rocky area called Sheephead Rock, in about 10' surrounded by 20' to 25' (you'll be able to spot it on any decent chart; 33'56.353 x 77'54.830 will put you in the zone). This is a good place to fish for (surprise!) sheephead, as well as flounder and sometimes red drum. Troll the edges from spring through fall, and you'll also find bluefish and Spanish mackerel here, along with kingfish at times.

PART II
Saltwater Gamefish of the Mid Atlantic

Every species along the Mid Atlantic coast fills a specific niche. Each has its own unique ways of acting, feeding, and migrating. Naturally, these variables will determine which way to best target the specific species you're trying to catch. While each and every fish that lives in the ocean isn't covered in these pages—that would be nearly impossible—all of the major sportfish harvested on a recreational basis are examined in detail. Ready to catch more of them? Here's the scoop on each different type and how to best attack them, both inshore and offshore.

CHAPTER 4
Black Drum

Pound for pound they may not be the world's greatest fighters, but what black drum lack in will they make up for in brute strength. These fish can grow quite large and the world record, caught in Delaware, hit 113 pounds, 1 ounce. Many of the blacks caught along the coastal bays and inlets hit the 50-pound mark, and these fish offer a big-game opportunity to anglers with boats too small for the offshore run. From New Jersey south blacks are more or less common, but on occasion they will be caught in waters farther to the north. Drum aren't fish that are caught here and there by accident very often. Since they move around in tight pods or at times in large schools, often around localized structure, drum are usually caught by anglers specifically targeting them when they are known to be in the area.

Their reputation as poor eating fair is a little overemphasized, but since it has surely accounted for a lot of released fish, is a good thing. If you keep and fillet a black you'll usually find worms in the meat, particularly near the tail end. They are quite obvious and large, so they are easily cut out of the fillets, and in any case won't survive in humans. But, they are a bit of a gross-out for a lot of folks.

Another black drum trait that is overemphasized is their poor eyesight. Many anglers believe that blacks hardly use sight at all, and it is true that they have unusually well developed senses of smell and vibration detection. However, studies by marine biologists in Florida have proven that, at least down south, black drum do use their sight extensively when feeding.

Soft and peeler crab, or in some northern areas shucked sea clams, are usually accepted as the best black drum baits. Regardless of the specific bait you choose, black drum are notorious for grabbing and spitting the hook. They have sensitive mouths and if they feel tension or excessive weight on the line, are said to drop it immediately. For this reason, most folks fishing for black drum use a fishfinder rig. Despite this fact, it's interesting to note that some CBBT anglers regularly catch black drum near the rock islands at the mouth of the Chesapeake Bay on spoons.

Conventional gear in the 30- to 40-pound class range is appropriate when targeting black drum, but oversized spinning gear rigged with superline will also do the trick. Most of the blacks caught along the coast come from near the inlet rock jetties, wrecks close to shore, and from bridge pilings close to or inside of inlets. Usually they'll be in water shallower than 50', and often the action comes in just 15' to 25' of water. Black drum are easy to spot on fishfinders since they provide such a huge target relative to water depth. Even in 20' of water, on your fishfinder a school of drum appears to take up half of the water column. On quality color units they appear as huge red triangles, sometimes just off and sometimes attached to the bottom. Want to target big blacks? Here are 10 tips that'll make you a more

The mighty black drum can top 100 pounds and is one of our largest inshore targets.

effective drummer.

1. When you feel a solid hit, don't give the fish a terribly long time to eat. A three count is plenty and a five-count is simply too long. Let the fish play with the bait for that much time and there's a fair chance it will feel tension or weight on the line at some point, and spit the hook.

2. These fish like a big meal. To make a single drum bait, cut a soft or peeler crab down the middle and use the entire half-crab. Fishing clams? Thread several big, gooey ones onto your hook.

3. Always net a black drum, never gaff it. These big fish have very thick, strong scales which are the size of a quarter. They're thicker and tougher than your thumb nail. Gaff shots will sometimes bounce right off of them. Meanwhile, their slow-but-steady method of swimming and fighting makes them an ideal fish to net. Note, though, that you need a really large net—a standard hoop won't cut the mustard, and a 3-footer is the minimum diameter net you want onboard. You're on a friend's boat, and his net isn't big enough? Go to the gaff, but carefully target the soft meat in the middle of the fish's lower jaw. There's no gaff onboard, either? Get the biggest spoon or bucktail in your tacklebox and duct-tape it to a scrub brush handle.

4. Along the coasts, bridge pilings account for a lot of black drum. When you think blacks are in the area, approach pilings from the up-current side, and drop anchor so your boat comes to rest 50' to 60' away. Use the lightest weight possible to drift baits back to the piling, close to the base.

5. Use a thick shock leader when drum fishing, made from a hard monofilament. Since you'll usually go after these fish around piles, rocks and wrecks, there's a good chance the fish will drag the line against an abrasion at some point during the fight.

6. Drum will usually be caught at or near the bottom, but occasionally you may spot one lazing near the surface. If this happens, toss a whole soft crab rigged without any weight in front of the fish, and let it slowly free-fall.

7. Keep a jigging rod or a spinner with a Trout Scout handy when you go drum fishing. After you catch some black drum work the area for trout and stripers. You'll often find these species playing clean-up behind the drum.

8. Drum can move large distances in short time periods. One day they can be in spot A and the next be in spot B, 10 or 20 miles away. If you return to a place that proved hot the day before, but you see absolutely nothing, don't hesitate to expand your search area to other near-by bridges, wrecks and inlets.

9. Remember drum's enhanced ability to smell. Make sure your hands are clean, free of fuel or other contaminants, and treat your baits with care. Keep them in the cooler until used, and never leave them in direct sunlight. It's not a bad idea to wash your hands in saltwater before handling baits.

10. Surf fishing for drum can be productive, mostly at the North Carolina inlets but occasionally farther north, as well. When surf casting and drum are in the area, be sure your reel is in freespool or the drag is exceptionally loose, before dropping your rod into a holder. The brute strength these fish possess is more than enough to rip a sand spike right out of the beach.

CHAPTER 5
Bluefish

Blues are about as vicious a fish as you'll find on the Atlantic seaboard—they will continue to slash through schools of bait even after they have eaten so much that they're constantly regurgitating shredded baitfish. Of more interest to anglers, blues fight with the same violence and vigor that they feed with. They provide spectacular jumps, and don't tire until they've fought to a near-death state. They also are dangerous—let a 10-pounder get to close to a finger or a toe and you'll have a very nasty cut to deal with, thanks to the bluefish's razor-sharp teeth.

Bluefish are known by several different names, according to their size. Small fish up to a pound are called snappers; these make good live baits for shark, tuna and billfish, and small ones (or strips of their belly meat) are good flounder bait. They can be caught in coastal bays and inlets in large numbers, usually by chumming menhaden. From 1 to 3 pounds, blues are commonly called tailors. These fish are also available in large numbers in both bays and inlets, and can be caught off the beach quite often. Large 15-pound or better blues are known as choppers. Choppers are caught in good numbers near inshore wrecks, lumps and other structure up and down the coast. In fact, in some years they are so numerous as to become a nuisance fish to inshore tuna anglers. Chunking for tuna during the summer months at inshore lumps like the Jackspot, 24 miles from Ocean City, Maryland, an angler can lose dozens of hooks in a single day to bluefish bite-offs. The common way to end bite-offs is to go to a wire leader, but this discourages the tuna from biting. Thus, most anglers who fish the inshore lumps for tuna need to come prepared with a fresh box of hooks (chunkers) or a full cooler of rigged ballyhoo (trollers) or they may run out of gear. On the other hand, anglers targeting these fish can enjoy hours of constant action, and often, will be able to watch the bluefish attack chunk baits within a few feet of the transom after teasing them in close with butterfish bits.

The spring appearance of blues, ranging from April to June depending on your exact location and the weather patterns each spring, also is a harbinger of the shark migration up the coast. Look for blues to follow shortly behind Atlantic mackerel, and for mako, blue, and thresher shark to follow closely behind the bluefish. There's also a yearly fall run of large blues in the surf. (There used to be a reliable spring run as well, but in the past decade it has deteriorated to a scattering of fish.) The fall run can start as early as September in northern areas, and usually peaks off the Carolina Outer Banks some time around Halloween.

Bluefish are unusual in that they are found nearly worldwide. They grow to be 20 to 30 pounds, and the world record, caught off Hatteras, NC, was 31 pounds. Blues will feed on anything. All finfish—including other blues—clams, crabs, eels, you name it. If you put it on a hook, a bluefish might eat it. Blues are one of the

Watch out for those teeth! Bluefish are vicious, and have a set of chompers that matches their attitude.

easiest species to target in near-shore waters, because as well as their desire to eat whatever is at hand, they're almost always willing to bite regardless of the time of day or tidal cycle. In fact, more blues are probably caught by accident than on purpose, by anglers targeting other species. Again: remember to be careful of those teeth. I've had them jump out of the water from several feet away to bite into my hand, and ended up needing stitches on two fingers—the danger factor presented by those choppers cannot be over-emphasized. Not only will blues bite right through skin and monofilament, they'll also bite the hairs off your bucktails, scrape the paint off your plugs, and shred the teasers off of rigs. If you have a favorite striper lure and the blues have moved in, you're best off saving it for another day. Use these bluefish-specific tips to hook up with more of these feisty, voracious predators.

1. Blues will be found feeding at or near the surface more often than many other sportfish. As a result, if you want to catch them in a chum line or under working birds, focus your effort on surface baits.

2. Bluefish love to chop baitfish right in half. This makes live-lining for them almost impossible, as they constantly take the tail-end off of your livies. Instead, cut the head and tail off of your live bait, toss them over the side for chum, and thread the middle of the baitfish on your hook.

3. Blues don't slurp, nibble, or inspect baits—they kill and eat them with the utmost urgency. Accordingly, when you feel one strike set the hook immediately.

4. Blues love flashy lures. Troll a spoon next to a bucktail, and bluefish will hit the spoon twice as often. Whenever choosing a lure to be trolled, jigged or cast to bluefish, pick out something that shines.

5. Bluefish have a good sense for feeling or hearing vibrations in the water. As a result, lures such as Rat-L-Traps which put out constant vibrations are very effective on them. It is downright dangerous, however, to catch blues on plugs with multiple gang hooks. It's nearly impossible to get the trebles out of their snapping jaws, and the blues tendency to go absolutely crazy while being held means that the second set of trebles will often end up in the anglers' hand or finger. Before casting a plug like this to a school of breaking blues, swap out the trebles for single hooks.

6. Smaller bluefish are much better eating than large ones. Although it's not as much of a thrill to catch a 3-pounder as it is to catch a 20-pounder, the 3-pound fish actually tastes a whole lot better—so don't feel bad about taking home the smaller ones, and throwing the choppers back.

7. Chumming with menhaden in bays and inlets at night with a set of night lights out will bring swarms of bluefish to your boat. Don't try this if you're hoping to catch stripers or trout, because they'll be overwhelmed by the blues.

8. Blues are jumpers, and fish in the air have a much better chance of shaking out a hook than those in the water do. When fighting a bluefish it's best to keep your tip low and off to the side, which will discourage jumping. If the fish does make it into the air, reel like a madman to keep maximum tension on the line.

9. If you jig for trout under working birds or breaking fish, you'll often encounter blues, too. Occasionally, you'll be reeling in a fish, feel a sudden tug, and pull up the front end of an undersized trout, dripping blood. When this happens lower the half-trout back into the water immediately, and let it sink 3' to 4'. Often the marauding bluefish will still be right under the boat, looking for the other half of his meal.

10. When the tails to your plastic baits keep getting bitten off, you'll know there are blues in the area. Swap the plastics for a spoon, to put them in the cooler.

CHAPTER 6
Cobia

Of all sportfish available in near-shore waters, cobia are serious contenders for top ranking when it comes to sheer strength. These fish fight with long winded, determined runs and they usually won't give up the fight until they've been in the cooler for quite some time. They commonly swim right through nylon mesh nets, strip the gears on spinning reels, and as often as not, swim away free while an angler curses his luck.

Cobia can be particularly frustrating because they can often be spotted on the surface, finning about near buoys, sea turtles, or other flotsam. When seen up on top, cobia are usually not in a feeding mode. Anglers might cast lure after lure to these finning fish, without generating one iota of interest. In this situation, live baits are the way to go, with live eels topping the list. Spot, croaker, peanut bunker and peeler crab will also put finning cobia into feeding mode.

Although most cobia along the coast are targeted after being spotted on the surface, chumming with baits set at all levels in the water column is better way to actually hook one of these fish. They usually feed near shoals, humps and wrecks which are relatively shallow, and often the best cobia fishing often takes place in 25' to 100' of water. At times, however, you'll spot cobia finning along or materializing in a chunk line as far as 45 miles from shore, usually from the waters off New Jersey to the south. Although they do pop up farther to the north some seasons, for the most part this is the northern end of their range and they will only appear here during the summer months. In the Carolina area, however, cobia can begin showing up early in the spring and may be available through late fall.

There's no mistaking a bite with cobia—usually they will suck down the bait then rip line off the reel for a solid 10 to 20 seconds before slowing down, if they ever do slow down. As a result 30-pound gear is minimal, 40-pound class is appropriate, and 50-pound class gear is not out of line. Although spinning gear can be used, conventional star drag reels are much more common. When it comes to cobia stay away from automatic level wind reels, however, as large fish will have the brawn to burn out the worm gear which drives the level winder.

When cobia fishing you should be prepared for multiple hookups, as these fish often travel in pairs or small pods. When one is being brought to boatside, a second rod should be kept at the ready in case another fish or two are following the hooked fish, providing the opportunity to get a second cobia on the line.

So, just how big a cobia can you hope to hook into on the Atlantic coast? The IGFA has recorded a fish that topped 135 pounds. Want to beat that mark? These tips will help.

1. When you spot a cobia on the surface and do not have any live baits onboard,

The author holds up a cobia that was spotted tailing a ray.

you can sometimes get the fish to strike a bucktail dressed with a twister tail (or similar lure) by casting it between 5' and 10' in front of the fish, and allowing it to free-fall. If the cobia chases the lure as it falls, wait to feel a slight bump on the line (that's the fish sucking it into its mouth) then set the hook. Cobia on the surface will hit free-falling lures about twice as often as those cast and retrieved along the surface.

2. Once you've fought a cobia up close, it will often swim parallel to the boat just out of gaffing range. The fish will attempt to hold its position, and rest. Don't let it—if you allow the fish to recover its breath, it will dart away and you'll have to start over again from ground zero. Instead, when you see the fish use this tactic tighten up on the drag and force the cobia closer to the boat. Usually, this will trigger the fish's final run.

3. Never cast beyond a cobia on the surface and bring the lure from the fish's tail towards its head. This is not how a baitfish will commonly act, and it often spooks cobia.

4. Most chummers use menhaden for cobia, but it's an accepted fact that cobia usually prefer shellfish to finfish. Take advantage of this by going to your local sea-food store, and asking if they have any "die-off" hard crabs. Usually they are happy to hand you a bag full of dead crabs for free; if not a few dollars should be all it takes. Smash up the crabs and mix them in with your chum flow. Setting out a half of a peeler crab as bait is a good idea, too. In southern areas of the Mid Atlantic, shrimp are also an effective chum and bait.

5. If a cobia comes to boatside quickly, don't attempt to land it right off the bat. Instead, pressure it one way and another, tap it on the tail with a gaff, or otherwise aggravate it so the fish fights harder and tires itself out. If you gaff and land a "green" (energetic) cobia, you are in for a big, big mess—these are powerful fish, and will go absolutely crazy in the cockpit of a boat if they aren't bone-tired.

6. Cobia will attempt to roll off of a gaff hook, often with success. If you strike and the cobia rolls off the hook, try aiming for a point farther forward on the fish's body. The underside of its head and gill area are good targets. Also, strike and lift the fish into the boat in one fluid motion. This way, if the fish rolls off the gaff hook, at least there's a good chance it'll land in the cockpit.

7. Cobia love live eels. Anytime you'll be fishing for cobia or foresee the possibility of lucking into one, it's a good move to toss a few live eels into the livewell before leaving the dock.

8. Cobia don't have sharp teeth, but they do have many small abrasive ones. As a result, you should use a stiff, abrasion-resistant leader. Considering its nearly invisible nature, fluorocarbon is the natural choice.

9. Whether chumming or casting to finning cobia, superlines or braids are generally not the best choice for line. Remember that these fish are real bulldogs. They will put an unbelievable amount of pressure on your tackle. If you're using a superline, there's a pretty fair chance the fish will break a rod or strip the gears on your reel.

10. Cobia are one of the best and most unique eating fish in the ocean. For a real treat, try this Floridian recipe: Mix 50% blue cheese salad dressing with 50% may-onnaise. Coat the cobia steaks, and bake until the mixture turns brown on top. It sounds strange, but tastes great!

CHAPTER 7
Cod, Pollock, Haddock, and Hake

Cod, pollock, haddock and hake are bottom fish that enjoy relatively cool water, and will usually occur from New Jersey waters northward. These three fish will often be caught in the same area on the same baits, and thus provide a mixed bag for bottom fishers. Small hake can be found year-round as far south as Virginian waters, but most of these fish are under a pound and are not targeted by sport angers. (Note—if you're trawler chunking and you see the trawler discarding by-catch with hake mixed in, use a dip net to scoop a few up for bait. The tuna love 'em.) During some winters cod can be caught as far south as off the mouth of the Chesapeake Bay, but again, this is a fishery that is iffy at best and is not utilized by sport anglers. Haddock tend to range even farther north, and are far more prevalent in the Gulf of Maine than in New York waters. In the northern regions of the Mid Atlantic, however, cod unquestionably rule the world of bottom fishing. They taste awesome, are relatively easy to catch, and grow larger than most other ground fish.

The biggest cod ever recorded by the IGFA was 98 pounds, 12 ounce, and was caught all the way back in 1969. Most of the cod caught today are significantly smaller, and a 50-pound fish is considered a trophy. Fifty pounds is the world record mark for pollock, and a 10-pounder is a good fish in anyone's eyes. White hake can get close to this size, with the established record hitting 46 pounds, 4 ounces, but fish in this class are few and far between. Silver hake run much smaller—the record is a mere 4 pounds, 8 ounces—but are usually available in good numbers. Haddock have been reportedly caught on commercial vessels up to 25 pounds, but the hook and line sport record rests at 14 pounds, 15 ounce. Most of these bottom dwellers prefer water temperatures in the 50's (although hake will accept water temperatures into the mid-70s) and can be caught in waters of 50' or better (they tend to move shallower in the winter months, and at times can even be taken while surf casting), but most are taken from 120' and deeper. Haddock are the exception, preferring 200' to 400' depths and temperatures in the 40's.

Sand eels and squid are top baits for all of these fish, but they can also be taken by jigging. Cod in particular are suckers for large, heavy diamond jigs, jerked erratically up and down from the deck of a rolling boat. Cod, pollock and haddock tend to be found near structure ranging from drops and bumps to wrecks, with a preference for rocky ledges and shelves. Hake, on the other hand, will be found over open sand bottom as well as around structure. Probe the depths and use these tricks, to land more of these tasty bottom fish.

1. Most of the time cod, haddock and pollock are caught it will be in water deep enough that the fish's air bladder can not adjust to the pressure changes as you reel

it in. Thus, all fish caught and released will probably die. If you're catching a lot of undersized fish, the best thing to do is simply move on to another spot. The bright side of a bloated belly? It makes larger fish easy to gaff; by the time they reach the surface, particularly pollock and haddock will have little fight left in them.

2. For all of these species, a modern braid or superline is a major advantage. Monofilament stretches too much to effectively feel the fish in deep water, but with superline you'll feel a 10" hake nibbling on a squid strip 100' below.

3. When you're catching haddock, avoid vigorous hook-sets and jerks on the rod during the fight. Their mouths are relatively soft, and it's all too easy to rip the hook out if you move the rod violently.

4. Although it usually occurs farther north than the areas covered in this book, pollock will on rare occasions chase bait up to the surface, and remain there while feeding. If you spot this behavior, rig a spinning rod with a twister tail jig, and cast and retrieve it past the fish—they'll usually eat it up.

5. During the warm summer months, if you want to catch large cod head for the deep. As the inshore waters warm the bigger fish move to depths of 200' to 300', to find cooler temperatures. If you want to hook them, you'll have to move farther out, too.

6. Cod in particular like clams. If you're targeting these fish, cut large chunks or strips out of surf clams and thread them onto your hook. The clam's foot is tough and stays on the hook well, but the body often is stripped away by small nibblers. Avoid this problem by salting your clams prior to leaving the dock. The salt will toughen them up, and make it harder for small bait stealers to rip the clam off the hook.

7. Catch small hake prior to a day of trawler chunking (see chapter 28) for tuna fish, and keep them kicking in the livewell. Often, the trawlers will be shoveling loads of dead or dying hake over the side when they cull their catch, and tuna looking for a free meal will focus in on these fish. They may ignore squid, butterfish and other offerings, but eat the hake with abandon.

8. Cod inhale a bait and swim away slowly, providing a more or less dead-weight kind of tug. Smaller ground fish like hake, however, nip at the bait with a twitch-twitch-twitch. If you feel the twitching strike and try to set the hook, you'll usually just yank the rig off bottom. Leave it in place, however, and the larger cod will sometimes chase the smaller fish off the bait and eat it themselves. When you feel the slow, steady tug, it's time for the hook-set.

9. When wreck fishing for these ground fish with diamond jigs, don't cast away from your boat. If you do, as the jig swings back towards you there's a good chance it'll become fouled in the wreckage. Jig straight up and down, however, and you have less chance of hooking bottom.

10. When fishing for Pollock, let the time of day dictate your tactics. Early in the morning and late in the afternoon, jigging will usually out-produce bait fishing. But during mid-day, bait will usually out-produce jigging.

CHAPTER 8
Ocean Panfish: Croaker, Porgy, Spot, and Sea Mullet

While croaker and spot decline in number the farther north you go, the sea mullet (also called kingfish or whiting) is available in good numbers along the entire Mid Atlantic coast and porgy get more numerous as you head up the coast. Sea mullet are unique in that they are most often caught in the surf. Not just close to the beach, but practically on it, right inside of the breaking waves. These are relatively small fish, with the world record being a mere 2 pounds, 7 ounces. On this flip side, these are some of the best eating fish available in the suds. Croaker grow larger—the record is 5 pounds, 8 ounces—and are usually present in great numbers from Delaware south. This makes them a good fish to target when fishing with kids, as the action is often non-stop once you've located a school of fish. Porgy (called scup by some) are plentiful in northern waters, and also provide good entertainment for the little ones. Spot are another small bottom fish, more often of interest as bait than food, although they are quite tasty. The record rests just over a pound, but this is only because no one ever bothered to enter a spot into the books until 2003; many in the 3-pound range have been caught along the Mid Atlantic coast, and if you want to put your name in the IGFA book, catching a large spot would be one relatively easy way to do it.

Pound for pound, all of these panfish are good fighters. Croaker hold a special place for many anglers because of their kid-friendly nature; the easy catching, great eating, and on top of that, they even talk to you—wonderful entertainment for the little ones. They are close relatives of drum, and the croaking noise they make is similarly formed in the air bladder. A quick glimpse at a croakers' mouth is all it takes to see how they feed; with jaws pointed down towards the bottom, croaker eat worms, grass shrimp, small crustaceans, bivalves and similar critters living in the mud or sand. Same goes for both spot and kingfish, which also have the down-turned mouth. When targeting any of these fish, bloodworms, peeler or soft crabs are probably the best baits, followed by squid. All of these fish are also available from late spring through late fall in this region, with longer seasons in Virginia and North Carolina. Some years, this far south it's possible to catch kingfish through the winter.

Spot are usually the last of these species to head north; however, anglers targeting larger game fish should be well tuned to their arrival as they're excellent live baits. The day before an offshore trip, savvy anglers will get a dozen bloodworms and find a channel or mud bottom in a coastal bay, anchor up, and load the livewell. Just about every gamefish found offshore will eat a live-lined spot without hesitation. Use these tactics to keep your livewell—and your cooler—full of croaker, porgy, spot and sea mullet.

They may not be huge, but coastal panfish like this croaker are usually willing to bite—and they're great eating.

1. Don't give croaker or spot a lot of time to eat baits. Usually, by the time you feel the fish it has eaten the bait and is leaving town. They aren't careful, dainty or hesitant in the way they eat, they just suck it down and keep on going. So as soon as you feel it on the line, set the hook and bring the fish in.

2. A croaker die-hard I know has developed his own secret weapon for catching croaker, which out-fishes anything else I've ever seen. Here's how to make these special croaker baits: Cut squid into 1", 3"-long strips, and spread them on a cutting board. With an ice pick, punch numerous holes into each strip. Then put them into a plastic container, like an old margarine tub, and set it in the refrigerator. Next, place a soft crab into a cheese cloth or strainer, and smash the juices out of it. Pour the crab juice into the tub of squid strips, stir, and let it percolate in the fridge for a few days before you bait your hooks with it. Yummy.

3. If you're fishing for spot or sea mullet use exceedingly small hooks. Both of these fish have tiny mouths, and when fishing for them hook size #6 or even #8 is about right. Similarly, use tiny bits of bait.

4. When surf fishing for sea mullet, over-casting is common. You'll catch most of these fish right in the breakers, and long casts aren't only unnecessary, they actually will reduce your catch.

5. Night fishing is the most effective way to catch large numbers of croaker, but when fishing for croaker in the dark don't bother with illuminating the water. This is one occasion when lights won't help you, and there's no reason to bother with all the batteries and wires. Instead, depend on the scent of your baits to bring in the fish. Make sure your baits are fresh, and replace them often.

6. Make sure you get a firm grip on a croaker's gill plates before you try to remove the hook from their mouth. Croaker have a way of flaring their gill plates, and they have a very sharp outer edge. If you're not careful, they'll cut your hand. Porgy are another that can hurt you, because of their sharp spines. Watch for them, when taking fish off the hook.

7. When you're fishing in the surf and your line suddenly goes slack, there's a good chance you've just been hit by a sea mullet. Even when you think you're casting short, these fish will grab your bait and run towards land. A line that goes completely slack all of the sudden is a sure indication of sea mullet in the area.

8. Spot feel like a jackhammer when they hit. You won't get a single nibble or a thump-thump-thump, it will be a series of quick, sharp taps. If you feel this style of bite yet don't hook any fish, down-size your hooks and baits.

9. In southern areas like the waters of North Carolina, catch sea mullet with this trick: instead of baiting up with bloodworms, buy some small, fresh shrimp. Cut off the last section of the shrimp before the tail, then cut off the tail itself, being careful to leave the shell intact. This elongated section of shell threads onto a #6 hook easily, and the tougher meat here will hold up better to repeated strikes. Added bonus: When pompano are around in good numbers (during the summer months, about one season out of four or five) they will also go crazy for this bait.

10. When fishing for any of these species in the surf during a moving tide, do away with the floats on your rigs. Yes, bait-stealing crabs will often become a problem in slack tides and calm seas. But remember how most of these fish feed: on or at the bottom. Those floats are not only keeping the baits away from the crabs, they're keeping them away from the fish, too.

CHAPTER 9
Dolphinfish (Mahi-Mahi)

Dolphinfish are a real crowd-pleaser: they are some of the most colorful fish in the sea, they fight vigorously and jump repeatedly, they are usually present in good numbers once they show up in any given area, and they taste great. During most years they are available in the offshore waters of this entire region during July, August, and into September. North Carolina and Virginia anglers will get to enjoy mahi-mahi a month earlier and a month later most seasons, perhaps even longer, as water temperatures dictate. Expect them to be present in any area with a water temperature of 70-degrees or better. Although they are essentially deep water pelagics, during the summer months they will often move inshore to waters as shallow as 80' and sometimes even less. Dolphinfish are free swimmers but are usually associated with some type of floating object, either flotsam, weedlines, sea turtles, or commercial fishing gear such as polyballs marking lobster pots or longlines.

Mahi-mahi school by size and usually the largest schools are composed of 5- to 10-pound fish, with larger fish traveling in pairs or triples, often a male (bull) and a female (cow) or two. The difference is apparent at a glance; males have nearly flat, vertical foreheads, while females have rounded, sleek heads. The largest in the record books is 87 pounds, however, larger fish are reported to have been caught on commercial fishing vessels.

These fish can be caught in massive numbers off the North Carolina coast in mid-summer, often around large mats of seaweed, by bailing or trolling. This is also the time when they are available to northern anglers, though their exact range and distribution will change from year to year depending on weather and water conditions. When those conditions are right—usually triggered by a warm water eddy splitting off from the Gulf Stream—mahi-mahi can be caught under just about anything that floats, including small crab trap and sea bass trap floats, just a few miles from shore. Note, however, that these will usually be relatively small fish in the 2- to 5-pound range. Larger dolphinfish tend to remain farther offshore. These are said to be some of the fastest growing fish in the sea, and even large ones are relatively young. Old or young, small or large, at times these fish will strike anything you offer them without hesitation, and other times they seem spooked and won't take any bait or lure. Hopefully, using these tactics, you'll catch more than your fair share.

1. Bailing is without a doubt the most effective way to rake in large catches of mahi. In fact, it's easy to accidentally keep too many. Set a reasonable limit for yourself, and stick to it. Bailing is an easy tactic to master (see chapter 28) and can be performed any time you come across an object floating on the water's surface. It's

Few pelagics are as numerous or as beautiful as mahi-mahi, and they provide plenty of opportunities for light-tackle battles.

worth checking out anything as large as or bigger than a five gallon bucket. Ignore balloons, cardboard tops from flats of butterfish, and plastic bags. You'll see plenty of these offshore, but they'll rarely if ever hold fish.

2. Use either a long shank hook or a thick, abrasion-resistant leader when going for dolphinfish. They have numerous jagged little teeth, and although they can't bite through monofilament, they will slowly wear it away. Long shank hooks will provide a hair more protection for your leader (unless the fish swallows the hook all the way into its gut) and 30-pound fluorocarbon with a short-shank hook can not be expected to hold up in a fight lasting longer than 15 minutes.

3. When trying to tempt mahi-mahi with lures, remember they like things fast—very fast. A jig or plug retrieved by one of these fish should be cranked every bit as fast as the reel will go. Don't worry, you can't reel fast enough to take the lure away from the fish if he decides he wants it. But reel in slowly, and the chance of him wanting it diminish greatly.

4. For whatever reason, dolphinfish like pink above all other colors as a general rule. Sure, there will be days when light and water conditions conspire to make other colors more effective. But all other things being equal, they will strike pink lures or ballyhoo rigged on pink skirts before any other color.

5. Swing mahi-mahi directly into the fishbox or cooler. Let them hit the deck of your boat, and they will go completely berserk. Don't fool yourself into thinking they are "fought out" because these fish don't stop flipping and flopping until they're completely dead. Keep the boat neat and in one piece by opening the fishbox hatch before they are in the boat, swinging them directly into the box, and slamming the hatch shut immediately. Then cut off the leader, and tie on another one.

6. When you bring a mahi-mahi up to the boat, keep it in the water for a moment or two and look around to see if any of his friends followed him. Often, an entire school will follow a single fish right up to you. Pull the hooked fish out of the water now, and the others will disappear. Instead, keep it in the water until someone else on the boat can hook another fish. By keeping one hooked fish in the water all the time, you can hold the school indefinitely.

7. When trolling for tuna or billfish, you can often add a mahi or two to the catch by running a 3" to 4" pink squid rigged with a single hook and no bait, right behind your transom. Set it on a flat line clip, about 20' to 25' from the boat.

8. When approaching a good-looking floating dolphin-attractor, like a cargo net or a large board, don't give up hope if you don't spot fish right off the bat. Sometimes, for whatever reason, dolphinfish will hover 40' to 80' below a floating item. When you find something good always try fishing deep as well as near the surface, before moving on.

9. Large dolphin—called "gaffers"—often hang around the periphery of a school of smaller fish. They'll often be deeper than the other fish, as well. Whenever you locate a large school of "chickens" in the 3- to 10-pound range, rig up a line with a large, fast sinking lure like a 10-ounce, stainless-steel diamond jig, or a wahoo bomb. Cast it beyond the school and let it sink to 100' or so, then rip it back to the boat as quickly as possible. Larger mahi may not hit this lure all the time, but they will often follow it back to your boat. When you see a big boy follow the lure in, throw a handful of chunks over the side to keep him interested, then drop in your bait.

10. Contrary to popular belief, mahi-mahi will spook if you drive your boat right over them. In fact, two good drifts on a school that's hanging around flotsam is really all you can expect; by the third drift, the fish are usually starting to wise up. Accordingly, suppress the urge to go charging up to an item you spot on the surface. Instead, throttle back when you're still 100' away, and approach at an idle.

CHAPTER 10
Flounder (Fluke: Summer and Winter)

Summer flounder are one of the most popular inshore sportfish along the Atlantic coast, with good reason: they are excellent table fare, with sweet, firm, white meat. Plus, they have unique ways of striking and fighting, and anglers must use species-specific tactics to be successful with these flatfish. As a result, there are hordes of anglers along the coast who "specialize" in flounder-pounding. Winter flounder is a smaller, much less sought after relative of the summer flounder. Because of the difference in popularity, this chapter will focus on summer flounder and a short winter flounder section will follow.

Most coastal bays offer the opportunity to catch fluke, so long as they fill a few requirements: good water flow, both deep channels and shallow areas, and sandy or shell bottoms. Sand bottoms are usually best. The largest of the species tend to stay close to the ocean, and most "doormats" (fish more than 6 or 7 pounds) will be caught in the ocean or within a few miles of an inlet. The IGFA's largest-ever doormat was weighed in at 22 pounds, 7 ounces, and was caught in New York waters. That's a truly giant flounder; for most folks, a 6-pound fish is a trophy and a 10-pounder is a once-in-a-lifetime catch.

Flatties feed mostly on small fish, which explains why bull and silverside minnows are the number one all-time flounder bait. Still, some anglers swear by squid, and the favored flounder rig along much of the coast is a Fluke Killer or Flounder Pounder (a bucktail-like skirt dressed with beads and a spinner) baited with both—a squid strip/minnow combination. The minnow used are the biggest possible, and squid strips are usually cut at about 2" wide and 5" long; flounder are not afraid of large baits. Still other dedicated flattie freaks stand by bucktail/minnow/squid combos, and another sect prefers bouncing jigs. Of one thing there is no doubt: all of these techniques are effective.

Unlike most fisheries, there are a good number of dependable constant factors when it comes to catching flounder. One is that they like clear water. In churned-up, muddy water it's not a good choice to focus on flounder. Low-light days can be productive, though less so than bluebird days, and when it's cloudy or raining it's doubly important the water be clean and clear. Flounder are also predictable in that they like moving baits. Motionless baits usually go untouched (which is why most people either drift or slow-troll for these fish, and anchoring is uncommon), and when jigging, the motion should be so fast it's almost violent. 99 times out of 100 flounder will hit lures as they fall, and you won't know it until you sweep the rod tip up to jig it. For this reason, always keep a firm hand and be ready to apply maximum pressure when you go to jig upwards. One final regularity: flounder hold tight to the bottom. If you want to hook one, you must keep your bait

An early spring flounder from Wachaprague, Virginia, which lays claim to the title "Flounder Capitol of the World."

or lure as close as possible to dead-on at all times.

Trolling for flounder is an especially productive method in deep water where the current is so strong it's tough to keep a bait down. At the Chesapeake Bay Bridge Tunnel, for example, wire-line trolling for flounder is a top technique. The down-side to wire-line trolling? Lots of weight is necessary to keep that bait down deep. Remember—if it leaves the bottom, you're not in the flounder zone.

In the open water of coastal bays, you'll usually find flounder on edges and drop-offs between 5' and 20' deep. Note, however, that you'll catch 75-percent of your fish within a 5' depth spread, through a tidal period. Accordingly, check the depth when you catch one and focus your efforts in that same depth range for a while. When the tide shifts expect that the flounder will too, and try to move with them. As a general rule of thumb expect flounder to move deep during low and out-going tides, and expect them to move into the shallows during flood tides.

Near the peak of a flood tide flounder may be found in good numbers in water as shallow as a foot. When fishing these shallows, casting dressed bucktails or jigs is the most effective technique. Three specific shallow-water features will draw in flounder. First off, anywhere rip-rap lines the shore you stand a fair chance of finding flatfish, and in some seasons, light tackle anglers casting to points and drops right on the shoreline will strike it rich with flounder. Secondly, cuts are another flattie hotspot. Any that drain marshes or salt ponds can be productive, even if they're just a few feet across. Cast to the mouths of cuts like these during the very beginning of the ebb tide until it's dropped about half-way, and you stand a good chance of finding fish. Thirdly, large sandy flats directly adjacent to deep water channels will attract flounder on the hunt for a meal.

This type of shallow-water flounder fishing is usually the most productive early in the year, when flounder first move out of the ocean and invade the bays. In southern waters this may occur as early as mid-March, and in northern areas it usually takes place by May.

More commonly, flounder anglers will be working channel edges. Here, when bait is employed, very specific techniques must be used to effectively catch flounder: when a fish first grabs the bait the angler will feel the rod tip quiver. Set the hook now, and the fish will go free. The angler has to wait until he feels a "thunk, thunk, thunk" on the end of the line. This is the time to set the hook. It could take anywhere from 1 to 10 seconds to go from quiver to thunk, but you must wait for the thunk to catch these fish. Conversely, jig and bucktail anglers need to set the hook immediately and solidly upon feeling the strike. Usually the lure will either hit home and set solidly in the fish's jaw, or pull free with little resistance. The stronger the hook-set, the better off you are. If it pulls free immediately drop back to the bottom, because sometimes the flounder will strike it again.

Flounder—especially large ones—can also be targeted in inshore ocean waters. Humps, wrecks and reefs in 25' to 150' of water attract flounder, and although heavy tackle is needed to combat the strong currents and deep water, the pay-off can be extreme. To target flounder in oceanic waters either fish shoal or hump edges while on the drift, or try fishing the outer edges of wrecks and reefs. Unlike other fish caught at the wrecks—sea bass and tautog, for example—flounder aren't usually caught while fishing directly over the structure itself. Instead, they're more often hooked on the periphery of the structure. Fish for them in these areas with the same baits and rigs you'd use in the bays, though you will need a beefier rod and reel to handle the heavy the extra weight.

Once on the line, another unusual trait of flounder is the way they fight. Large flounder often fool you into thinking you've hooked bottom—they don't move, not even an inch, when you pull on them. Then, as you apply more pressure, you'll feel the fish's head slowly lift off the bottom. The slow-but-steady pull generates a feeling similar to the sensation of hooking a large mat of weeds, which holds fast to the bottom for a second or two before slowly ripping away. Once you've lifted the fish off the bottom, it will suddenly come to life and pull with hard, twitching jerks. Then you'll get the slow tug again, maybe a run or two, and more of those hard jerks. The feeling is very unique, and you won't mix it up with other fish when you have a big flattie on the line.

One final bit of uniqueness from our flat friends: filleting a flounder is also different than cleaning other fish. Split the fillets by slicing down along the lateral line, all the way to the backbone, then slide the knife along the top of the bones working from the center of the fish out towards the edges. You'll come away with two delicious strips of meat from each side. Ready to target some flatties? Use these tips.

1. Flounder usually show a preference for bright colors. White, chartreuse, and yellow are usually best. One exception: in slightly off-colored water, purple will often be the top producer.

2. In discolored water, choose Fluke Killers, Roadrunners, or other rigs that have a spinning blade. They seem to do better than other lures in this situation, the prevailing theory being that the fish can hone in on the vibrations produced by the blade as it spins.

3. Some knowledgeable fluke sages drag a weight or a length of chain as they drift. Many people believe that flounder will follow the trail of puffing, disturbed sand, right up to your lures.

4. Save some of a flounders' white belly meat for bait. Strips of flounder belly sometimes out-perform all other baits, and they are amazingly tough. You may be able to catch a half-dozen fish on the same bait, and it won't be any the worse for wear.

5. Never let a flounder hang in the water while someone's going for the net. It's imperative to keep a constant tension on the line with flounder, or that jerky head-shake will rattle the hook loose. As soon as someone hooks up, someone else onboard should immediately go for the net and stand ready.

6. When choosing a plastic jig for flounder, go with the paddle-tail style. Who can say why they like them better? Not me—but there's no doubt that flounder show a clear preference for paddle tails over twister tails of the same color.

7. When wire-lining for flounder and you get a fish on, don't slow or change the boats' speed. Again, it's that jerky head-shake thing. As soon as a flounder feels a change in the tension on the line or the least bit of slack, he'll give it that shake. So keep the boat speed steady as the fish is brought up.

8. Flounder have sharp teeth. Of course you should handle them with care, but this also means you should use slightly thicker leaders than would be the norm for fish that commonly top-out at 10 pounds. Use a line that has good abrasion resistance, such as fluorocarbon, and feel it for nicks and cuts after each fish you catch.

9. To hold a flounder pinch it with a couple of fingers on the top of the gill plates, just behind the eyes. Trying to grab it by the tail or body will only provide entertainment for your crewmates.

10. When jigging for flounder in deep water use superline. Remember the need for that fast, firm hook-set? With mono, it just won't be fast or firm enough because of the stretch in the line. Fish with superline, and you'll increase the number of solid hook-ups by 25-percent. Similarly, choose a rod with a firm, fast-action tip.

Winter flounder are far less popular than summer flounder, especially in southern areas because their numbers dwindle as you move south. These fish used to be prevalent all the way down into Virginia waters, but in the past decade their numbers have been low from the Chesapeake region south. Winter flounder also don't grow nearly as large as fluke, with the IGFA record set at a mere 7 pounds for a fish caught off Fire Island, NY.

Still, winter flounder are extremely tasty fish and their presence during late fall and into the winter, when summer flounder have departed from coastal bay waters, makes them an excellent off-season target. Winter flounder are almost exclusively caught in the bays and are rarely found in deep waters, and unlike summer flounder, show a preference for mud bottoms.

Catch a winter flounder and the first thing you'll notice is how much smaller their mouths are than those of summer flounder. As a result, tackle and baits must be tailored specifically for this species. Very small (#6) hooks rigged on a top-and-bottom rig are the norm when targeting winter flounder. Anglers usually bait up with grass shrimp, or bloodworm, squid, and clam bits. Many winter flounder specialists like to anchor up and chum clam mixed with corn or shrimp bits over 12' to 20' deep mud flats, to draw the fish in.

CHAPTER 11
Grouper

There are few fish in this world as tasty as fresh grouper. Although they only inhabit the southernmost waters of our range, regularly in North Carolina and to a lesser degree Virginian waters, they still constitute an important game fish which are highly sought-after by a dedicated following of anglers.

Although there are many varieties of grouper, in our region two species will make up the bulk of the catch: gags (also known as black grouper) and red grouper. Both fish will be found in relatively deep water, rarely less than 50' and more commonly in 100' or more around hard structure. Most often, that means wrecks and reefs. Remember that the closer to shore a wreck lies, the more likely it is to receive constant fishing pressure. As a result, the largest grouper will almost always be caught farther from shore in deeper waters.

The IGFA lists an 80-pound, 6-ounce gag and a 42-pound, 4-ounce red grouper as the world record fish, but most will run in the 5- to 20-pound class. Interestingly, gags start off life mostly as females and change sex as they grow larger. These fish are ambush predators with huge, bass-like mouths, and they sit in cracks, holes and crevices, before popping out to inhale their prey in a single gulp.

Groupers are purely bottom fish. Although trolling for them with large lipped plugs is effective in Gulf coast passes, where they move into shallow water, in the Mid Atlantic region bottom fishing is the only well-established way of effectively targeting them. Baits are commonly cut fish or squid. Many anglers feel live baits work better than cut bait, but in depths beyond 300' or so live baits won't be alive for very long after you weight them down with lead and drop them to the bottom—the near-instant pressure change is just too strenuous. Most anglers use some variation of the standard top-and-bottom rig when fishing for grouper, though as you'd expect leaders and hooks must be up-sized from the norm. 6/0 hooks are minimal and many grouper fanatics use 8/0 or even 10/0 size hooks. Most also agree that circle hooks work extremely well when fishing for this species. Get more grouper to eat your hooks, using these tricks.

1. Since grouper are ambush predators they will have some time to eyeball your offering closely before deciding whether or not to go for it. Unfortunately, this allows them to be a little more finicky than some other fish. Hide your hooks in the bait as much as possible, and stick with fresh baits, not frozen, whenever possible.

2. Carry some fresh shrimp in the cooler. Some days it seems like grouper will eat any offering you drop to the bottom, but others it's a real challenge to get them to bite. If this is the case, try putting fresh shrimp on the hook.

Anthony Ng, of Fish-Ng Accessories, with a couple of pretty North Carolina grouper.

3. Grouper rarely peck at cut bait, they usually gulp it down. Accordingly, if you feel a strike set the hook immediately (or, if you're using circle hooks, you'll want to simply begin taking up line). If you feel lots of pecking but can't seem to set the hook into anything solid, you're probably being hit by small snappers or sea bass and may want to consider trying a new spot.

4. Like other smart wreck dwellers, a grouper will attempt to wrap your line in the structure once he's on the hook. Combat this in two ways: first, use relatively heavy leaders and rigs. 80-pound or even 100-pound leaders are not out of line. Secondly, the moment you have a fish on apply maximum pressure. Try to put some distance between the fish and the wreckage as soon as possible.

5. If a grouper tangles you in the wreckage, don't yank until the line breaks. Instead, release all pressure. Sometimes the fish will swim its way right back out of the tangle, and you can resume the fight.

6. If you catch an undersized grouper and its air bladder is popping out of its mouth (a result of the quick pressure change often seen when you're fishing deep water) pop it with a pin before releasing the fish. Most scientists agree that the fish has a better chance for survival if you deflate the air bladder before putting it back over the side.

7. The best way to catch truly huge grouper is to locate your own chunk of wreck or reef, far from the inlet. Yes, I know this is a tall order. But try to keep an eye on your fishfinder as you troll, bail, or fish in other ways. If you can find structure that no one else knows about, you have a much better chance of bringing in the big one.

8. If you're getting nipped by lots of "beeliners" or vermillion snappers, up-size your baits. Remember—that grouper has a huge mouth. Even if you have to go to whole 8" or 10" baitfish, it will be able to choke it down. In this case, however, you may want to allow the fish a few seconds to eat before setting the hook or reeling up.

9. If you're anchored over a wreck or other hard structure you can excite the grouper by jump-starting the food chain. You'll need a cannonball-type weight tied to the end of a heavy rig (at least 50-pound test). Before you start fishing, drop the weight down to the structure and let it free-fall until it hits. Then raise it 10' or so, and let it freefall again. Repeat the process a dozen or so times, then reel it up and drop your baits. Banging on the structure will dislodge all kinds or organisms and sediments, which creates some easy pickings for small fish, which will in turn attract the big fish.

10. If you're fishing at anchor in relatively shallow water, it's possible to excite the grouper with chum. Sink a weighted chum pot with frozen chum balls, which will release tidbits as they thaw, and place your baits as close by as possible.

CHAPTER 12
King Mackerel

King mackerel—often simply called kings or kingfish—have grown in popularity by leaps and bounds in recent years, thanks to the Southern Kingfish Association and its tournament trail. As the name of the association suggests, kings are mostly a southern species. During the summer months they will be encountered with regularity as far north as Delaware waters, however, and their range officially includes territory clear up to Maine.

Kings are mostly inshore oceanic fish; they can be caught within sight of the beach on occasion but in our region they mostly range from 80' to 200' deep waters between five and 30 miles off the coast. They can be found near wrecks, reefs, ledges, or open water when there are large shoals of bait near by.

While the IGFA record posts a 93-pound fish caught off the coast of Puerto Rico, most kingfish caught recreationally range from 5 to 30 pounds. These fish have extremely toothy mouths and wire leader is a must-have when going for kings. They can be taken while chunking but more commonly are targeted by slow-trolling, often at speeds of just two to three miles per hour. Many serious kingfish anglers slow-troll with a chum bag in the water and live menhaden, mullet, ribbon-fish, or other baitfish on the hook. When live baits aren't available, spoons, plugs, and plastic ribbon fish are all good choices. The venerable Clark Spoon is probably the number one artificial used along the Atlantic coast.

Most kingfishers use a very specific rig, with a 4' to 5' wire leader terminating in a single short-shank hook and a stinger treble hook 4" behind it. The single hook is run through the bait's mouth and the stinger treble is placed far aft on its back. Interestingly, you'll also see this rig with the hooks reversed—treble up front, single hook aft. This rig is very effective considering a kingfish's feeding method: they charge a bait and often cut it in half, then turn around and look for the sinking fish parts. If you get a strike and the fish misses both hooks, simply shift into free-spool so your bait sinks naturally. Often, the king will come back and inhale one half or the other, getting a hook in the process.

Another factor unique to kingfish fishing is their soft mouths. Often hooks will rip free from a kingfish when a lot of pressure is applied. To account for this problem kingfishers like long, slow-action rods that have a lot of give, and they set their drags very lightly. They also use extremely long gaffs (10' is not uncommon) so they can reach out and stick the fish before it gets close enough to the boat to trigger a final burst of energy.

Kingfish often respond well to sub-surface baits pulled behind planers. Ballyhoo and Clark spoons pulled 15' to 20' down will sometimes out-fish those same baits dragged along the surface. Ready to catch a fish that's fit for a king? Check out these tactics.

This king fell to a trolled ballyhoo rigged on mono—but nine times out of ten, the lack of wire leader means the fish swims away free.

1. If you want to seriously target kingfish, take a lesson from Floridians and fly a kite. Kite fishing on the drift allows you to get out several down-wind lines. At the same time, you can trail several up-wind lines off the front or side of the boat, so you're covering a huge swath of water with baits.

2. When you're on the search and you don't know exactly where the fish are located, troll artificials. This allows you to go a bit faster—and cover more ground—than slow-trolling with livies or rigged dead baits.

3. Use black or dull-finish swivels when fishing for kings. When they see the flash of a silver swivel, they'll often take a shot at it and cut your line.

4. If you can fill the livewell with peanut bunker or bull minnow, bounce one off the back of the boat every minute or so. Toss it hard enough to stun it, but not hard enough to kill it. The trail of struggling baitfish has an obvious result.

5. When drift fishing, lower a chum bag on a downrigger cannonball. Try setting it at about 20' and often you'll attract more fish than a chum bag set on the surface.

6. If you're fishing with rigged ribbon fish, brine them in rock salt the day before. It'll toughen the bait up, and otherwise, there's a good chance it will get shredded the first time a king hits it.

7. Kingfish caught on the standard two-hook bait rig will often come up hooked in unusual places—the top of the head, the back, the outside jaw, or the bottom of the jaw, for example. When you're playing in a fish keep an eye out for the hook placement. If it's in one of these unusual areas take pains not to over-pressure the fish. Hooks set in the meat of the fish, as opposed to the jaws, often pull free if the fish tries to dart away.

8. Those long-handled gaffs work great for kings, but wide-gap gaffs do not. A 3" gap is usually considered the maximum you'll want when targeting these fish. Because of their narrow, torpedo-like shape, larger gaff hooks lead to missed gaff shots—and missed opportunities.

9. Clear water/dirty water breaks with visible rips on the surface are good areas to hunt for kings. Regardless of the surrounding structure, when you find a rip that stands out clearly, it's worth giving it a shot.

10. Keep an eye on your temperature gauge. Kings like water that's warmer than 68-degrees. If you read temps that are chillier than this, you may want to scout for a different location.

CHAPTER 13
Mako Shark

You want an adrenaline-pumping thrill that will be etched in your mind for years to come? It's time to take a shot at catching a mako. Not only are these fish fast, powerful, and dangerous, they're also one of the few shark species that's likely to go airborne as you fight it.

Mako is the one and only shark targeted by sport anglers for its food value. While small threshers and dogfish are edible, mako is the one species that shines on the dinner plate as brightly as it does in the deep blue. Though the IGFA's heaviest listing for mako breaks 1,200 pounds, fish of over 500 pounds are extremely rare these days. In fact, a 300-pound mako is considered a good catch.

Mako fishing begins along the Mid Atlantic coast as early as May to the south, and as late as July in the north. As usual, the timing depends on the weather patterns. In the case of mako, however, you can always get an early indication of their presence by keeping an eye on the other fish migrating up the coast. First come the mackerel, then the bluefish, and mako follow close behind. In fact, both mackerel and bluefish are good mako baits. Blue shark are usually present in the same areas as makos during the same time frame, and usually in larger numbers. At times, you'll have to weed through several blue shark to find a single mako. And since you don't want to gaff a blue—which is more or less inedible—you'll want to pay close attention to the shark's pectoral fins. They are notably longer on blue shark. A good look at their jaws is another way to differentiate between blues and mako. Mako's teeth are dagger-like, while a blue's teeth are wider and serrated. Thresher shark will also be in the mix though in fewer numbers, but there's no mistaking them for other species—their tails make up half of their body length. Fishing for thresher is no different, but additional care must be taken to keep clear of those tails. They can sweep them through the air hard enough to knock a full grown man to the deck, and more than one injury has
been sustained by anglers handling thresher shark.

During slow springs when the mako bite is anemic on the inshore grounds, they can sometimes be located in better numbers at the canyons. Most years, however, it's not necessary to run far from the inlet to get in a shot at these awesome fish. Note that unlike most other shark, mako are aggressive enough that they can be targeted effectively on the troll. They often hit ballyhoo, mullet, and other baits traditionally run for tunas, marlin and other species. So when mako fishing has been slow, don't hesitate to go on the troll for other species and keep a sharp eye peeled for fins on the surface. If you see a mako finning, make a slow circle around the fish to drag your baits past its nose.

When chumming for mako—the traditional and most effective way of targeting them—specific rigs are a necessity (seen in chapter 34). Not only do these

Bringing a mako onboard is dangerous—shark appearing to be dead can suddenly spring to life.

predators have a mouth full of dangerously sharp teeth, they also jump clear of the water and spin during battle. All-wire rigs will often kink and break when the mako spins, and if these fish get their rough skin in contact with monofilament, the fight is usually over quickly as the line chaffs and breaks in short order.

Of course, we need to add in a few words of caution when it comes to fishing for mako. These are one of the most dangerous fish sport anglers in the Atlantic may face, and could also hold the number one spot for causing serious injury. The golden rule: never bring one into the boat. Dead, alive, whatever—these fish can appear to be dead for hours, then suddenly spring to life. Instead, once you have one on the gaff work a tail rope over it, and either hang or partially hang the fish from a cleat or stanchion for the run home. You've probably heard that some people shoot mako then haul them into the boat, but bringing a gun onboard undoubtedly introduces more danger than it mitigates. I can't speak to bang sticks as I have no direct experience using them, but if you keep the fish on the outside of the boat, you eliminate the danger—so why try anything else?

Rule number two when mako fishing: don't reach anywhere near the fish to un-hook it, get another line on it, or for any other reason. They can bend in ways that boggle the imagination, and that toothy set of jaws can travel 6' or 8' before your brain can even register the movement. When you have an undersized fish that needs to be released, simply cut the line. Now, ready to fight a mako shark? Here are some tips to help you get one on the line.

1. When the current is lame, extend your chum slick by power-chumming. Bump the boat in and out of gear or putt along at idle speed, while spooning chum over the side liberally. Spread the chum out thickly for a mile or two, then shut down and go on the drift.

2. If the action is slow, try cutting off the chum. Every once in a while a mako will hang in the slick, but won't approach the boat. By stopping the chum they'll some-times move in to investigate, and take a bait.

3. Give a mako plenty of time to eat. If the shark is holding your bait in its jaws and you lock up the reel, you'll miss the fish—you can't set a hook into the teeth, you need that bait to be fairly far back in the mako's mouth. Usually a 10-count is about right, but when smaller fish are eating larger baits, you may want to give it a solid 20-count.

4. Never, ever try to gaff a mako with a fixed gaff. It will simply spin right off the hook, and probably break your line at the same time. Flying gaffs are an absolute necessity when trying to land mako shark. And when you do strike the fish, note that the gaff will often bounce off of the shark's rough skin. Usually, the best place to hit is in and around the gill slits.

5. Mackerel, tuna, and bluefish chunks are good mako baits, and mackerel chum works well, but chumming blues is ineffective. In fact, serious sharkers will usually put out menhaden (bunker) chum, which creates a huge oily slick, while fishing either bluefish or mackerel baits.

6. Shark are attracted by noise, and one popular method of bringing them in from afar is to cup your hand and whack the side of your boat, to create a hollow clap-ping sound. Many anglers swear by this method, and beat the side of their boat every few minutes.

7. Shark are also attracted to the vibrations and electrical fields put out by strug-gling fish. If you see flashes in your chum line, toss out a chunk bait or two and see if you can catch a false albacore or skipjack. Bring in the fish, make sure the hook is embedded in its jaw, then cut a slice or two in the fish's sides or back where you won't do any immediately fatal damage but you will cause the fish to bleed and struggle. Then let it back over the side, and allow it to (hopefully) bring in the sharks. If you can catch one small enough, live-line the fish on a shark rig—and hold on tight!

8. Drift before you fish. Most of the time drifting as opposed to anchoring is the better move, but you want to ensure that your drift takes you over structure, uneven bottom, and the like. So, before you fish, take the boat out of gear and turn on the track line function on your GPS/Chartplotter. Prep baits and rig lines for five minutes or so, then look at the track you've established. As often as not, the direction of your drift will not be exactly what you expected—but now you know exactly how to position your boat to drift right over the hotspot.

9. While fillets and chunks are the norm, live baits will get the mako feeding with more vigor. Snapper blues, tinker mackerel, bunker, and false albacore will all do the trick. The livies should be just a couple of pounds, unless you're specifically targeting a trophy-sized shark. In that case, the sky's the limit.

10. As with other forms of offshore chumming or chunking, most anglers will suspend baits beneath balloons set to different depths to cover the water column. When you do so, keep an eye on those balloons. Often mako will "play" with the balloon—nudge it with their nose, kick at it with their tail, and sometimes even outright attack it. In all of these circumstances there's a good chance the fish will either bite through or abrade your line. If you see a shark approaching the balloon, reel like crazy; this will bring your bait up near the surface, where the shark will be more likely to spot it, while lowering the chance it bites off your line.

CHAPTER 14
Marlin (Blue and White)

Marlin are, without question, doubt or argument, kings of the sportfishing world. Along the Mid Atlantic coast you're likely to run into two types, blues and whites. The whites are far more plentiful but much smaller; although the IGFA lists a 181-pound white, a 70-pounder caught in our region is a nice one. Blue marlin, on the other hand, aren't really considered "big" until they break 500 pounds or so and the record stands at a hair over 1,400 pounds. How do you tell the two species apart? It can be quite tough at a glance, as their coloration and markings vary from fish to fish and even fight to fight—like mahi-mahi, tuna, and some other pelagics, their colorations change depending on what situation the fish is in at any given moment. So don't try to see if the billfish is white in color, or blue in color. Instead, look at its dorsal and pectoral fins. White marlin have rounded dorsals and pecs, while blue marlin have points on the ends of these fins.

Blues are rarely seen inshore of the canyons, but white marlin have a habit of wandering in to the near-shore lumps as close as 25 miles from port, in 100' or so of water. Of course this isn't the "normal" place to find them most of the time, but some seasons weather and water conditions conspire to make whites more plentiful inshore than they are offshore. Their tendency to pop up close to home is how Ocean City, Maryland became known as "White Marlin Capital of the World". The Jack Spot, a mere 24 miles from the inlet, had whites on or near it quite often decades ago, and it became the destination for many sport fishermen. These days you'll still sight whites at the Jack Spot, though with much less frequency.

Whether you're chasing whites, blues, or both, trolling is the normal method of fishing. You will take them on occasion while chunking, but not with any real regularity. Most anglers will troll fairly slowly at four to six knots with rigged dead baits—small ballyhoo for whites, and large for blues—some naked and some skirted with different colors. You'll find that the many will come up on squid spreader bars and bat the baits around with their bill without taking the hooked bait. This is a classic opportunity to pull the old bait-and-switch with a rigged ballyhoo.

For both species, keeping your cool and running an effective bait-and-switch is imperative when a billfish appears in the spread. Most of the time these fish don't just slam a hook, they swipe at baits or teasers with their bills and wait for a crippled baitfish to drift back from the "school." Anyone trolling the canyons, be it for tuna, marlin or mahi, should always keep a "pitch bait" (a rod ready to go with a rigged ballyhoo) handy so they can drop it back to a hot marlin in the spread.

Exactly where and in what numbers marlin will appear has a great deal to do with warm water eddies which break off from the Gulf Stream. You can keep an eye on such eddies by subscribing to a temperature charting service, such as Terrafin (www.terrafin.com). For about $100 a season, you'll be given a password and

The mate of the Project Boat, Rocky Calia, wrestles with an angry white marlin caught in Baltimore Canyon.

can log onto their web site, to get a satellite's view of ocean water temperatures. Identify an eddy with a nice sharp edge within your cruising range, and you have a shot at one of these billfish—or maybe more than one.

If you do hook into a marlin, be prepared for the fight of your life. They will tail walk, pull 180-degree hairpin turns, charge the boat, and fly through the air in dazzling displays of speed and power. And, it's just as important that you be prepared to release the fish at the end of the fight. No one that I know of keeps marlin these days, since their numbers are low and their value as sport fish to the charter and recreational fleets is high. The thrill, however, is worth the effort. Get in on the action, by applying these marlin catching tricks.

1. If a marlin shows up in the spread and focuses on one bait or lure, bills it but does not eat it, and won't be drawn by a pitch bait, try cranking in the item it's focused on as quickly as you can turn the reel handle. Often this fools the marlin into thinking dinner is escaping, and triggers a full-blown attack.

2. Looking for a blue marlin? Make sure you have this traditional bait somewhere in the spread: a blue and white Ilander bullet-head lure trailing a horse ballyhoo.

3. Pull at least one dredge teaser, such as a Strip Tease, made up of several strands of reflective Mylar fish. Okay, so maybe you already do—but how do you run the dredge? Most people allow them to run too close to the surface. To draw the attention of marlin, particularly whites, put several pounds of lead in front of the teaser so it runs 5' or 10' below the surface. Then run a naked ballyhoo on the surface, about 10' behind the teaser.

4. If you don't know where the fish have been biting, start the day off by trolling lures at relatively high speeds; eight or nine knots. When you spot your first bill and you don't have to worry so much about covering lots of ground to locate the fish anymore, kick back the speed and let out your rigged baits. Note—if you're trolling specifically for blue marlin, keep the speeds on the higher side. Use four to six knots as a rule of thumb for whites and seven to eight as a rule of thumb for blues.

5. When a white marlin takes a rigged bait give it several seconds to eat before you lock up the reel. If you strike it immediately, the hook will probably pull free of the fish's bony jaws. But if you give it a 10-count, you'll end up gut-hooking the marlin. A five-count is usually about right.

6. Many people believe they need to yank the rod back and strike hard to set the hook into the bony jaws of white marlin. I don't know why people think this, but in my experience it's completely wrong. Try using the count method described in tip number 5, and instead of setting the hook just lock up the reel and bring the line tight—your hookup to missed strike ratio will soar.

7. When rigging up for blues, use extremely tough leader—300-pound test is about right. Blue marlin bills are 10 times rougher than white marlin bills, and as a result, they chaff leaders significantly during battle. Drop the leader size, and you'll have a lot of break-offs. Conversely, you can safely drop down to 100- or even 80-pound test leaders when fishing for white marlin.

8. You spotted a school of 2- to 5-pound skipjack tuna on the surface? You now have the opportunity to set up specifically for large blue marlin. Clear one side of the boat's spread, then drop back a 2" pink or white squid skirt and troll around the school until you hook a skippie. Drop back your speed to two or three knots—just as slow as you can go while still making headway—put the fish on a live bait rig or "bridle" it (use a rigging needle to run a piece of string through its nose, and tie it to the hook) and set the skipjack about 50' behind the boat. Then make a loop in the line and twist it several times before running it through the rigger clip in the long position, on the side you cleared. (Twisting the line will keep it from running freely through the clip.) Once it's set, strip out 30' to 40' of line and let it create a bow between the rod tip and the rigger clip. If a blue comes up and eats the skippie, the bow in the line will create the perfect amount of drop-back. As soon as you get a strike, put the reel into gear and prepare for battle.

9. Want to try catching a marlin on spinning gear? It's a lot of fun, and can be effectively done by sight-casting to fish you see finning on the surface, or on fish that appear in the spread. The secret? Put a couple of live eels in the livewell before you leave the docks—white marlin love to munch them up, and with spinning gear you can toss the bait right at 'em.

10. Any time you're fishing live baits for marlin, either rig them on a bridle or hook them through the nose (in one nostril and out the other). Never hook them through the upper and lower jaws; this pins the bait's mouth closed, making it nearly impossible for the fish to breath, and it will die quickly.

CHAPTER 15
Red Drum

Red drum, also called redfish or channel bass, are another seasonal visitor to the inshore waters and coastal bays of southern areas of the Mid Atlantic region. You can count on them making a showing in Virginia waters every season but whether or not they venture very far into Maryland is a toss-up any given year. Sometimes they don't, and sometimes they are caught as far north as Delaware.

No matter how far north or south they range during any particular season redfish are near-shore fish. They are often caught from the surf and in inlets, but rarely from boats that are more than a mile or two away from the beach. They invade most coastal bays as well, particularly those with healthy weed growth and strong currents.

Since they are an excellent food fish, grow large and put up a significant fight, red drum are a highly sought-after gamefish. Just how big do they get? The IGFA recorded a whopping 94-pound, 2-ounce fish—so far as inshore fish go these are serious bruisers. Big drum in this category are usually called "bulls," a somewhat ironic term as most larger drum are females. Of course, fish of this size are the exception, not the norm. Most drum range between 2 and 20 pounds. These are the best for eating anyway, as larger, older fish sometimes have coarse flesh.

Red drum are easily differentiated from their black drum cousins by body shape and markings. Reds tend to have more elongated bodies, and they don't have the small whiskers present on blacks. Their body is more orange than black, with a white underbelly, and reds have a spot located on or near the tail. In some cases, they may have two or three spots. Overall and aside from sheer size they look very similar to croaker and anglers have been known to mistake horse croaker for puppy drum.

Redfish have down-turned, tough mouths, which gives you a clue as to their favorite foods. They like crustaceans, especially shrimp and crabs. They also feed on finfish, and are commonly caught on live baits. Many anglers believe that drum have a keen sense of smell and poor vision, but studies by marine biologists have more or less debunked this theory—in fact, their eye sight is average. When you're ready to set your sights on redfish, use these 10 tips and tricks that will help you hook into that bull of a lifetime.

1. For whatever reason, big reds like fish heads. Fresh mullet, menhaden and spot heads are all exceptionally good redfish baits. Peeler crabs are also excellent bait, provided they are fresh. Both baits are most productive when reds are gathered in small schools around cuts, channels and other fish-attracting features, as opposed to when they are scattered across the flats and shallows. When fishing the shallows for single redfish it's usually important to keep moving and cover a lot of

Ahhh, soon-to-be blackened redfish. What could be better?

territory, which makes bait fishing more or less ineffective.

2. Puppy drum love riprap. If you want to cast light or ultralight gear to pups in the 1 to 10 pound range, try tossing 3" twister tail soft plastic grubs right up to rip-rap jetties, and bounce the jig back along the bottom.

3. When fishing in shallow water for redfish keep an eye out for "tailing" fish. You will occasionally see the tip of the redfish's tail just breaking the surface of the water, as the fish roots around on the bottom. When you spot a tailing fish, cast at least 5' in front of it (10' is better) and give it a slow, steady retrieve.

4. Gold spoons are a favorite of shallow water redfish. Cast and retrieved through shallows with a slow wobble, they can be deadly. Those with rattles, such as the Nemire Red Ripper, often out-perform other styles.

5. Particularly in southern waters (and for our purposes, that includes Virginia and North Carolina) weedbeds are a favorite feeding area for red drum. Look to catch drum in the "potholes" (circular holes in the weedbeds). They tend to move into these holes during falling tides, and can be caught either by cast and retrieving through them or by tossing a bait into the area of open water. If the hit doesn't come within a minute or two move on, as reds hanging in the grassbeds are usually on the feed and will bite if given the opportunity. If nothing happens, chances are there aren't any fish around that particular spot.

6. An effective way to pry reds out of weedbeds is to troll alongside of them with un-weighted gold spoons, screwtail jigs, and Sluggo-style lures. Keep your boat just far enough out that you don't drive through the weedbeds, and keep it at idle speed. If you have several people onboard it's a good idea to post one on the foredeck armed with a spinning rod and a lure; when he spots depressions or near-by potholes in the weeds, he can take a shot at them.

7. Popping with a cork, a Floridian technique for catching bull reds, can be used just as effectively along the Mid Atlantic as it is down south. The rig is amazingly simple: just tie a couple feet of 30-pound leader to your main line, and attach a hook on the end. Then secure a large bobber with a concave surface—the cork— to your line just above the leader, so it sits about 3' above the bait. Add a couple of split shot just above the hook to keep your bait down. Cast this rig into any area that looks like a winner for redfish, and let it sit for a few seconds. Then jerk the line quickly and violently, so the bobber makes a popping noise. Wait 15 to 20 seconds, and pop it again. Reds seem attracted to the commotion, and with a little luck, when they come to investigate they'll find your bait.

8. When rays are thick, fish with lures. Many of the areas you'll find redfish also have a lot of rays, and usually, they will find your bait before the fish do. If you catch a ray or two when bait fishing, consider switching to lures before you find yourself inundated with these large, flat, anti-fish.

9. Reds respond well to noise makers and vibration producers. Add chuggers, rattling lures and lures with vibrating blades to your list of red-friendly lures. If you're casting bucktails tipped with bait, add to their attraction by clipping on a rattler tube (available at any tackle shop for a dollar or two, these small plastic rattle-filled chambers snap onto the shank of your hook).

10. In off-color, stained or muddy water, try lures that are root beer colored. For some reason reds seem to have an easier time spotting root beer in discolored water. Remember to slow down your presentation, and you'll sometimes catch just as many reds in dirty water as you will in gin-clear conditions.

CHAPTER 16
Sea Bass and Tautog

Tog and black sea bass are regular customers throughout this entire region. The IGFA record sea bass (10 pounds, 4 ounces) was caught off Virginia Beach, and the record tog (25 pounds even) was taken off the Ocean City, NJ coast. Both of these fish are easily distinguished and they're unrelated, so why lump them together? Because they're both ground fish which are often found in the same places at the same times. Anglers will commonly enjoy a mixed-bag with these species, even though there are a few particulars that serious anglers take into account when targeting one over the other. Sea bass and tautog are reef dwellers, and if there isn't a wreck, reef or shellfish bed on the bottom, you won't find either one of them around. The biggest difference in their behavior is that bass tend to hang around the edges of and over the top of structure, while tog dwell literally inside of it, in holes, nooks and crannies.

Black sea bass are an excellent eating fish, with firm, white meat. Interestingly, sea bass are hermaphrodites—they begin life as females, then change to males as they grow older. They are voracious predators which will eat just about anything from squid to fish. Because it stays on the hook well and works as well as anything else, squid is usually the favored bass bait. Since sea bass have very large jaws and suck a bait straight down without hesitation, they are relatively easy to catch once located. Like spot and croaker, this trait makes sea bass an excellent target when you have kids onboard and need fast, constant action. Although bass bites will ebb and flow with the tide, they will feed to some degree during almost any tidal cycle, adding to their reputation as a cooperative fish. During the peak fishing seasons of spring and fall you'll find them near just about any inshore structure in the ocean, most commonly in 50' to 150' of water. In the slightly warmer waters off the coast of Virginia and North Carolina, however, sea bass will bite right through the winter in these depths. In the northern areas of the range they seasonally migrate and during the winter months will be found in depths of 200' to 300'. They also are found in good numbers in most barrier island bays during the warmer months of the year, although the vast majority of the bay-caught sea bass are juveniles and often, an angler could catch a dozen in a day without ever seeing one close to keeper sized.

Another interesting quirk of the sea bass is its appearance when mature and well fed. Large, healthy fish will develop a hump on their forehead, just behind their eyes. These fish are nicknamed "humpbacks" or "humpies" and usually weigh 5 pounds or better.

Tog are a little less cooperative than sea bass. They use their thick, tough lips and front buck-teeth to crush their meals, before sucking them down. Those large, tough, puffy lips—which look like they are always puckered up for a kiss—

This husky hump-back sea bass was yanked from the African Queen wreck site, off the Maryland coast.

are also the key to understanding how to catch these fish. As often as not, when a tog bites he will suck the meat right out of crustacean baits and leave you with nothing but the shell in the blink of an eye. So anglers intent on togging need to stand at the ready at all times, with their hook-setting motion on a hair-trigger.

Like sea bass tog do migrate seasonally, but to a lesser degree. You won't catch them in water over 200' very often (look to find them in deep waters during winter), and at times you'll pluck them from as little as 10' of water in inlets and near bay-side rockpiles (usually early in the fall). Now, ready, set, go bottom fishing.

1. Big sea bass are aggressive and will often beat the smaller fish to the bait, so the largest fish holding on any one wreck or rockpile are usually caught early in the game. Accordingly, when you catch small fish after small fish without any larger ones mixed in, after a half hour or so it's reasonable to expect that there are only small ones in that area and you may want to consider moving on to a new location.

2. Because they have large mouths and feed voraciously, sea bass are one of the wreckfishes in the Mid Atlantic region that can be targeted effectively with artificials. Jigging spoons, soft plastics on heavy leadheads, and large bucktails are all effective. Conventional wisdom calls for tipping such lures with a squid strip or a slice of fish, but this isn't entirely necessary and there are days when screw tail plastics out-fish cut bait by a wide margin.

3. Both of these types of fish like to stick close to structure. To target them effectively you need to anchor directly over the structure the fish are holding on, or repeatedly drift over it. Anchoring over a small wreck or rockpile may be challenging, but it will result in fewer snags than drifting. Savvy anglers will locate a good spot with their fishfinder, and drop a float marker on it. Then they will take the time to anchor so the boat holds right next to the float, and the structure is directly below.

4. Watch the gill plates on sea bass. They're every bit as sharp as those found on croaker, and will result in nasty cuts if you're not careful. Children should not be allowed to handle sea bass. Their dorsal fins can stick you as well, but always look out for those gill plates.

5. Sea bass seem to be more apt to blow their air bladder when reeled up quickly than many other fish. In fact, if you fish near other boats and everyone is catching small sea bass in water deeper than 30', you will often see numerous released fish floating by in the throes of death. When you get into a large number of undersized bass, the best move is to relocate. When you feel a small fish on the line, reel it in very slowly to give it a chance to adjust to the pressure changes, and there's a better chance it will survive.

6. Sea bass like a little flash. Even when fishing bait like crab chunks or squid strips, you'll increase your catch by using hooks dressed with beads and spinners. When dropping jigging spoons, choose those with a bright silver finish.

7. It's best to use break-away weights when wreck fishing for these species. Because of the need to fish close in to structure, wreck anglers encounter a lot of snags and lost rigs. When you set up your top-and-bottom rigs—the standard for sea bass and tog—tie a short length of light leader between the bottom of the rig and your sinker. This way, if the weight becomes wedged in the wreck or rocks it will break off before the entire rig does.

8. Small moves can mean a lot when you're fishing for a species that holds so tightly to structure, and shifting your boat a few yards will sometimes change the action completely. While anchored over structure in a strong current, it's possible to shift the position of your boat without re-anchoring. If you've fished a specific spot for a while and it seems that the best fishing is over, crank your steering wheel all the way to one side or the other. In a stiff current this can move the boat as much as 15 or 20 yards, which will give you virgin territory to try. If the results are unsatisfactory—or fast action becomes slow again—crank the wheel all the way in the other direction and try again. For an even greater change run your anchor line off of a spring cleat (sea conditions permitting). Although this may hold your beam into the sea, increasing the rocking and rolling of your boat, it will change your position even more than cranking the wheel hard over does.

9. If you want to specifically target the bass, stick with squid strips. If tog are your main interest, however, you'll do better with green crab, peeler crab, calico crab, and clam chunks. When fishing in inlets, sand fleas are also a good choice.

10. Although sea bass and tautog are more or less sedentary, you can draw them into catching range with an unusual method of chumming. The day before you go fishing, you'll need to go to a seafood store or crab house, and ask them if they will give you (or if you can purchase for a reduced amount) their day's die-offs. Most are more than willing to point you to the dead crabs. So long as they haven't gone rancid in the sun, die-offs work just fine for this tactic. Smash a few crabs, and put them into a wire basket or a mesh bag with lots of weight. Usually, several pounds is needed because you want that chum to sit directly under the boat, right next to your lines. Every half hour or so add another smashed crab, and you will draw hungry bass into striking distance. This tactic also works well for weakfish, spot, and croaker. Even flounder pop up sometimes when chumming with die-offs.

CHAPTER 17
Spadefish

Spadefish don't have much tolerance for chilly water, and won't be caught north of Maryland many seasons. Even in southern Mid Atlantic waters, they are not an incredibly popular sportfish. The number of anglers targeting them has been growing, however, for about a decade now. And where they are found spades usually pack in tight, making for exciting fishing. Schools of adult spades usually number 500 or more and are oriented to wrecks or other significant structure—catch one, and you're probably in for a heck of a lot of action. You'll find schools over any significant wreck of reef, from the Delaware or Maryland coast (again, weather plays a key role in just how far they'll range during any given season) south to Virginia Beach during late July and August. Along the North Carolina coast, look for them from late June through September. Most of the time they'll be relatively close to shore, and can be found around any wreck 35' or deeper out to 20 miles or so from the beach in 100' to 120' of water. Spades will also gather in the mouths of major bays like the Chesapeake, but don't expect to find them in serious numbers in coastal bays behind barrier islands.

Spadefish are unusually tough to hook because they have tiny mouths. A number four hook is the largest you'll want to use, and sixes are better. Strangely, unlike most other inshore oceanic sportfish, spadefish prefer to bite on a slack or dying tide. This makes them an excellent option when other fish you've been targeting shut down after feeding on a strong tide.

Although spadefish look like some type of tropical angelfish, they are quite good on the grill. The meat of a spadefish is firm and white, but has an unusual taste. While unique it is considered excellent by most, and spades are a desirable food fish. That angelfish-like body has another consequence: spadefish can turn their wide, flat sides into the water, and put a lot of pressure on the line. Because of this attribute, even though spades are relatively small fish (the IGFA record is 14 pounds and most you catch will be in the 3 to 5 pound range) they often feel like a real trophy fish on the end of the line.

Most anglers will pursue spadefish with relatively light spinning gear in the 15- to 20-pound class. Heavier gear is useless because you can't catch spadefish using leaders heavier than 20 or 25 pounds, since anything larger is simply too thick to tie on those tiny hooks. Ready for a change of pace? Maybe it's time to target spadefish; use these tricks to ensure your success.

1. Chumming clams over wrecks or other significant structure is unquestionably the best way to catch spadefish. Most anglers will smash a dozen or so large cherrystones together, then hang them off the transom in a wire mesh basket or a cloth chum bag. Give the bag a shake now and again to make sure plenty of clam tidbits

Spadefish were once an under-fished species, but they've
become much more popular lately.

are entering the water, and add a fresh clam or two as necessary. Baits should be thin strips—not chunks—of the clam.

2. When attracted to a boat by chum, spadefish will often hold about 10' below the surface. Accordingly, use a small amount of weight to get your bait into this zone when there's a current. When the tide is dead-slack, it's usually more effective to ditch the weight and allow your bait to drift back naturally in the chum slick.

3. Never cast a spadefish bait away from the boat. Spadefish will usually stick tight to that chum line, and baits a mere 5' or 10' out off to the sides may go untouched.

4. When the tide goes completely slack, spadefish will sometimes hover right under the surface. Whenever you are targeting spadefish, keep an eye out for a thin stick-like dorsal fin just breaking the water. If you see one, try to drift your bait back close by and you should get a strike.

5. Many savvy anglers will find a good wreck then target sea bass and tog while the tide is running. When it quits and the bite drops off, swap the bottom rigs for spadefish appropriate gear, and drop the clam bag over the side.

6. Don't set out lines, stick the rods in the holders, and expect spadefish to attack. They don't usually like static lines, and want bait that appears to be drifting naturally. The most effective way to get a bite is to fish with an open bail, letting line fall out slack as the current carries it away from the boat. Watch the line closely, and when you see it jump, close the bail and reel it in tight.

7. Anchor according to the wind, not the tide, to get your boat set right over the wreck. Remember—spades will bite during slack water. If you anchor up when the tide is flowing, your boat is likely to swing off of the wreck as soon as the good bite begins.

8. Keep the clam bits in good supply. Once spadefish arrive in your chum slick, they will usually hang around until the clams stop flowing. The key here is—just like with stripers, blues and other gamefish—to keep the flow of chum steady.

9. When a spadefish takes a clam bait, allow it a three-count before setting the hook. They will sometimes grasp the strip of meat and turn before sucking it all the way into their mouth, and if you strike right away, you may pull the hook and bait away from the fish.

10. Since spadefish require fairly specific rigs (particularly, the tiny hooks) and you're likely to encounter a wide variety of other gamefish in the same areas they frequent, whenever you go spadefishing it's a good idea to keep rods rigged with standard chumming rigs ready to use in extra rodholders or hard top rocket launchers. If you start experiencing sudden, jolting strikes or break-offs, place a larger bait on the bigger hook and rig, and lower away.

CHAPTER 18
Spanish Mackerel

Spanish mackerel are another coastal raider that appears from Delaware waters south most seasons, but can range farther north when the water is warm enough. Still, these hard-fighting fish have a pretty limited time frame during which they range north of the Carolinas. Usually they will head north in the mid summer and pop up off the coasts of Virginia and Maryland starting in July, but the first cool nights of September send them scurrying back south. During very warm summers they have been caught as far north as Cape Cod, but this is a real rarity.

Spanish mackerel are good eating fish, but their soft meat must be treated gently and quickly drops in food value if frozen. In fact, many anglers eat them fresh or not at all. Although a 13-pound Spanish holds top world-record honors, most are a far cry from this size. Two- to three-pound fish are average, five-pound fish are nice, and a 10-pounder is a real lunker. They can be caught in major estuaries like the Chesapeake, but don't expect to encounter these fish very often in barrier island bays.

Spanish mackerel are good fighters, which jump more often than stripers but less often than blues. Since most are relatively small the hectic fight comes from their speed, not their bulk. On light gear they provide an exceptional battle, zipping back and forth as quickly as any sportfish. Many anglers like to target Spanish Macks when they're schooled and mixed with bluefish feeding under birds, when it's possible to throw light lures on gear in the 8- to 10-pound class—the perfect recipe for an epic light tackle battle.

Spanish mackerel eat mostly fin fish and usually feed at or near the surface. As you might expect this has a lot of influence on fishing methods, and usually Spanish mackerel must be specifically targeted to produce decent catches. You may pick up an oddball fish once or twice a season while chumming or bottom fishing, but to be consistently successful with mackerel you'll have to concentrate on them. Target these fish close to shore—they're rarely caught in waters deeper than 80' or 90' and are often caught by trolling just a mile or two off the beach—and in areas where bluefish are known to feed with regularity. And, use these 10 tricks to put more mackerel in your fishbox.

1. For whatever reason, more often than not Spanish mackerel prefer gold over silver. The standard methods of catching these fish—trolling or casting spoons to breaking fish—works best when lure color is gold. Clark spoons are the gold standard, so to speak, but Tony Acettas and Crippled Alwives are also good choices.

2. Bump up the throttle to catch Spanish mack. Trolling speeds of four to five mph won't produce any fish. Speeds of six or seven mph will produce some, but an

Spanish mackerel are seasonal visitors along most of the Mid-Atlantic coast.

eight-mph troll is better for these speedsters. Naturally, this means that you would need a ton of weight (and the heavy gear to support it) if you wanted to run your trolling lines anywhere but right on the surface. Luckily, right at the surface is where these fish usually feed. Use just enough weight to keep your spoons from flipping out of the water and skipping across the surface. When the mackerel do seem to be sub-surface feeding, slow down a hair and use a #1 or #2 planer to get your offerings down deeper.

3. When casting spoons to breaking fish, you'll do best on Spanish if you rip the spoon across the surface as quickly as you can. Don't be afraid to crank the reel at maximum velocity—that's how these fish like it.

4. One other effective method of taking these fish is with live baits. Peanut bunker and finger mullet will both work. They can be drifted and live lined anywhere Spanish mackerel are present, but quite often bluefish will be mixed in with mackerel—and will chew the majority of your baits to pieces.

5. You may be able to find breaking fish and working birds, but that doesn't mean there are Spanish mackerel in attendance. They are usually mixed in with bluefish, but just as often, you'll locate a school of breaking fish and catch blues, only. Finding out if there are Spanish mackerel around is easier than you might think, however. Simply watch the feeding fish. If there are mackerel around you will see them jump clear out of the water, often in small groups of twos and threes. They will jump in an arc, and often "greyhound," or perform several of these jumps in a row. Bluefish will absolutely, positively, never exhibit this behavior, so if you see the arcing fish in greyhounding mode, you know Spanish mackerel are around.

6. Spanish mackerel have teeth that are fairly sharp, though they don't match those of a bluefish. They are sharp enough, however, to cut through monofilament leaders. Save your gear and land more fish by tying a 6" trace of wire leader ahead of your lures.

7. Whether casting or trolling, any time you fish for Spanish mackerel with spoons you stand a good chance of encountering massive line twist. Trolling spoons at high speed is the worst case scenario when it comes to twist, and ten minutes is sometimes enough to trash a spool of line. Accordingly, whenever you troll for these fish make sure you use high-quality ball-bearing swivels between your main line and leader.

8. When breaking fish aren't visible, try trolling along tidal breaks and scum lines. Often, Spanish mackerel will orient along changes in the water and any tide line or color change is a good bet when you're in search mode.

9. These fish are always on the move. If you've located a good bite which dies out after 15 or 20 minutes, don't spend a lot of time working the area. Chances are, the Spanish have moved on.

10. On slick calm days, try increasing your trolling speed even more than usual. Conversely, in rough seas drop it back a bit. You'll find you get just as many strikes. For whatever reason, the mackerel seem to have a tougher time catching the lure when the water is riled, yet they show less interest when it's glassy out.

CHAPTER 19
Speckled Sea Trout

Speckled sea trout—specks, as they're often called—are very similar to weakfish in body shape, possess the same delicate flesh and they have the same set of vicious looking teeth. But when it comes to catching them, the differences are much greater than the similarities. Specks are shallow water feeders, and will be found in coastal bays where the water is just waist-deep, in many cases. On occasion (usually during spring and fall, when the fish are migrating along the coast) specks can also be taken in the surf.

Speckled sea trout average 1 to 3 pounds, but occasionally "gators" in the 10 pound range are caught. The largest ever taken on hook and line was more than 17 pounds. Specks are very popular gamefish in Florida and along most of the Gulf coats, especially in Texas. They can be caught all the way up into New York waters but as with many warm water transients, this is the northernmost extent of their range. Once you get north of Delaware, most seasons their population is sparse. Down in the Carolinas, speckled trout are a favorite target of many anglers and can be caught in healthy numbers, to say the least. Their favored diet consists of shrimp, crabs, other crustaceans and small baitfish.

Specks hit a lure with vigor, and they may be caught at different levels of the water column. That's part of what makes fishing for them so interesting—during different tidal cycles, you may catch them up near the surface, then at mid depth, then down near the bottom. They're rarely caught in water over 20' deep, most are caught in 10' or less water, and the very best spots are usually in the shallows near points, creek mouths and tidal rips, or along channel edges where large shallow flats meet well-defined drops.

Speckled sea trout will establish patterns in their feeding techniques, which may hold for a week, month, or even a season at a time. If you can figure out the patterns the fish are feeding on, you'll catch a lot more fish. Let's say you find that at the flood tide they're feeding near the surface, and on a dropping tide, they feed near bottom. The next time you go fishing, note the current tidal cycle, and stick to fishing according to the pattern you saw the previous trip—if the tide is dropping, cast and retrieve near bottom, and if it's flooding, try retrieving near the surface. More often than not, you'll find that the pattern holds, at least until the next major shift in weather patterns or forage availability. Here are 10 tips that are sure to help you catch more trout.

1. Specks usually like a vigorous, moving bait. Instead of slow and steady retrieves, stick with erratic, faster retrieves. When hopping jigs along the bottom, make them jump up quickly then freefall. Constantly vary the speed, and keep that lure moving at all times.

Four inch chartreuse/pumpkinseed twister tail grubs are killers when you're going after speckled trout.

2. When casting lures to speckled trout in bays, it's tough to beat a 4" curly tail jig, either chartreuse, pink or white in color. Rig it on a half-ounce jig head, and you can use it for all ranges through the water column in the areas you're likely to locate trout.

3. Never stop the retrieve short of the boat. Specks will often follow a lure right up to the surface. If you stop reeling when the lure is 5' or 6' away, you will end up missing some fish that would have charged and struck in the final seconds.

4. Moving water is key for locating speckled sea trout in the shallows. Anywhere the current creates a rip or is visibly moving, you're likely to find these fish. Points, cuts and rips are prime speckled trout territory.

5. Don't be afraid to search out cuts barely big enough to get your boat into. At times, you'll find the largest speckled sea trout inhabiting 5' wide, 2' deep cuts that run into marshland. When patrolling a shoreline or marsh in search of specks, cast as far up into those little cuts as you possibly can. Remember that most of them will have slightly deeper patches of water on the inside of a bend, where you'll often locate the best fish.

6. Multiple specks will congregate in the same spot, even if the productive water is only a few feet across. Often, you'll find a point or bar that creates a tidal rip, which attracts specks. You'll find that you must pinpoint cast to the very tip of the rip, or the very base of the rip, to get a strike—anywhere else, and your bait gets ignored. Yet if you cast to that spot over and over again, you'll catch fish after fish. So don't move on simply because you've already caught a fish from a very small hotspot—keep working it until you're sure there aren't any other hungry trout around.

7. Bang the shoreline with your lures. Especially in areas where there's a sharp drop-off, speckled trout will often be feeding within inches of marsh grass or sandy beach. Make your casts as close to the shoreline as possible, and whenever you can, cast parallel to shore and retrieve along it.

8. Oyster bars that come within a few feet of the surface are another good spot to cast for specks. On a high tide try ripping your lure directly over the bar, and on a low tide, allow it to drop down next to the bar on whichever side has deeper water.

9. Specks are strong fighters, and pound for pound, will out-fight weakfish. However, they have that same weak jaw that's easily ripped. So it's even more important that you fish with a loose drag when you're after specks. Don't over pressure the fish, and allow them to run as much as they like. Also, as with weakfish, make sure you have a net ready before the fish is sighted and get that net under the fish well before you lift its head out of the water.

10. If you're fishing plastic tail jigs, make sure you have plenty of extra tails onboard. As with bluefish and other toothy predators, specks will often short-strike and "tail" the jig (eat the last 1⁄2" off.) When this happens, immediately swap out the tail. It may look like it will still work, but that last 1/2" provides some critical motion. Fish with it and you'll eventually realize that the trout will not strike a tailed lure half as much as they will hit a fresh one, with the whole curl.

CHAPTER 20
Striped Bass

Striped bass are the king of the Mid Atlantic inshore sportfishing world. They're the most popular gamefish, can be caught throughout the entire region for much if not all of the season, and they're good fighting, good eating fish that are available in good numbers. They're one of the few success stories in fisheries management and barring any natural disaster or legislative stupidity, stripers are back in force for the foreseeable future.

The striped bass is commonly called rockfish, or striper. They average 1 to 5 pounds, but 10- and 15-pound fish are relatively common and much larger fish—up to 60 pounds and above—will be encountered in near-shore waters, coastal bays, inlets and the surf. The world record striper was a hair over 78 pounds, but catches nearing 100 pounds have been claimed by commercial netters. By some estimates, up to 50 percent of all the stripers along the Atlantic seaboard are born in the Chesapeake, and return to it to spawn. After spawning, most of the large stripers migrate back to the ocean and travel up the coast to feed in bait-rich northern waters of New Jersey, New York, and Massachusetts. Several rivers in Virginia and North Carolina also have strong striper runs, however, and during the winter months there's usually good striper fishing in the southern Mid Atlantic.

Stripers have sandpaper-like teeth, which makes handling them by the jaw relatively easy. Note to catch-and-release anglers: hoisting large stripers by the jaw and holding them vertically can do internal damage to the fish; they should be supported with a second hand (wet it first, so you don't remove the fish's' protective coat of slime) behind the anal fin.

Stripers feed not by biting and cutting their pray, but by sucking it in and grabbing it; most meals are swallowed whole. Some favorites of the striped bass include: eels, soft or peeler crabs, menhaden, spot, bloodworms, clams, and herring.

Stripers can be taken with dozens of different methods, many of which are discussed in this book. Whichever you choose to use, remember these striped bass tips—they're applicable to all methods and modes of angling.

1. In most conditions, stripers feed like clockwork in relation to the tides. Commonly the change of tide is the best, from one hour or so before the slack tide to a half hour or so after. In coastal inlets the tide is particularly important, and will often mean the difference between catching dozens of fish versus never having a strike.

2. Striped bass are light-sensitive fish. On bright, bluebird days look for them in deeper water, and on cloudy low-light days, look for the fish in shallower water or close to the surface over deep water. Sunset and sunrise are good times to target these fish.

3. Stripers are schooling fish, and they often school by size. When you're catching

The most popular recreational sportfish in most of the Mid Atlantic is the striper.

14" fish one after the other, consider changing your game plan entirely or move to a different location. Otherwise, you're likely to catch throw-backs all day.

4. When the stripers are in migration mode during the spring and fall, hit the near-shore shoals. Any shoal within 10 miles or so of shore which has a significant depth change can attract them. Note that both state and federal regulations will severely restrict where and when you can target stripers and these regs change from year to year—so do your homework before you go fishing.

5. A rockfish's metabolism changes with the water temperature, and successful anglers will have to adjust lure retrieve speeds, jigging techniques and trolling speeds accordingly. In the hot summer months provide lots of action and speed, but early and late in the year, keep it slow and lethargic.

6. Particularly in the fall, eels are the number one bait for stripers. Live eels drifted over structure and trolled artificial eels will both produce fish.

7. Stripers like to grab their prey, and squeeze the life out of it. This means that they often will grab a baitfish and swim with it clenched tightly in their jaws for several seconds, before sucking it all the way in. As a result, whenever in doubt, give the fish a 5- or 10-second count from the time you feel it pick up a bait to the time you set the hook.

8. When fishing in a chum slick, use the same variety of fish for bait as you are using for chum. Stripers seem to become focused on the type of fish or chum that attracts them, as they peruse the baits offered to them. Speaking of bait—in an interesting geographical split, many anglers north of the Mason-Dixon line like to use the head of bunker as baits, and throw the rest of the fish away when targeting large stripers. Yet most anglers south of the Mason-Dixon line do the exact opposite. They toss the heads overboard, and fish with fillet or chunk baits.

9. Stripers love rocks and rips. Look to find them around inlet jetties, rock piles, and where visible rips form on the surface of the water.

10. Stripers are slow, steady fighters that do not burn themselves out on single, spectacular runs. When catching large ones on light gear, give them their head. Do not attempt to muscle or push the fish, which often leads to break-offs. Instead be patient; the fish will eventually wear down.

CHAPTER 21
Swordfish

Swordfish is one of the ultimate offshore catches. These fish are incredibly strong, incredibly hard to locate and catch, and taste incredibly good. Full disclosure: I still haven't caught one. Every year I take at least one overnighter in the hopes of hooking a sword, and although tunas, shark, and mahi have come up to the gaff under our night-lights, it still hasn't happened with a swordfish. So all of the sword-fish information in this chapter comes from outside sources.

Swords can get big—really big. The world record fish weighed in at 1,182 pounds. This is a long-standing record, which was set way back in 1953. What are the chances of catching a swordfish in this class? Not great. Sword stocks have really been pounded by longliners, and catching them in the Mid Atlantic region is still a long shot, although their numbers have been on the rise in southern waters. Running out of Miami or Islamorada a good captain can hope to get two or three bites a night, and a few years ago, swords were just as rare down there as they are in our region today. So hopefully, the recovery will work its way north and the catch rates will pick up in our area soon.

These are strictly offshore fish, with most being taken along the edge of the continental shelf in 100 fathoms or more of water. Canyon tips and edges, temperature breaks, and sea mounts are all features that will attract these fish. They're usually taken by anglers drifting through the night, while illuminating the water around their boat with artificial lights. Similarly, a chemical light stick is se-cured to the lines about 10' away from the bait, to help draw in the fish. Lines are set near the surface, 100' down, 150' down, and so on, staggered throughout the water column, suspended under balloons.

Like marlin and other billfishes, swords slash at a bait with their bill before attempting to eat it. Since squid is their main fare—and by far the bait most com-monly used to catch them—an angler's baits will often be slashed in half by the fish. Thus, it's extremely important to sew the squid's mantle to its tentacles to en-sure it remains whole when the swordfish turns and eats it, after the initial attack. Want to try and catch a swordie? Hopefully, you'll have better luck than I've had to date. Use these tactics to get one up to the gaff.

1. Bring squid jigs with you when you're going swordfishing. Often squid will swim up to the lights around your boat, where you can catch them. Fill up the livewell, then start live-baiting with the squid.

2. Some captains prefer blue lights, some prefer green, and some just use regular white halogens. The lights set from your boat will attract baitfish, which in turn attracts predators like swordfish and tuna. But testing I performed for magazine ar-

The night angler wistfully awaits a swordfish bite.

ticles proved that green attracts more baitfish, while blue (the color which out-lasts others that fade as distance from the source increases) attracts fish from a longer distance. So set out both—a green light to which the critters will swarm, and a blue light to call them in from afar.

3. Watch your balloon bobbers for lateral motion. Often a fish will take a bait and swim while remaining at the same depth. The balloon won't go under, but will seem to slide across the surface of the ocean.

4. Swordfish have relatively soft mouths, and hooks rip free of them with regularity. Apply as little pressure as possible to move the fish, and never crank the drag down hard.

5. During daylight before an overnighter for swords, keep an eye out for squid boats. These huge steel factory ships will be towing massive nets off the edge of the shelf, and they definitely indicate the presence of squid. Since you'll find the predators where you find the bait, if you see one of these squid boats keep it in mind when choosing where to set up for the evening.

6. Try to set baits that are near the surface at the very edge of the lightline surrounding your boat. Whatever type of lights you choose to use, you'll see an edge where they fade out into blackness. This is where the predators often hunt, and this is where you want your bait to be waiting for them.

7. Lunar cycles are extremely important when swordfishing. The last quarter moon leading up to a full moon is usually considered the best. Some captains like to fish on a full moon but some others claim there's too much natural live bait swimming around for the swords to find your hooks, because squid often rise to the surface to mate under the full moon. All agree that the last few days of a disappearing moon and the first few days of a new moon provide the slowest action of all.

8. Temperature breaks are considered very, very important when hunting for swords. Many serious captains will cruise for miles, to reach the edge of a Gulf Stream eddy where there's a nice change. So before leaving the dock, check your offshore temp chart and see if there are any good breaks within cruising distance.

9. Get good squid. Swordfish can be picky, and the cheap box of squid you buy for sea bass bait won't cut it. Larger, 1' squid which retain their outer skin are best. These are usually sold for trolling and command top-dollar, but the better bait is worth the extra bucks.

10. Chunk with squid and/or butterfish as you drift. There's debate over how much effect this has on drawing in swordfish, but there's no question it will lead big eye and yellowfin to the boat. Plus, everyone I know who has landed a sword at a Mid Atlantic canyon has done so while chunking.

CHAPTER 22
Tilefish (Golden, Sand and Blue Line)

Few fish taste as incredible as the golden tilefish—and few are as tough to harvest with a rod and reel. To catch tilefish you'll have to deep-drop in water 600' to 900' deep, with 2 to 4 pounds of lead. You'll have to wait five minutes for your rig to hit the bottom. And the real challenge will be cranking up the fish plus all that lead, a half-hour endeavor that will leave you winded and with sore arms. The reward is well worth the effort: golden tilefish tastes like lobster. I don't mean it tastes sort of like lobster, or that it has a lobster-ish taste. It tastes just like lobster. If it weren't for the consistency, you'd never know the difference. And considering that you can haul up a fish that will dress out with 10- or even 20-pound fillets of lobster-yum, all that cranking suddenly seems like a good thing.

Golden tilefish is another species that was decimated due to longlining, but they are well on the road to recovery and can be caught in decent numbers these days. Find a good spot and loading the cooler is not out of the question—if you're in shape. These fish can grow upwards of 50 pounds (the IGFA hook and line record is 51 pounds, 2 ounces) and have a body shape similar to that of a grouper. So while you're looking at cranking up hundreds of yards of line, there's a serious contender trying to swim in the opposite direction.

Sand and blue line tilefish don't grow nearly as large; 4-pound fish are whoppers. Nor do they taste like lobster, but they do have an excellent firm white meat. They're usually caught in much shallower water, in the 250' to 400' range, and just above the edge of the continental shelf they can be taken in large numbers.

All tilefish bite well on squid (use whole squid for the big goldens and squid chunks for smaller tilefish) and they'll also take fish chunks. If you have unlimited bait funds, however, put lobster on the hook and you'll catch even more. Their diet explains the taste of their meat—tilefish love eating lobster and lobster-like crustaceans. Cut open their bellies and you'll often find these shellfish inside. When you're ready for a real change of pace give tilefish fishing a shot, and use these tricks to put more in your cooler.

1. Tilefish of all varieties live in burrows in muddy bottoms. You can spot these burrows if you have a high power, good quality fishfinder. Crank up the bottom zoom as far as it will go, and look for a series of unusual depressions while searching for a spot.

2. Monofilament is nearly useless when deep-dropping. You'll need to be spooled up with braid or superline like Magibraid or Fireline. These no-stretch lines will let you feel every nibble from 800' above, even when 1-pound fish are eating the hook. With monofilament, however, there's so much stretch you won't know a fish is on the line until you have it half way in.

It'll take a lot of work to crank a golden tilefish up from 750' but the taste of this fish's meat makes it all worthwhile.

3. Many anglers won't have fishfinders potent enough to find the hotspots in such deep water. If this is your predicament, note that you'll be able to feel the difference between sticky mud bottoms and sandy bottoms (sticky mud is better). That 2- or 3-pound weight will sink in and stick, just like smaller weights do on mucky bottoms. While drifting, allow your weight to bounce bottom and let out line for a few seconds so it stays there. Then tighten up and lift the rod tip. So long as you're fishing with braid you'll be able to feel whether the weight pulls right off of sand, or is stuck in mud until it slingshots free.

4. Multiple hooks are the rule when tilefishing. With all that reeling and dropping, you won't want to wonder if your baits have been cleaned off by small fish, or if a shark bit it off. Drop with five- or six-hook rigs, so you can miss a few strikes and know you still have baits on the line.

5. Boost the chances a fish finds your bait in the dark, deep water, by adding small glow-in-the-dark sleeves to your hook shank.

6. Tilefish stay near bottom, so hooks set 5' or 6' up the leader usually don't get hit. To increase the odds, place a 1-ounce weight where your swivel and main line meet the rig. If you've drifted for a while and felt strikes but don't have any fish on the line, every few minutes try dropping your rod tip and allowing the line to go slack. The small weight will pull down the top of your rig, pulling those baits down to the mud.

7. Fishing for tilefish after dark requires lots and lots of extra hooks, and is usually a long-shot. Although tiles are awake and feeding, shark also become very active in the deep at night. Often, within seconds all the hooks will be bitten off of your rig.

8. Look out for lobster pots along the canyon edges. Their drop lines are so long that you can be a quarter of a mile away from the nearest polyball, yet still become fouled on the line. Always set up on the up-tide side if they're in the area, to prevent tangles.

9. Circle hooks are must-haves. There's no way to set the hook from 600' or 800' away, so you need hooks that self-set with steady pressure. 8/0 circles are a good choice. Most found on rigs sold as "grouper deep-drop rigs" will do the trick.

10. When you cook up tilefish, don't mess with that meat! Adding spice will only change the flavor. Instead steam it plain, as you would lobster, then dip it in drawn butter. You'll be amazed at how good this meat is all on its own! You want a full-blown tilefish recipe? Then you'll have to get *Off The Hook, Rudow's Recipes for Cooking Your Catch,* available from Tidewater Publishers (800/638-7641 or www. cmptp.com.).

CHAPTER 23
Triggerfish

Triggerfish are probably one of the most under-harvested fish in the Atlantic. You can catch them both inshore and offshore, usually under flotsam when in the deep but also off of the bottom or around wrecks in inshore waters. Their meat is firm and delicious, they bite readily, and when you find one you often find a school of a dozen or more fish. So, why don't people target them? At least in part because they've had triggerfish nibble at their baits time and time again, without ever catching one. The reason why is simple: these fish have tiny mouths filled by two huge buck teeth, and they are experts at removing bait from hooks without ever getting stuck.

Triggerfish don't get incredibly large and the IGFA's biggest was just a hair over 6 pounds. Most you find in the Mid Atlantic will range from 1 to 3 pounds. They'll be found off the Atlantic coast from May or June through October, and most seasons they start popping up beneath floating logs, buoys and other items several weeks before mahi-mahi make their initial appearance.

Once hooked triggerfish put up a great fight. Like other fish with rounded bodies they can turn broadside and apply a lot more pressure against the rod than you'd think. Once in the boat, look out for those buck teeth—they can cause some serious damage. Give fishing for triggers a try, with these tricks.

1. The most common problem people encounter when trying to hook trigger fish is that they don't have small enough hooks on the boat. Size 6—not 6/0—hooks are as big as you'll want when trying to get a trigger on the line.

2. Just about any bait will do; squid, fish chunks and the like all generate strikes. But taking triggerfish on artificials is nearly impossible. You may notice, however, that when casting soft plastic baits to flotsam in the hopes of hooking a mahi-mahi, you may feel a bite and discover that there are small round divots in the plastic. When you see these, reach for the little hooks and bait chunks—it's a sure indication of triggerfish.

3. This may not appeal to the sportsman in you, but...if you see a triggerfish under something offshore and want to harvest it, yet it will not take a bait, drive the boat right up next to it and try free-gaffing the fish. Most of the time triggerfish will refuse to leave the cover of what they are hiding under, right up until the gaff strikes them.

4. If you're wreck fishing and triggerfish are near by, you can often chum them right up to the surface. Tiny squid bits work best, but they'll rise for just about any form of chum so long as it's cut into very small pieces.

This triggerfish was baited with a tiny piece of butterfish, and pulled out from under a lobster pot float.

5. Look out for the spike—the "trigger"—on the back of the fish. It will inflict a nasty wound if you're not careful.

6. If you catch a small trigger and there are larger pelagics in the area, consider live-baiting it. Studies have shown that trigger fish are eaten by all of the major predators, including tunas and billfish. Particularly near thick weedlines, it's worth sacrificing the catch to make a bigger one.

7. Triggerfish love the small shrimp and crabs found in weedlines. If you don't have any natural bait onboard but there are weeds near by, scoop up a bunch in a dip net and spread it across the deck. Pick out the critters, thread them on a hook, and the triggerfish will start biting.

8. Careful when cleaning triggerfish—they have extremely tough scales and they're incredibly slimy, too. The combination often leads to slips with the fillet knife.

9. Like mahi-mahi, triggerfish will sometimes follow each other up to the boat. Particularly when you're fishing inshore wrecks and hooking these fish, keep an extra rod at the ready. If one trigger follows another to the surface, be ready to pitch it a bait at a moments notice.

10. Triggerfish can be leader shy. 20-pound test is usually about the maximum you can use when fishing for them, and at times, you'll have to go down to even thinner line to get them to bite. If you see the fish swim right up to a bait, stop, hover for a moment, then swim back under cover, you know it's time to go lighter.

CHAPTER 24
Tuna (Albacore, Big Eye, Bluefin, and Yellowfin)

Tuna fish mean power. Big power. Enough to tire out a boatload of anglers. Enough to break rods, snap leaders, bend hooks and strip the gears in a reel. Battles can go on for hours, and the longer they last, the greater the chances the fish will win. But catching tuna also means great meals, sometimes enough to last for months. Their meat is highly prized, and can be prepared in a multitude of ways. Of course, each of the tuna species is fairly unique. So let's look at them one at a time.

When it comes to tuna, a single fish may be all it takes to excite an entire boatload of anglers.

Albacore

Albacore—often called longfin tuna, thanks to their oversized pectoral fins—are virtually always caught in canyon waters. When they're not, it's a sure bet the edge of the shelf isn't far away. They range throughout the Mid Atlantic and well beyond and can be found seasonally in our waters from summer through fall, with numbers usually increasing later in the year. The largest hook-and-line caught albacore weighed in at 88 pounds, 2 ounces. While most you're likely to encounter will run in the 20-pound range, 40-pounders are not at all uncommon. Often they'll be mixed in schools of yellowfin, and when it comes to albacore, it's just as common to have sudden multiple hook-ups as it is to hook single fish.

Albacore are easily identified not only because of their long pectorals, which may stretch all the way beyond their anal fin, but also because these fish lack the colorful mottling other tunas may display, and commonly have light sides with a darker colored back. They're easy to identify from the cockpit, too. After being hooked on the troll and fought to the boat, much of the time they'll swim along just 10' or so below the surface and won't budge an inch. A glance over the side is all it takes to see those long pectorals spread wide, providing plenty of water resistance and making life tough for the angler. And since these fish travel in packs and often strike several lines at once, it's not unusual for two, three or even four anglers at a time to dance around the cockpit in the throes of battle.

Another trait albacore are known for is their reputation as a "white" tuna, a reference to their meat. It's light color, firm texture and awesome taste puts it at or near the top of just about everyone's list of favorite food fish. Put some on your plate using these tactics.

1. Albacore like green lures, and the Green Machine holds the number-one spot as the most effective albacore lure around. If you want to target these fish, keep an ample selection of Green Machines on hand; I never leave the dock with less than a half dozen of them. As a back-up or for a change, try pulling a chartreuse or off-green Sea Witch rigged with a 'hoo.

2. Make single hook-ups into multiples by staying away from the throttles when a rod goes down. It's hard, but force yourself not to react. Leave the rod in the holder and don't vary your speed one bit for at least 10 seconds. Often, another one or two or three will hop on the lines. Some captains swear that turning towards the side the strike came from improves the odds.

3. Although it's tough to locate them by chunking, once albacore have been located while on the troll it's possible to switch over to chunking. You'll have to pitch a lot of bait over the gunwales, and it'll have to happen within seconds of the initial strikes. But if you can get those chunks in the water and keep them flowing you have a shot at loading the boat.

4. Stay in water at least 250' or deeper if you hope to catch albacore. Come inshore much more than this, and your chances go way down.

5. Look to find albacore where hard weedlines break up into scattered weeds. Often, where the structure begins to disintegrate these fish will be on the hunt.

6. Large albacore have a habit of zig-zagging from side to side as they near the boat. For this reason, if you have a dredge in the water it may be tough to keep the fish away from it. Instead of trying to force the fish's direction you're better served by pulling the dredge and any other lines that could cause tangles.

7. Squid are an albacore's favorite food. If you're going to attempt to chunk for them, you're better off doing so with squid than butterfish.

8. Birds rigs are another good albacore lure. But with this species it's important to modify the rig by replacing the string of lures running behind the bird with Green Machines.

9. Albacore don't usually go into a "death spiral" like yellowfin and bluefin. This

Albacore are also called longfin tuna, for obvious reasons.

sometimes throws off inexperienced gaffers, who are waiting for that perfect side shot. Don't wait—strike it across the back, just behind the head, as soon as it's within gaffing range.

10. Albacore like lures with a lot of action, and pre-rigged Green Machines sometimes come with very heavy leaders that squelch the lure's motion in the water. Buy them un-rigged, and try using 100-pound or even 80-pound test. You'll see the difference in action the first time you watch it from the cockpit.

Big Eye

Big eye are probably the toughest Mid Atlantic tuna to catch, for two reasons: they're only found in the canyons and beyond, and they rarely bite during full sunlight. Most big eye are caught at night or right at sunrise and sunset—hours that are tough to fish when you need to be 50 or more miles offshore.

These fish are real beasts, too. The IGFA record is 392 pounds, but catching 100- to 200-pound fish is as or more common than catching smaller big eye. Once hooked they fight as well as any other tuna, and as table fare, they're at or near the top of the list. A big eye's meat is usually relatively fatty throughout, making these great fish to eat as sushi.

Because of the fact that big eye are never found close to home, they don't account for a large proportion of the recreationally caught tuna in the Mid Atlantic. Just how healthy are the stocks? Who knows—big eye have never been caught in huge numbers but the catch rate for those targeting them seems to be more consistent through the years than it is for bluefin or other species known to be highly pressured. Very little is actually known about just how many big eye there are in the Atlantic. Identifying a big eye is not always as easy as it seems, either. Their eyes do tend to be larger than those of a yellowfin. Their second dorsal and anal fins don't grow as long as they do on yellowfin, making them look somewhat like bluefin. Plus, any 100- to 200-pound tuna caught in a Mid Atlantic canyon is more likely to be a big eye than a yellowfin or bluefin. Big eye also tend to have a more squat body shape than the other tunas. That said, sometimes the only way to figure out for sure which species a particular fish belongs to is to check the liver, which is striated in big eye but smooth in yellowfin. Of course, before this ever becomes an issue you'll have to hook one. Boost your chances using these tactics.

1. If you really want to target big eye, plan on doing an overnighter. You can catch them chunking in the dark (one of the best ways to catch a big eye), but you can also target them on the troll during low-light times like sunrise and sunset, when most anglers are still cruising for the fishing grounds.

2. Big eye do much of their feeding down deep, but they must surface occasionally to warm their blood. If you spot masses of squid hundreds of feet below and you know big eye have been found in the area, stick with the spot. Even if there aren't any big eye around at the moment, those fish will come up near the surface sooner or later. Note—this fact accounts for the big eye that are caught during daylight hours. Even though most of their feeding during the day takes place hundreds of feet down, they will still pop up to the surface waters to warm up.

3. Look for whales. Often, a pod of them will indicate big eye near by. If you're fishing during the day, even if you go hours at a time without a strike, stick around them. As mentioned earlier, sooner or later they'll come up to the top.

4. If you're after big eye during the day go ahead and up-size your leaders. Don't

This big eye was caught from around a pod of whales in Washington Canyon, off the Delmarva coast.

worry about the fish seeing the line—they won't. One of the reasons big eye stay deep during full sunlight is that they can't see very well in bright light because their eyes are tuned to low-light conditions. In fact, you'll often have several hits and misses from big eye, simply because they're having trouble targeting your bait or lures. Accordingly, 200-pound test is not out of line.

5. Use squid, and squid imitations. Spreader bars are good, as are natural rigged squid. These are the big eye's favorite food—so give them what they want.

6. When chunking for big eye at night, go full blast with the night lights. Green fluorescents are best for holding lots of bait, but blues attract fish from farther away. So if you can, put out both.

7. If you can attract live squid to the boat at night (with your lights, of course) catch some and live-bait them. You can "hook" squid on squid jigs, and at times, they'll come close enough to the boat to scoop them up with a dip net. When live baiting them, put a single short-shank hook through the mantle, near the top.

8. Up-size your tackle when targeting these fish. In the areas where you find big eye you'll be so deep that if the fish decides to dive and you can't stop it, it'll spool you. 50's and larger are appropriate.

9. When night fishing, the first time you bring a big eye near the boat be prepared for a sudden run straight down. Often they seem to act as though they don't even know they're hooked, and will allow themselves to be led up near the boat. When they get an eyeball on it and realize they may actually be in danger, the real fun begins.

10. Big eye tend to run in packs as opposed to large schools, so multiple hookups beyond two at a time are not as likely as they are with some other tunas. If you hook one or two, clear the other lines and concentrate on the hooked fish, instead of focusing on generating multiple bites.

Bluefin

When it comes to sheer size and power, bluefin are the kings of the ocean—the world record is an astonishing 1,496 pounds. Unfortunately, their popularity on the dinner table (especially in Japan) has made them a prime target of commercial fishermen on both sides of the Atlantic. As a result their numbers are relatively low and catch regulations are tight. Some seasons the fishery may be shut down or cut to a mere one fish per boat limit, others it may be as high as four or five fish per boat, and it can change at a moment's notice. Before targeting bluefin it's always a good idea to check the NMFS web site for the latest regulation updates.

That said, the reality of the matter is that bluefin are one of the easiest of the tunas to catch in certain areas of the Mid Atlantic region. During the summer months they'll be found in good numbers from Virginia north, and during the winter months, North Carolina often sees a run of giant (300 pounds and larger) bluefin. Plus, these fish can be caught close to home. Early in the season as smaller bluefin migrate up the coast and large schools of them can be located, they may be extremely close to shore. At all times they're around, bluefin will be caught inside of the canyons and are rarely targeted in waters deeper than 200' or 250'.

Bluefin can be found around structure such as humps, drop-offs, current rips and even large wrecks. This makes chunking relatively effective, since you can often park your boat right on top of the fish. Trawler chunking is also extremely effective on bluefin tuna (see chapter 28 for a detailed run-down on the tactic). Trolling for them is effective as well, particularly during the early season. Ready to do battle with one of the largest, toughest fish in the Atlantic? Use these tactics to hook into a bluefin.

1. When chunking at anchor, always un-tie your anchor line from the boat after you have dropped the anchor and cleated it off. Then, tie an orange polyball (large

Big bluefin like this one can often be plucked from behind a scallop dragger. This fish fell for a goo-ball of squid tossed into a dragger's wake at the Sausages.

fenders will work, too) on the end of the line. If you hook into a big fish and have to chase it down with the boat, you can un-cleat the anchor line, throw the polyball over the side, and pick it up later.

2. When chunking for bluefin with butterfish, always put a whole rigged squid on a weighted line and set it 10' above the bottom. You'll be amazed at how often this line is the one that gets hit.

3. When bluefin over 100 pounds are around, up-size your tackle. There seems to be a breaking point at about this weight, where it becomes impossible to turn the fish's head with 30-pound or lighter gear. Fights on 90-pounders with 30s may go a half hour or 45 minutes, but a 110-pound fish may take two or three hours to beat. So if you know some big ones are around, consider bumping the gear up to 50s.

4. If you hook a large bluefin on light gear and can't force it up to the boat, back off. The fish will usually come up to the surface 100' to 200' away and thrash around, trying to spit the hook. Then it will usually start swimming in one steady direction. When it does, parallel it with your boat. Slowly work your way over closer and closer to the fish. It will often dive when you draw near, but each time you repeat the process, it will wait a little longer before diving again. After three or four attempts, you should get a gaff shot.

5. When you know bluefin are in the area and can't buy a bite, drop your leader size. Sometimes, 30-pound fluorocarbon leaders will draw hits just seconds after the bait enters the water while 50-pound leaders get ignored all day long.

6. If you have a hookup while chunking, dedicate a crewmember to continuing the chunk flow no matter what. A school of bluefin will stick with your boat all day long, if you just keep feeding them.

7. When trolling for early season bluefin, stick with cedar plugs, spoons, and other traditional lures. Blue and white combinations or the natural cedar finish are usually best. The Dancing Squid rig (see chapter 34) is also very effective on these fish. Note—in the early season you may see schools of bluefin on the surface, "pushing" water. These fish usually ignore your spread. If you find yourself in this position, try casting a spoon in front of the school and ripping it across the water as fast as you can reel. Sometimes, this breaks the bluefin out of their lockjaw.

8. When trolling for large bluefin, always run a blue and white Ilander rigged with a horse ballyhoo, waaaaaay back behind the boat. How far back? Dump a third to a half of the spool of line on a 50. It sounds ridiculous, but try it and you'll discover that large, smart, boat-shy bluefin will slurp it down when they won't hit anything else.

9. When chunking on the drift, try weighting a rigged ballyhoo and dropping it to the depth the fish are feeding at. While butterfish chunks often spin and cause tangles on a drifting boat, the rigged 'hoo does the trick.

10. When anglers chunk butterfish all day, run out of bait, and want to keep fishing, it's not uncommon for them to cut up a skipjack or bonito they caught and use it for the chunks. This will work, but beware—if you cut the fillets off the fish and drop the still-quivering body over the side, the bluefin will disappear in a flash. I don't know if the dying fish sends out a danger signal or what, but this is the quickest way I know of to instantaneously shut down a hot bluefin bite.

Yellowfin

Yellowfin tuna are probably the most sought-after member of the tuna clan. They're available up and down the coast in the entire region at one point or another during the season, and although sometimes they stay far offshore, other times they can be caught at inshore lumps and sloughs. Yellowfin are the mainstay of the charter fleets, and it's no wonder—they fight hard and are among the best fish in the world when it's time to fire up the grill.

Yellowfin will usually be found near one type of structure or another, from sudden changes in the bottom contour to temperature breaks to weedlines. Rips, diving birds, and color changes are all items one should look for when on the hunt for yellowfin. They can be taken both trolling and chunking, and will strike a huge variety of lures. Interestingly, tactics used to target these fish vary wildly from port to port. Anglers in the Carolinas usually troll rigged ballyhoo, anglers from Maryland and Delaware often focus their effort on squid spreader bars and bird rigs, and some New Yorkers do one or the other as well as high-speed (10- to 12-knots) lure trolling. Yellowfin can be successfully targeted up and down the coast with any combination of these methods, as well as by slow-trolling live baits suspended from kites, running Dancing Squid rigs and a plethora of other methods. Bottom line: these fish feed hard, and often.

Although yellowfin can't compare with bluefin for sheer size (The IGFA word record is 388 pounds, and most caught in the Mid Atlantic region will range between 20 and 80 pounds) they certainly can compete when it comes to strength per pound. There's a running debate as to which fights harder. Every time I play tug-of-war with a bluefin I tell myself they fight better, and every time I pull against a yellowfin, I swear they are the stronger fish. This is one debate that will never, ever be settled. Want to see if you can decide for yourself? Use these tips to catch more yellowfin tuna.

1. When yellowfin tag along behind a scalloper, as a rule they seem to hold a little

Hot dog! Another nice yellowfin falls for a chunk bait at the Hot Dog.

deeper than bluefin do. If you're targeting them while trawler chunking, weight at least one line with 3 to 5 ounces, and let it fall to at least 60' or 80'.

2. When chunking for yellowfin, reel your stripper baits back to the boat slowly. For some reason, often they'll take a chunk that's headed the wrong way through the current.

3. Always run a naked rigged 'hoo about 10' behind your sub-surface teasers. A ballyhoo swimming on the surface, just behind a Strip Tease dredge set about 10' down, will account for a heck of a lot of the yellowfin you catch.

4. Keep an eye out for common and spinner dolphin. Remember that it's against the law to run up to and harass these marine mammals. Sometimes, however, they will approach your boat as it trolls along and play in the wake. As a law-abiding citizen, of course you will try to get away from them. But a lot of the time you simply can't. When the dolphin are jumping and playing around you, yellowfin will often strike your lines.

5. At other times, you may find that the porpoises are playing amongst several boats. Yellowfin that were on the feed earlier, however, have shut down thanks to the thick boat traffic. If you find yourself in this situation, run a sub-surface planer line 20' to 30' down, with a rigged ballyhoo on the hook. This will usually get those yellowfin back into eating mode.

6. Check out the Squidly rig in chapter 34. When yellowfin are in town, run this rig in the Shotgun position back about 100 or 120 yards. Some seasons (especially when pressure is strong and this fish are acting skittish) this simple rig will account for half the yellowfin in your box.

7. Occasionally you'll spot yellowfin churning on the surface, and troll around the breaking fish without a single touch. Frustrating, isn't it? Damn straight, but you may be able to get these fish to strike by switching tactics. Pull to within casting distance, and throw the biggest surface plug you have in your box. You'll need one about 10" long, as heavy as possible, with a large concave popping surface. Make it splash, and the yellowfin will often pounce on it.

8. Yellowfin usually travel in large schools, and you'll out-catch the competition if you capitalize on this fact. When a rod goes down don't pull the throttles back immediately. Instead, keep your speed constant and initiate a slight turn to bring your other lures in and out of the propwash. Everyone in the cockpit should grab a rod, and start jigging it. Keep up the jigging and swerving until the rod that got hit in the first place has lost half of its line—many times, by then a second or second and third fish have struck.

9. When a yellowfin takes a chunk bait, don't give it time to eat. These fish charge up and attack so quickly that by the time you realize you've been hit, the tuna's already looking for something else to eat. Half the time it's already swallowed the chunk when you reach the rod, so as soon as the reel goes off lock it up and start cranking.

10. Unless there's a crowd of boats, yellowfin are usually not incredibly boat-wary. In fact, many anglers believe your boat is the biggest, best teaser you have—and sometimes it seems like that is the case. Often flat lines set a mere 30' behind the transom are the ones that yellowfin hit first, so always run a bait or two in close when targeting these fish.

CHAPTER 25
Wahoo

Wahoo are seasonal visitors to Mid Atlantic waters, and most years, won't be present in large enough numbers to specifically target them in much of our region. But by tweaking your spread just a bit you can boost your odds of encountering one or two each season, and perhaps one season out of five they will show up in good numbers in one area or another. The one exception: North Carolina's waters, where more often than not wahoo will be scattered about in decent numbers and there may be a strong spring and/or fall run.

Wahoo are usually either solitary or found in twos and threes. They may be found in open water, around structure, near weedlines, and often around large floating items similar to those you'll find mahi-mahi holding under. Most of the time they'll be in the 20- to 40-pound range, but occasionally bruisers twice that size pop up and you never can tell when or where a fish approaching the IGFA's mark of 158 pounds, 8 ounces will make a showing.

The most important thing to remember about wahoo: they have incredibly sharp teeth. They will slice through mono without even realizing it's there, and it's not uncommon for a single fish to clip off two, three, or four lines in a single dash through your trolling spread. Once they're brought into the boat, obviously, keep your body parts clear of their mouth. And if you hope to land one, wire leaders are a necessity.

Wahoo are incredibly fast fish, and can go from one side of the boat to the other in the blink of an eye. Accordingly, it's a good idea to clear the lines, dredges and teasers when you have one hooked up. Keep your drags relatively light to accommodate for their speedy runs. And when one comes up into gaffing range, the angler must be ready for a mad dash at all times. Because of their torpedo shape these fish are tough to gaff, and inexperienced gaffers will often take a swing and a miss before making a good strike. As you might guess, this gets the wahoo a little riled up. Like to experience it first-hand? Use these tricks to hook more wahoo.

1. Wahoo like to feed a little deeper than most pelagics. While they certainly will hit lines trolled on the surface, you'll boost your odds of hooking one by running a sub-surface line either on a planer or a downrigger. Many anglers also like to troll diving plugs for their wahoo line.

2. Wahoo hit dark colors more often than most other fish you're trolling for offshore. Purples, purple/black combinations, and orange/black combinations are usually most effective on them.

Wahoo like this one caught at The Point, off Oregon Inlet, have razor-sharp teeth, and must be treated with respect.

3. When wahoo are in the area, they will pop up in chunk lines intended for tuna. If you see one slurping down chunks behind your boat, get any near-by lines out of the water quickly—serving up a mono-rigged bait will do no more than aggravate the fish. Instead, always keep a chunk rig tipped with a 10" trace of wire leader at the hook ready and close at hand. Better yet, rig one on an extra rod and leave it up in the rocket launchers, just in case a wahoo suddenly appears. When one does, bait the wire rig and pitch it over the side.

4. Wahoo like speed. If you want to dedicate yourself to catching one, rig up with baits and lures that can take some abuse and troll them at 10- to 14-knots. Experienced wahoo buffs use sash weights to keep their lines in the water at these speeds. Serious die-hards run them on wire line rigs, either stainless-steel or monel.

5. Diving plugs intended for wahoo often run to one side or the other, and can cause havoc in the spread. If you have this problem use a pair of pliers to bend the eye of the plug slightly in one direction or the other, to "tune" which way it runs.

6. Whenever you approach a large floating item to bail for mahi, try tossing a wahoo bomb, diamond jig, or other heavy, fast-sinking lure next to it on the initial approach. Let it free-fall for at least 100' (if you feel a bump as it falls, lock up and reel), then crank it back as fast as you can make your reel turn.

7. Wahoo like flash. When rigging a skirted ballyhoo to sub-surface troll, it's a good call to use a skirt that has a few strips of reflective tinsel in the mix.

8. Like king mackerel, wahoo will sometimes slice a baitfish in half, then turn around and eat the sinking halves at their leisure. If you see one chop a bait, grab that rod and throw the reel into freespool. Allow the bait to sink for several seconds, and the wahoo will often pick it up as it drops.

9. If you're trolling around a thick weedline—a great place to find wahoo—make sure you pull and check your deep-running lines often. Otherwise, it's a good bet they'll become fouled with weeds at one time or another, and the wahoo won't touch a weeded bait.

10. If you discover there are wahoo around flotsam because a lure or two gets bitten off, re-rig with wire and give it another shot. The fish will probably still be in the area, since it's orienting to a specific item. And unlike some other fish, a wahoo doesn't always seem deterred from feeding by a lost rig or two hanging from its jaws.

CHAPTER 26
Weakfish

Although weakfish take a back seat to stripers and blues in the hearts of many Mid Atlantic inshore anglers, these fish top the list in several other areas of the country. They're especially popular from the Chesapeake region down to the Carolinas, and after eating one you'll understand why.

These fish are known as weakfish because of their tender, easily-ripped mouths. Some also call them yellow-fin sea trout, gray sea trout, or simply sea trout. They are very similar in body shape and appearance to speckled sea trout, but they feed in different ways and are usually not found together. Both species are easily identified as members of the trout clan by their "canine" teeth—two long, sharp fangs centered on the top jaw, and two slightly smaller fangs on the lower jaw. While these teeth can cause injury to unwary anglers, on the whole they don't hold a candle to bluefish when it comes to making anglers bleed.

One other important feature shared by both weakfish and specks: Their meat is incredibly good eating when cared for properly, but turns to mush when cared for improperly. Occasionally, you'll hear people say trout are not good to eat. Ask them how the fish were chilled after they were caught. Most of the time, the answer is that they were placed in a wooden or fiberglass fishbox with a block of ice, or a bag of ice shoved into a corner. For sea trout, this kind of treatment just does not cut it. Two key factors must be addressed if you want your trout to taste good.

The first is temperature. Being stowed in a cool box is not good enough. The second factor is pressure. Stack large fish, ice blocks or large chunks of ice, soda cans, or bottles on top of a trout, and its meat will be smashed. To keep your trout in prime shape first dump a bag of ice into the cooler to provide a bottom layer. After you catch a few trout, rip a hole in a second bag of ice and put a thin layer of it over the fish—after dropping the bag on the deck a few times, to make sure that it's broken up and no large chunks remain. Treat trout with this much care, and you'll find that the meat is so sweet, you'll be tempted to fish for them every time you go out. Hickory-smoked weakfish is so good it's mind-blowing, and if you place trout fillets skin down in the oven and spread crab imperial over them, the fish will take on the taste of the crab.

A 10-pound or larger weakfish—called a "gator" trout—is extremely rare these days (they were more numerous several decades ago, but followed the usual pattern of an over-harvested species). The IGFA recorded a 19-pound, 2-ounce fish caught in Delaware as the largest recreationally caught weakfish ever. But these days, finding a school of weakfish over 1 or 2 pounds is tough sometimes and a 6- or 7-pounder is a trophy. These fish will feed on most small baitfish including bay anchovies, peanut bunker, and small spot, but their favorite meals are soft or peeler crab.

Weakfish can be caught throughout the Mid Atlantic region, and are a favorite of many bay anglers.

Trout aren't as tolerant of low salinity as some other species are, and during years of heavy rainfall their presence in some coastal bays drops notably. On the flip side, when this occurs the fish are often present in larger than usual numbers in the inlets and around near-shore wrecks or shoals. They range throughout the Mid Atlantic region during the summer months, with the best bites usually taking place in the fall. Late in the fall when these fish disappear from coastal bays look for them along the coast, as they migrate south.

Because of the trout's weak mouth membranes, you'll have to take special measures in the way you hook, fight and land these fish. For starters, remember that if you hook trout, you will lose some. Don't take it personally. At times, usually when jigging in deep water, you'll have two or three hits for each solid hook-up. Since their mouths tear so easily, you need to make sure you're fishing with a light drag. Don't over-pressure a weakfish, or the hook will pull every time. Similarly, don't try to slam it home when you set the hook. Just use a smooth, authoritative motion. Once the fish is on don't jerk the rod tip, and prepare a net well before it reaches the surface. Don't even bother trying to lift a trout out of the water and swing it onto the boat; you may as well just shake your rod until the fish falls off the hook.

Let's say you get the fish to the surface and for whatever reason a net isn't ready. Let the line go slack, and the fish will fall off the hook. Lift its head out of the water, and the fish will fall off the hook. The best way to handle this situation? Swing your rod tip fore or aft and force the fish to swim back and forth at the surface, maintaining tension, until you can get a net under it. Of course, in order for this to be a problem, you'll have to hook up with some weakfish in the first place. Use these tips to get them on the end of your line.

1. You'll often find trout holding in surprisingly deep water—even down to 100' at times. This makes jigging for them tough, but you can make it easier by using a superline or braid. The lack of stretch and better water-cutting properties allow you to use half as much weight to get down deep, and stay there.

2. Trout are just about the only fish you'll find along the coast that sometimes prefer a static bait. Dead-sticking—dropping your jig or lure into the strike zone, putting your rod into a holder, and leaving it there until a fish is on—works sometimes. This isn't the norm, but it happens often enough that you should try dead-sticking whenever there are trout around but you're not catching them.

3. Trout school seasonally. Early in the year during the spring run of sea trout, they'll usually be traveling in pods. This is when you can catch one or two, then you'll have to move on and try to re-locate the pod or hunt for another one. In the summer, large numbers of these fish will scatter out in the bays and locating schools can become very difficult, if not impossible. This is when you either have to peck them out one at a time, or focus on night fishing. In the fall the trout will stack up again, but not in pods—this time the fish will form huge schools. Now you can park on top of 'em, and load up.

4. Trout are ambitious eaters, and will try to chow down baits half their size. If you're over a big mass of trout but keep catching undersized fish, don't be afraid to swap up to a lure that seems ridiculously large. A 6"-long, 6-ounce jigging spoon, for example, is not out of the question when catching barely legal trout.

5. Match the hatch. Weakfish will show a strong, sometimes overwhelming desire to eat only the lures or bait that imitates the prey they are feeding on at the moment. When they are feeding on 3" bay anchovies, for example, that big spoon will may go untouched. Switch to a 3" feather jig, however, and you might just load the cooler.

6. Look for caterpillar-like markings right against the bottom, on your fishfinder. For some reason, maybe the way that trout form schools or because of their body density, they appear on most quality fishfinders as caterpillars crawling across the bottom. Often, the caterpillar will be connected or partially connected to the bottom. A caterpillar-like shape that extends 5' to 10' off the bottom indicates a nice solid mass of trout.

7. During the summer and early in the fall, you might find trout on the fishfinder but they won't touch a bait or lure, regardless of the tidal period. When this happens, return to the very same spot after dark and set up to night fish. During the dog days, weakfish will often feed exclusively or nearly exclusively after dark. Look for channel edges and bulkheads that are hit by a lot of current to be good places to give this a shot.

8. In the early spring when trout first make a showing in the coastal bays, they'll be organized in fairly small, tight pods. Don't spend a lot of time drifting along, or focusing on an edge or hump. Instead, spend your time milling around with a close eye on the fishfinder. Drop only when you're sure your baits are going to fall right on top of the fish. You'll spend more time hunting and less fishing, but in the long run, you'll catch more fish.

9. Gator trout in our region often come from inlets or coastal bays with very close inlets. Fish right around the rocks or in near-by channels, and to seriously target these fish, do it at night.

10. Be very gentle when handling trout you plan on releasing. Their bodies are as delicate as their mouths are, and if you squeeze them slightly when removing the hook, you may give the fish internal damage.

PART III
Tackle & Tactics

There are as many different ways of fishing as there are fishermen. Are all of you going to agree with all of the tackle and tactics I suggest? Heck no. Does that mean they're any better or worse than those of other anglers? Heck no. The tackle and tactics included on these pages are an eclectic mix accumulated over thousands of fishing trips, including hundred taken with professional anglers—charter captains, lure and tackle manufacturers, outdoors writers, and tournament anglers. Because of regional differences, one or another is sure to seem strange to just about every angler out there. Others will undoubtedly be familiar to even the most novice anglers.

So: Which tackle and tactics should you apply? All of them. I'm a firm believer that there aren't right and wrong ways to catch fish. There are different ways, and one can be more effective than others on any given day, due to the particular mix of variables being encountered. Maintain an open mind, try new things, and you'll catch more fish.

CHAPTER 27
Offshore Trolling

Trolling is without a doubt one of the most popular and effective ways of taking bluewater gamefish—everything from billfish to bluefin tuna can be taken on the troll, and at times, trolling will be the only game in town. There are a number of different specific types of trolling, but more commonly, people use a combination of different techniques at the same time to try and catch whatever pelagic they can locate—tunas, marlin, dolphin, or wahoo.

Pelagic Trolling Spreads

Pulling a mixed spread of skirted and naked rigged ballyhoo at six or seven knots is one of the most popular methods of trolling in Mid Atlantic blue water. No wonder—throughout the region this is usually the most effective way to catch a mixed-bag of pelagics, regardless of seasonality. Tuna, billfish, wahoo, mahi, kingfish, and just about any predator you'll encounter in the Mid Atlantic will strike a swimming ballyhoo.

For most experienced anglers, at the start of the day a mixed spread might include a couple of naked rigged 'hoo, a couple with dark pattern skirts, and a couple with light pattern skirts, run on 15' long 100-pound to 200-pound leaders, attached to the main line via a swivel connection. (Remember: the lighter the leader you choose the more strikes you'll get—and the more fish you'll break off.) As the day's color preference is determined, by noting which get struck and which get ignored by the fish, color patterns are swapped out accordingly. Black/purple, blue/white, and fluorescent green are a few of the old stand-bys for tuna. When targeting mahi-mahi, pink should always be in the spread. If wahoo are around send back at least one rig with orange, purple, or blood-red in the mix, and white marlin and tuna—particularly albacore—seem to prefer green many seasons. Always remember to mix things up until you identify just what the fish want to eat. Some seasons pearl or plain white is a killer, others it goes uneaten, and the same can be said for most different color patterns. The key is to keep changing things up until you can make something happen. Don't just send out your "favorite" spread, then kick back and wait. If you've trolled for an hour without a strike, pick something new out of the tacklebox. That goes for speed, too; kick it up a notch or drop it back when things are slow. Still no hits? Bring all of your lures 10' closer to the boat. That didn't do the trick? Drop them back 20' farther astern. Try dropping leader sizes, try jigging a line or two as you troll, and zig-zag the boat more often. Bottom line: If you are sitting on your butt yawning, wondering why the fish aren't biting, there's a good chance it's because you're just sitting there instead of going to work and making it happen.

One of the biggest mistakes people make is to rig up a ballyhoo, drop it over the side and send it back, then forget about it. Did you check out that 'hoo? Before deploying any bait, hold it next to the boat for a moment or two and watch it swim. If it drags without motion, lays over on its side, or (worst of all) spins, it needs to be yanked. Every bait should get checked 30 minutes to an hour after being set over the side, to be sure it hasn't deteriorated or started doing something funny.

Many anglers will add a few lures into the common skirted ballyhoo mixed spread. Green Machines are one old stand-by that should always be in the water, period. If albacore are in the area, that's the bait they'll hit nine times out of ten. White marlin often attack them (bait and switch for a ballyhoo, if you can) and tunas of all stripes do as well. Many guys also run cedar plugs regularly. I admit they're effective for early season bluefin but once mid-July hits, I say pack 'em away. Many good captains don't; you'll have to try them and decide for yourself. In any case note that cedar plugs must be run with ball-bearing swivels in-line, or you're sure to end up with a tangled mess at the end of the day. Another must-have lure is the bird rig. A bird is a large wood teaser that has an arm on either side. It wobbles back and forth as it's pulled through the water, creating one heck of a surface disturbance. It's commonly rigged with several trailing lures, the last one with a hook. Boone makes a good bird rig, but an even better one can be easily assembled by rigging three hookless Green Machines in-line on 200-lb. test, spaced at 3' intervals behind the bird and followed by a fourth Green Machine rigged with a 9/0 hook. This rig creates a lot of water resistance and will pop outrigger clips in any kind of seas, so it's usually best run directly off a rod tip.

Then there are the combinations of lures and ballyhoo, above and beyond the regular skirts. Mostly these consist of small metallic heads with rubber or nylon skirts, such as Ilanders. (The blue/white Ilander with a chrome bullet head is a killer, year after year. Don't pull off the dock without a couple of them in the boat.) These heads give the ballyhoo a little more action and the extra weight helps them stay in the water on rough days. While nylon skirted lures have proven effective, I have my doubts about running plastics in combination with ballyhoo. I'm not saying it doesn't work, but it hasn't for me and I don't know of any professional captains who use such a rig on a consistent basis.

One big question people ask all the time: How many lines do you troll? The simple answer is, as many as possible without creating a huge mess. With a set of minimal outriggers you can get at least six lines off of just about any transom. Most decent boats can support eight, and often can be brought to nine or 10 by an experienced captain. Recreational anglers who run more than 10 lines are probably pushing their luck. I know some pros who have run as many as 20 lines at a time, yet they usually run eight or 10 and don't use more unless they go into desperation mode.

One way to get additional lines into your spread is to send out some subsurface rigs. If you have downriggers this is easy. Otherwise, you'll have to use an in-line planer, a diving lure, or a "poor man's downrigger." Of these options, the poor man's downrigger is a must-try rig for several reasons: it doesn't take up gunwale and/or rodholder space (as downriggers do), it doesn't trip accidentally and have to be re-set (as in-line planers do) and you can use it to run any size or type of bait within reason. Diving lures, such as the Marauder, do produce at times and some guys swear by them.

So, what exactly is a poor man's downrigger? A large planer (Sea Striker's size five works well) rigged to 35' or 40' or 400-pound test mono instead of a rod. It should be run directly off of a cleat and deployed off the corner of the boat. Crimp a loop in the end of the line and slide it over the cleat before you begin to drop back the planer—the amount of pressure it will put on the line is astonishing, and it can easily pull the whole rig right out of your hands. Once the planer is deployed choose the rod you'll run on the planer line, and set it out about 20'. Next, bend a rubber band over the fishing line. Put both ends of the rubber band through the eye of a snap swivel, then push the other side of the swivel back through the ends of the rubber band so it's securely attached. Finally, clip the snap of the swivel onto the planer line. Place your rod into freespool, and water pressure will draw the swivel right down the planer line to the planer itself.

This is a great rig to set wahoo baits on and it will also draw a lot of tuna bites, particularly when there's heavy boat traffic in the area and the fish have been pushed down or become shy about coming to the surface.

I know some of you guys are just chomping at the bit—what about spreader bars? Aren't these the biggest invention since the hook? Yeah, spreader bars do produce a lot of fish. Yellowfin tuna in particular, and white marlin also love to pop up and bat them around. But these rigs are more than just lures. They act as teasers as well, and by treating them as such we're going to increase the overall effectiveness of our entire spread.

Teasers and Dredges

Teasers—hookless baits and rigs intended to mimic injured fish or entire schools of fish—are one of the most under-utilized tools available to recreational anglers. Does it seem like the big sportfishers always come back to the dock with more fish in the box than the small, trailerable boats? Sure it does—the guys on the 50-footers have some serious advantages over those in center console and cuddy cabin boats. But that doesn't mean you can't hang with the big dogs when you're hunting tuna, billfish and other pelagics from a small boat. What you need are teasers. Modern teasers give the little guy the ability to draw in fish just like the big boats, if you know which to run, when to run them, and how to use them to your best advantage.

Serious professional boats, running with unlimited budgets and hired hands who have the ability to spend days or even hours preparing for a single trip, often

The Mylar Strip Teaser dragging off the stern (after being pulled in for the fight) attracted this yellowfin—and three others at the same time—to rigged ballyhoo run near-by.

drag entire schools of baitfish along for the ride—literally. They will rig several dozen mullet, ballyhoo, or mackerel on an umbrella (wire spreaders with four or six arms); they will deploy double dredges from both sides of the boat; they will literally fill a 5' wide, 15' long swath of water with hookless fish, rigged to swim au natural. One mate I know rigged two 24-mullet dredges together for each side of the boat during the White Marlin Open one year, and all day long they drove around towing a school of 96 enticing bait fish along behind the transom. Of course, most recreational guys don't have the time or money for such endeavors.

There are, lucky for us, several artificial dredge teasers on the market today. My favorite (something I absolutely won't leave the dock without!) is the Strip Tease. It consists of holographic fish inlaid in plastic strips, and if you deploy it without warning the crew, it will fool just about anyone into thinking there's a school of fish shadowing the boat. These teasers roll up to the size of a four-arm spreader bar for easy stowage, and run from 33-fish models (about $100) to six-arm, 198-fish versions (about $500; www.alltackle.com). Rig a 4-pound sash weight in front of the teaser to keep the rig below the surface, pull the line from a stern cleat, and it will look like a real school of fish is trailing 30' behind your boat at all times. This type of teaser is designed to attract billfish and it's very effective for this task. Yellowfin tuna, however, also come to a Strip Tease in droves. To catch them both, run a naked ballyhoo about 5' to 10' behind the teaser, and a second 'hoo, either skirted or naked, on your short rigger clip on the same side of the boat. Often, yellowfin will pile onto these baits.

Another sub-surface teaser you may want to check out is Tournament Cable's bucket teasers ($250, www.tournamentcable.com). These dredges are rigged with plastic ballyhoo or menhaden, or mini bowling pins. The nicest thing about these rigs is that they drop into a 5-gallon bucket for easy instant stowage. You can keep several different ones onboard, without taking up a ton of space or creating an awful tangled mess. A new teaser on the market is the Holofish umbrella dredge ($265, www.alltackle.com) which has plastic fish with reflective strips embedded in them. These things emit a holographic glow, and like the Strip Teasers, will fool the crew into thinking live fish are tagging along.

Blue marlin teasers are an entirely different beast. These are usually large surface disturbers which chug, dart and smoke, and are run fairly close to the transom of the boat. Large bowling pins, mirrored Witchdoctors, and birds are commonly used for this purpose. Essentially, anything that makes a commotion will do the trick—Moldcraft even offers a painted fender as a marlin teaser, and I've been told by more than one knowledgeable captain that it works. Whichever type you choose, run it fairly close to the boat and keep a close eye on it. The billfish will often eyeball it without attacking, and if you're not on the lookout, it may disappear without anyone onboard ever noticing it.

When a blue marlin is spotted on a teaser it's time to pull the bait-and-switch: drop back a horse ballyhoo, or a ballyhoo rigged to a large blue/white Ilander (a marlin favorite in the Mid Atlantic region).

The final type of teaser commonly towed across the Mid Atlantic region is another form of surface teaser, intended to draw in tuna. These consist of spreader bars made of multiple squid, or of daisy chains of squid which are often capped off by a ballyhoo rigged on an Ilander or similar lure. Pink, green, blue/white and psychedelic colors are all effective on different days, but it's rare that they are all equally effective on any given day. Those run purely as teasers are usually deployed directly from the outriggers, but such a rig requires dedicated teaser reels operated from a flybridge. This is the traditional practice when running squid chain teasers in the Carolinas: a chain of pink runs down one side, a chain of green down the other, and both are capped off by a ballyhoo rigged to a blue/white Ilander with no hook. More commonly on recreational boats, you'll be running surface teasers which also act as lures—such as spreader bars with a trailing hook bait.

The ideal position for running spreader bars is off of a short rigger, 35' to 50' behind the boat. They should be positioned so the metal bar itself stays in the air, but the baits remain in the water. Finding where the spreader bar runs in this position will dictate the exact distance back it needs to be set. In calm seas it's fairly easy to find this sweet spot. But when it's rough, the bar may dip into the water and most small boat outriggers won't be able to take the pressure; the line will pop free of the outrigger clips frequently. In this case, run your spreader bars directly off the rod tips.

Both tuna and billfish (white marlin, quite often) will come up on the spreader bars, but sometimes the billfish won't eat the hook bait. Instead, they may merely whack the rig with their bill, over and over again. If a billfish pops up and attacks a spreader bar, immediately drop a rigged ballyhoo back to it and try to run the old bait-and-switch routine.

Now that your boat's ready to draw in the big ones with baits, lures and teasers, let's take the surface/subsurface teaser combination to a new level; it's a method my mate and I developed which has resulted in excellent success, particularly on mixed spreads targeting yellowfin tuna and white marlin—I call it the X Theory, and it helps an angler approach his spread with a three-dimensional attitude instead of the usual one-dimensional surface spread approach.

Let's say you're running a sub-surface teaser on the starboard side of the boat, and a surface teaser, a spreader bar, is on the port side. You have ballyhoo baits running along the surface just behind and above the sub-surface teaser. Good. Now, set a sub-surface bait in the port side flat line position. You can use the poor man's downrigger described earlier, a diving plug such as that Marauder (go with orange/black, if wahoo are in town), a downrigger bait, or a planer bait. Set this one back about the same distance as the teasers, so it runs 20' or so below the surface. Now, you've created an X shape with your lures and teasers, as it would be viewed by a fish approaching from behind the boat. One arm of the X is formed by the sub-surface and surface teasers; the other by the sub-surface and surface baits. No matter what depth or direction a fish approaches the spread from, it will be presented with both baits and teasers.

Now add in a couple of long rigger baits with varied skirts, which will give the fish some different color and contrast options. For a shotgun (a line run straight down the middle, way back) run your most reliable all-around bait far behind the rest of the spread—such as a bird rig, a Squidly, or a Green Machine. No matter how small your boat, if it has outriggers and is offshore-capable, you will be able to get this line/teaser spread including the X off the transom without too many problems.

Wait a sec—what's this "Squidly" thing? He's described in detail in Chapter 34. This little, nearly-invisible looking squid will get smashed by tuna when nothing else seems to work, and it is definitely most effective when run well behind the boat in either a long rigger or shotgun position. And there's one more reason to love Squidly: it's a nearly-instant re-rig. As soon as you swing a tuna into the boat, clip off the leader where it's tied to the main line, clip the tip off of a new squid, and thread it onto the leader just as you did earlier. After a couple of tries you'll be rigging a Squidly in 30 seconds or so. One note of caution: each time you send back a new squid it's only good for an hour, max, because they usually deteriorate quickly from water pressure and lose tentacles or fall apart altogether. So be sure to reel Squidly in often and give him a look-see.

High Speed Trolling

This is a form of lure fishing used to target yellowfin tuna and/or wahoo. Speed is set at 10- to 14-knots, and a spread of plastic chuggers, artificial squid, and/or daisy chains are deployed. The greatest advantage to this tactic is the ability to cover lots of ground in a short amount of time. Plus, strikes are usually savage and hook-ups are usually solid.

No dredges or spreader bars are used when high-speed trolling, as this gear creates too much water resistance. Some common lures used in such a spread would include Green Machines, Moldcraft chuggers, and an assortment of jet heads. A variety of colors is deployed initially, until the fish establish a preference.

High speed trolling is practiced by a relatively small number of anglers up and down the coast. I've tried it with extremely limited success and do not feel it is my most effective way to target tunas. Yet some highly respected and extremely good professional captains, such as John Raguso in New York, employ high speed trolling with a great deal of success. It should also be noted that a fair number of southern anglers use this tactic successfully when targeting yellowfin tunas busting water on the far side of the Gulf Stream. And Floridian anglers have proven that when targeting wahoo, faster is often better than slower.

When targeting wahoo as opposed to yellowfin, most high speed anglers try to get their lures to run sub-surface by rigging sash weights of 5 or 6 pounds on wire-line rigs. The wire line cuts through the water far better than mono or even superlines, and its effectiveness is unquestionable. On such gear, however, the fight is notably dampened. On top of that, wire line kinks and can break if not closely monitored, and trolling with this much lead on your line is a real pain in the butt—cranking up is a workout, even when there isn't a fish on the line.

Good high-speed wahoo baits generally consist of plastic skirted lures with

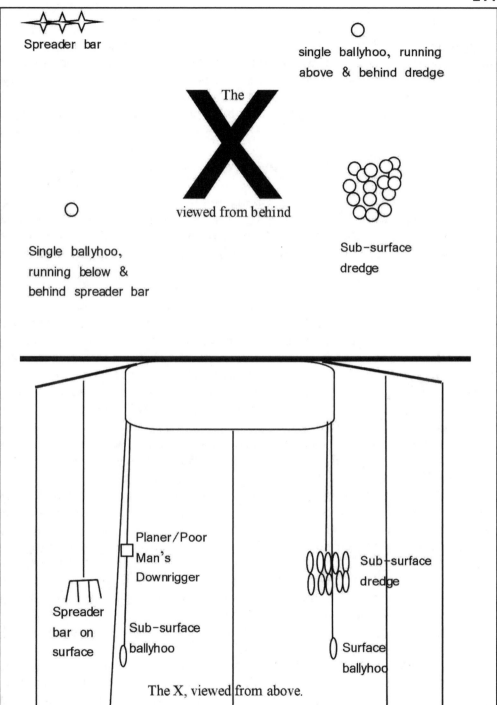

Spreader bar

single ballyhoo, running above & behind dredge

The **X** viewed from behind

Single ballyhoo, running below & behind spreader bar

Sub-surface dredge

Planer/Poor Man's Downrigger

Sub-surface dredge

Spreader bar on surface

Sub-surface ballyhoo

Surface ballyhoo

The X, viewed from above.

Picture a fish approaching from behind the boat, or from below. Any way it comes in, there's both a visible teaser and a visible tasty treat waiting for it.

heads in red/black, black/blue, or orange/black color combinations. If you're not near a good concentration of wahoo, however, this type of fishing is an exercise in futility. Tuna, marlin, and other game fish aren't likely to strike at these rigs very often. As a result, it has few applications in the Mid Atlantic region other than off the Carolina coast, particularly late in the fall when wahoo are present in good numbers and on the feed.

Trolling Offshore Structure

Now you know the how-to part of the equation, and in the first part of the book we covered the where-to and when-to. But, how do you make the specific where-to/when-to call on any given day? Judging where and when to troll offshore is, as with many aspects of fishing, part science, part experience and part black magic. But in the vast majority of cases, you should be trolling around or over structure. In deep offshore waters, structure can be very different than the inshore wrecks, ledges and rockpiles we tend to focus on. Temperature breaks, color changes, surface rips, and floating weedlines all count as offshore structure, and all should draw your attention as well as the physical features of the ocean floor.

It's simply not possible to predict what structure which fish will be located near, on any given day. They may focus on a specific color change for a week, but on day eight, disappear from the area completely. You may find a beautiful looking rip which is completely barren of life, and you're just as likely to find a minor-league one-degree temperature break and discover it's teeming with life. So why is it that, all other things being equal, charter captains seem so much better at locating fish on a regular basis than recreational captains? Because they're out there more often. The single best thing you can do to more accurately predict where and when you'll have success trolling is simply to fish more often. You'll be better able to keep tabs on where the fish are, where and when they seem to be on the move, and what types of structure they seem to be orienting to during that particular stage of the season. A good captain can usually follow the fish's basic movements from day to day, but trying to do so from week to week is impossible. So fishing more means catching more, with logarithmic increases in the success rate. When making your decision as to which spot to head for on any given morning remember that the patterns you've identified will be shaken up by significant changes in wind direction and speed, large or violent storms, significant temperature changes, and boat pressure.

Canyons at the edge of the continental shelf provide the most significant form of offshore structure. They cause abrupt changes in current patterns which in turn cause upwellings and force bodies of different color and/or temperature water to bump and grind. On any given day out of the year, if you have no clue as to where to troll and you're running through the inlet, the canyons are probably your safest bet. Plus, at the Mid Atlantic canyons (in-season, of course) you have the possibility of running into just about any pelagic predator. (Excepting bluefin tuna, which are not commonly found beyond the shelf.) We won't get into the dangers of making such a run in a relatively small boat right now—covering that topic would require an entire book on its own. Obviously, you have to pick your weather days and know for a fact that both your boat and your captaining skills are up to the job.

Humps and bumps inshore of the canyons are the next major item of structure. These include places such as the Hot Dog, off the Delaware/Maryland coast, where the bottom rises from about 150' to about 110'. Like the canyon edges, the shoal that is the Dog creates abrupt changes in current patterns. You'll often be able to see this with the naked eye, in the form of surface rips. They form often in the vicinity of the Dog and on some days you'll spot rip after rip after rip everywhere around it. But bumps like this do not attract yellowfin tuna, billfish, mahi-mahi or wahoo with the same season-to-season regularity of the canyons. Some years one particular bump will swarm with these pelagics, others that very same bump is a desert. The one exception here is bluefin tuna. Nearly every season they will be found on one hump or another or many of them, scattered up and down through the Mid Atlantic range.

Temperature changes are another major form of offshore structure, and these can be located with nearly as much accuracy as fixed features, thanks to modern satellite imagery. You can simply log on to http://marine.rutgers.edu/mrs/sat_data/?northumbs=1 and get a glimpse of the surface temps up and down the coast. But these are very generalized shots. If you want to zoom in close and get a more detailed view of exactly what's going on offshore, you'll need to buy into a for-pay site. There are many out there, but a good pick is Terrafin, at www.terrafin.com. This service is cheap ($100/year), you can pinpoint breaks with GPS coordinates, and it has a loop feature which allows you to play a week's worth of temp charts as a movie clip, making it clear which direction the different masses of water have been trending.

Yup—the different chunks of water out there fly around in different directions. Sure, they more or less head from south to north with the Gulf Stream most of the time, but it's anyone's guess as to whether they'll slide westward or eastward or change direction overnight. What the recreational angler is most interested in, however, are warm water eddies that spin off of the Gulf Stream. Some seasons several will split off and head towards shore, and other years we won't see a single one. In any case, when a warm water eddy can be identified you'll see a temperature break of several degrees, and often, a visible color change. Any edge where these changes take place is a good spot to try trolling. Marlin and swordfish anglers in particular will want to place significant weight on these features, since they account for much of the structure found beyond the shelf.

Color changes formed between inshore and offshore waters are another fish attractor. Again, it's anyone's guess as to when and where these will be found.

Sometimes you'll run through a significant color change 20 miles out, sometimes at 40 miles, and sometimes beyond the big drop. Whenever you're trolling one, however, be sure to investigate both sides of the change. You'll be surprised at how often tuna will school up on the dirtier side of a break, as opposed to in the cleaner water.

Surface rips are yet another form of offshore structure. Often they're actually an indication of solid structure, and you'll find them at or near bottom changes or in areas where currents collide. They're less reliable than physical structure or temperature and color changes, however, when it comes to finding fish. You may troll through 50 great looking rips before you find one that holds any life. Then on the next one, every rod goes down on every pass you make. It's frustrating to fish so much barren water that looks good to the eye, but don't ignore rips because when you do find fish (particularly yellowfin tuna) they're usually focused on feeding in that one specific rip. This gives you the rare ability to visually identify the fish's exact location—which in turn gives you the ability to pound on them, and load the boat. Considering these facts savvy captains will always pay attention to rips seen while trolling, but they won't stop short of their intended destination just because they see a rip unless some other indicator (such as birds, weeds in the area, or blow-ups) makes it too tempting to pass by.

Weedlines are sort of a mix between solid structure and structure created by changes in the water. Weeds are solid, of course, but the masses they form change and shift constantly. On occasion really massive ones will remain in the same general area for large stretches of time, but sometimes they'll be in one spot one day and miles away the next. Generally speaking, weedlines seem better for attracting billfish than tuna, and wahoo will pop up under them from time to time, but mahi-mahi are without question the most numerous predators found under virtually every weedline that circulates through the Mid Atlantic region.

When you encounter a weedline, don't try to zig-zag across it or you'll just load up your baits with weeds. Instead, parallel it and cross only when you spot a clear opening. Look for solid items bobbing about in the weeds—tree branches, planks and the like—which tend to concentrate fish in the area. And make sure that each and every bait or lure you have in the water remains weed-free. Weed stuck on the hook is the kiss of death, and even a 1" chunk of weed is enough to keep the fish from striking.

CHAPTER 28
Offshore Chunking & Bailing

There are several types of chunking, but they all boil down to this: tossing cut up bait into the water to attract fish to your boat, and hopefully hold them there. Some captains call chunking "going over to the dark side" because it's simplistic, boring, and messy. In fact, many of the captains will claim that they absolutely hate to chunk. But guess what—virtually all of them do it, sooner or later. Why? Because chunking catches fish, period. And personally, I've never found it necessary to make it any harder to catch fish in the first place—who cares if it's simpler and less "artistic" than trolling? Besides, if you want to get artsy just look at the swirly, red-brown-green stains you can make on your boat. As you toss the chunks overboard try bouncing them off your crewmember's white T-shirts, and you'll conjure up Rorschach-like patterns no troller has ever dreamed of. And sometimes chunking results in a cockpit running ankle-deep in tuna blood, which then dyes your white High-tops red—the finest art form of them all.

This tactic is commonly employed along the east coast when targeting tuna, although chunkers may encounter just about anything at any time. Dolphin pop up quite commonly in offshore chunk slicks, shark and (if you're inshore) cobia come by for visits, and even white marlin will sometimes suddenly appear behind the transom, swirling on butterfish chunks.

Speaking of butterfish—when it comes to offshore chunking, these are probably the most popular bait in our region. Menhaden (also called bunker or fatback) and squid are also good chunk baits. Bonus tip: Since they float on the surface, tossing peanut bunker of 3" or 4" over the side is a great way to bring hungry tuna right to the surface, where you can watch them boil. Double bonus tip: If you can toss a cast net and fill the livewell with peanut bunker, and dolphin are in the area, nothing gets these fish riled up like bouncing a handful of peanuts off the side of your boat. The stunned menhaden wiggle and swim in disoriented circles, while the mahi pick them off—and go into a feeding frenzy.

Squid are most often employed by chunkers on the hunt for albacore, at the canyons. A flat of squid costs a lot more than butterfish, but albacore love them. And truth be told, they're at least as effective as butterfish on all of the tunas.

Chunking at Anchor

Chunking at anchor is a very popular way to target both bluefin and yellowfin tuna, and this tactic can be employed anywhere you encounter these fish in 200' or less of water. Beyond that, you'll need an awful lot of anchor line to hold bottom. First, the bait: You'll need a 25-pound flat of butterfish to keep an average chunk line going for about four hours. If you plan on a full day of fishing, two flats will be needed.

All too often, you'll be sold sub-standard butterfish. Ensure the quality by pulling the top off the box before you leave the store, and eyeballing the baits. Chalky yellow spots—rot, which usually forms around the dorsal and anal fins first—indicates poor quality. Another thing to look for is sunken, dried out eyes, which also indicates poor quality. Size of the baits is less important, as long as there are enough butterfish the size of your palm to use as baits. Tiny ones are just fine for chunks.

Now that you have your flat of butters, it's time to turn them into chunks. But if you bought them at five o'clock in the morning, tossed them into your cooler of ice, and cruised out to the fishing grounds, those butterfish will be as hard as a rock and you won't be cutting anything for a few hours yet—make sure you open a flat and give it a blast from the washdown hose to start it thawing, the moment you load it onto the boat at the marina.

Once thawed, you can use one of three methods to cut the fish: the knife method, the shear method, or the chopper method. Most anglers simply put a few butterfish onto a cutting board, slice them into chunks the size of a pocket lighter, push the chunks into a bucket, and grab some more fish to chop.

Using this method, it will take about half an hour to go through a quarter of a flat, at which point the guy slicing butterfish either: A. Pukes, from breathing in the aroma of butterfish for too long while bobbing around at sea; B. Cuts himself with the knife or pokes himself with a butterfish fin and bleeds, or C. gets a blister, and asks someone else to take over. In case you hadn't noticed yet, chopping butterfish in this manner is a real pain in the butt.

Anglers with more experience are apt to carry a large pair of steel shears on the boat, grip a butterfish by the head, and hold it over the bucket as they slice the fish into chunks. This works better than a knife, but is still a pain in the butt. Luckily, shortly after the turn of the century a couple of companies started producing commercially-made butterfish chunkers, which look and function like huge egg slicers. Capt. John's EZ Chunk ($229, 302/359-5581, www.captjohn sezchunk.com) and The Chunkster ($178, 410/352-3360, www.thechunkster.com) both fit over the top of a five-gallon bucket, and chop the fish directly into it. The Chunkster is less expensive and looks a bit rougher around the edges, while Capt. John's EZ Chunk is more polished and priced accordingly, but I've used both and the bottom line is that either will get the job done far more easily and quickly than a knife or shears.

So—you now have a bucket full of chunks. What next? Cut some baits. Traditional theory holds that for yellowfin you should take the head and tail off the butterfish, turning the body into an extra-large chunk, and for bluefin you should use the entire butterfish. I've found both or either can be successful on any given day, and at times, both bluefin and yellowfin seem to prefer a regular small chunk to larger offerings. In either case, do your best to hide your hook in the bait. If you don't, those tunas will see it and you'll get fewer strikes, guaranteed. The least-aggravating, most effective baits are usually the bodies with the head and tail removed, and the hook threaded in from the tail end of the fish, next to the backbone. Once it's threaded on, turn the hook and push the point out through the other side of the bait so it's just barely exposed.

With a whole butterfish I find it best to break the bone where the tail meets the body, then run the hook in at that break, pop it through near the dorsal, reverse it, and bring it back through the fish until the point is exposed on the opposite side.

Once you thread a butterfish or a chunk onto the hook, drop it over the side and pull it through the water to make sure it's not spinning. If it does spin, rip it off and rig a new bait. Not only does a spinning bait look unnatural, it can put enough twist into your line to drive you crazy. Even if you have to re-bait five times before one comes out right, do it. Wait a sec—won't a swivel take care of this problem? It would reduce it, but I suggest tying a direct leader-to-line connection when chunking, with no swivel in-between. The simple fact of the matter is that a huge proportion of tuna that are hooked—especially on light leaders—are lost at boatside, during the wiring procedure. By going direct you eliminate the need for wiring altogether. (Some anglers do like to tie small "wind-on" in-line swivels between the leader and main line, and this works with most gear. This isn't an option with some 30-pound class rods and most smaller ones, however, because they have rod tips too thin for the swivel to pass through.)

To go direct from main line to leader simply tie a Spider Hitch in the end of your leader, forming a small loop. Then tie your doubled main line to that loop. This is a solid connection, and if the knots are tied properly, won't break. But if you don't mind wiring, by all means, tie on that swivel and worry less about spinning baits. Leader size used for chunking can vary radically, because tuna have great eye sight and can be finicky when it comes to heavy leaders. When possible, 80-pound or 100-pound test fluorocarbon can be used and it gives you the ability to muscle the fish around pretty well. But often tuna won't touch heavy leaders—remember that when chunking these fish are eyeballing a more or less static bait, and they can see the leader much better than when chasing a trolled bait—and you may have to scale all the way down to 30-pound test before fish start taking it without hesitation. If you have ever tried to wire a 100-pound fish on 30-pound test, then you now see the importance of eliminating wiring altogether.

8/0 is about the right hook size to use when targeting tuna on the chunk, and rig it to a 5' leader. How do you know what size leader to use on any given day? Most captains start out with the heavy stuff, and if bites don't come quickly, set out a line or two with light leaders. If those lines get taken, they will switch the rest of the gear accordingly.

Where to place your baits in the water column is one of the most important aspects of chunking. Bottom line: you will catch fish from surface baits, mid-depth baits, and bottom baits, at different times on different days. Trying to predict which will be the most effective ahead of time is impossible, so you should always try to cover all the bases. When one particular depth seems to be the productive one for that given day, switch your other rigs around accordingly. Start off by setting one line about 10' off the bottom, one at mid-depth, and one near the surface. Fill in the gaps with additional lines accordingly. Sink baits by attaching weights to the line with the copper wires you usually use for rigging ballyhoo. A couple of twists around the line and through the weight's eye will keep it in place until a tuna grabs the bait and swims off, which will create enough pressure to straighten out the wire and allow the weight to fall free. If you don't have copper in the tacklebox (shame on you!) attaching it with a rubber band has the same effect.

When it comes to suspending their baits, most anglers use balloons. Simply strip out the desired amount of line then tie the balloon directly around the main line with a square knot. Let the current or wind float the balloon out and away from the boat, and when you get a fish on, you can reel the balloon right up to the rod tip—then keep on reeling, and the line will slide through the rubber knot as the balloon is pulled snug against the rod tip.

Setting baits is all well and good, but "stripper" baits are often the ticket to a full fishbox. Strippers are baits you rig with no weight or balloon. When you lower one over the side, throw out an extra-large handful of chunks, trying to scatter them in the water all around your bait. Then set the rod into a holder, in freespool with the clicker on. Before the bait sinks enough to cause tension against the rod, grab your line just beyond the tip, strip out 5' or 6', and drop it on the water's surface so that your bait sinks unrestricted. As the line comes close to getting tight repeat the process, and keep it up for 10 or 15 minutes. Fished in this way, the bait will sink through the water column at the same rate as the chunks, and will look as natural as possible to the fish. One caveat: this tactic is all but impossible when large schools of bluefish are in the area. Usually, they'll chow on a stripper bait before it gets 20 yards from the boat.

Whether you get hit on a stripper, mid-depth or deep line, as soon as a fish takes the bait throw the reel into strike and smoothly start reeling, without any hookset; these fish are moving so fast that a yank on the rod has little to no effect, other than to occasionally jiggle the hook free.

Once your baits are set, what's the best way to chunk? The standard game plan is to toss out a handful of fish bits, and watch as they sink. Once the chunks disappear from view, send another handful over the side. This works. Make it work a whole lot better by throwing a few chunks as far off to port as you can, a few off to starboard, and a few right off the transom. Toss some to the bow, and toss some astern. The wider you broadcast the chunks the better the chance a fish or two will find them. Sweeten the pot by dumping some menhaden oil into the chunk bucket, so each and every piece of fish sends out a smelly stream of tuna attractant.

Any chunker's worst nightmare is a directly opposing wind and current. In this situation, both the chunks and the lines will drift back under the boat and it sometimes becomes literally impossible to fish—as soon as you drop a bait over the side, it heads for the props or the anchor line. In some cases you can mitigate the effect by running your anchor line to a spring cleat. This puts the tension off-center, and swings your boat partially across the current. Note that in rough seas this can be dangerous because the waves may start hitting your boat on the beam, and in all sea conditions it's bound to increase the rocking motion of the boat. In a very strong wind or current, even this tactic won't help. In this situation, it's time to try chunking on the drift.

Chunking on the Drift

Chunking on the drift will allow your lines to stay clear of the boat. It is not, in my opinion, quite as effective at attracting and holding fish as chunking at anchor. It can, however, be more effective at catching fish in two instances. First, when the aforementioned situation makes fishing at anchor impossible. And second, when the fish are holding over a particular rip or structure that you can't anchor your boat over, for whatever reason.

Chunking on the drift is really not very different than chunking at anchor, but you'll find it a bit more limiting in how many lines you can get out while still avoiding tangles. Since the boat constantly shifts position, four lines is usually the max. That means a bottom line, a mid-depth line, a surface line, and a stripper. If your boat can be fished from the bow you may be able to get an angler running a second stripper line from up front. Remember that you'll need to up-size the weights on your bottom line and mid depth line in order to keep the baits where they belong. When 3 ounces is enough for the mid-depth line at anchor in a moderate current, on the drift in the same current you'll need 5 or 6. And while 6 is usually enough for a bottom line set in 100' to 120' with moderate current, on the drift, you'll need eight or 10 to keep your offering down deep.

If spinning butterfish chunks are a pain in the butt when fishing at anchor, they're absolute death when on the drift. The increased drag and motion makes them spin twice as much, and sometimes, it seems impossible to make a decent bait. If you find yourself in this situation there might just be enough current to rig a ballyhoo for the bait. Try lowering one over the side and if the drift is fast enough to get it swimming, lower away.

Before you set up to drift on the chunk, always determine your exact direction of drift beforehand. Let the boat drift for a few minutes and keep a close eye on your chartplotter. Be sure to set it to show the "track" feature, so you won't be guessing at your direction of drift, you'll know without a doubt exactly which way it will be. Remember that you'll usually be doing this when the wind and current are opposed (since you can't drop anchor) and in this situation it's often impossible to predict the exact path your boat will drift in without the aid of electronics. Which direction you set the boat up in when you shift out of gear also has an effect. Particularly with powercats, the boat will often sit abeam to the wind and current and travel in the path of least resistance—directly ahead—as well as across these forces. So when you run up to start a new drift remember to stop the boat in the same position you did earlier, or it may travel in an unexpected direction.

One more note about chunking on the drift—in many cases, your chunk line will be relatively shallow when it crosses the area your set lines are drifting at. You can shrink this gap between chunks and baits, however. Simply remember to toss the bulk of your chunks up-drift, so they have a moment to sink before they even get to your boat. You may also want to slow your drift by deploying a drift anchor from a spring cleat; in a pinch, a 5-gallon bucket will also do the trick for relatively small boats.

Trawler Chunking

Trawler chunking is a form of fishing that's become extremely popular—and effective—for bluefin and yellowfin tunas along the Mid Atlantic region in the past few years. This tactic, while not exactly new, was kept more or less hush-hush by those who practiced it. But make no mistake, the fact that you can catch tuna off the commercial scallop boats has now become common knowledge. What seems to have escaped the attention of many anglers, however, is how to do it safely, effectively, and politely.

Unfortunately, this type of fishing can become an exercise in uninhibited insanity. Boats stop in front of moving draggers, drive so close they could reach out and touch the outriggers or cables, and cut each other off while jockeying for position. Several boats have been damaged in the past few years. Boats may run in tight on the trawlers and come close enough to trade food or beverages for scallop guts, which make excellent bait. Its effectiveness not withstanding, personally, I think you've got to be insane to try this maneuver. The payoff is simply not worth the risk. And guess what—you really don't need to. Yeah, yeah, I know, lots of captains will disagree with me on this one. But in my experience, butterfish works just as well as scallop gut. During many trips we've fished two lines with butterfish and two with scallop gut, the butterfish took just as many fish. If you're really stuck on the scallop gut thing, you can still avoid coming danger-close to trade for bait by getting some sea clams. Threaded on a hook they look and smell more or less like the guts. A big gooey wad of whole squid clustered on a hook is also very effective behind the draggers.

Another dose of insanity: Some anglers stop in front of the trawler and wait for it to pass close astern, then start chunking. This has to be the craziest thing I've ever seen offshore. It's like asking a huge steel boat to run over you. It's beyond foolhardy and it can't be discouraged strongly enough.

So, if you stay a safe distance from the trawlers, how are you supposed to catch any fish off of them? News Flash: Tuna following these boats will often be well behind the scallop boat. They're not necessarily following the boat itself, but are behind the cage the scallopers drag, scraping along the bottom. The tuna feed on the creatures it kicks loose, as well as the gut and trash fish the draggers pitch over their gunwales. Often fish will be directly over the cage, and only sometimes (specifically, when the commercial fishermen are shucking scallops—you'll know they're doing so when you see them tossing shells over the side of the boat) will the tuna be holding tight to the dragger's hull.

Give it a try, and you'll find you commonly hook up when the trawler is a quarter to a half-mile away. Don't pull up behind one of these draggers, chunk for five minutes then give up, as so many people do. Sometimes, the fish don't strike until the scalloper is a mile off in the distance. So stick it out for a while—you'll be surprised at the result.

Of course, before you can try trawler chunking you have to find a scalloper in the first place. They work different areas of the coast with differing levels of intensity from year to year, but can generally be found throughout the region. Word of mouth usually is good enough to gain a general sense of what area they've been working lately. Once you feel you have some idea of where the scallopers are simply point the bow eastward, a little to the south or a little to the north as your gut and the fishing reports advise, and cruise 20 or 30 miles out. Then fire up the radar, and as you continue offshore look for large returns on the screen. Once you locate one head for it, and as the shape appears on the horizon break out the binoculars and make sure it's a scalloper, not a tanker or a big pleasure boat.

You'll find both scallopers and net draggers in our region. While both hold fish at times, the scallopers do seem to hold them about twice as often as the draggers do. You can differentiate between the two when you are within sighting distance by looking at the cables they are dragging. Scallopers usually run a single cable directly off the side or back of the boat, while net draggers have two cables running from the ends of the booms.

Here's the drill: When you have located a moving scalloper approach from the rear, down-wind side. Tune your VHF in to channel 16, so you can hear the commercial captains if they attempt to contact you. Parallel the trawler from 50 yards or so, then turn directly towards the propwash trail of the boat. (Many captains believe that as you approach you should never drive through the propwash, however, as there are often tuna near the surface in this turbulent water and your boat may drive them down.) Come in at idle speed, and just before you hit the scalloper's propwash swing the wheel around hard so the stern of your boat turns towards it. Then, start chunking like mad.

I'm not going to tell you exactly how close to get, because that's a judgment call every captain is going to have to make for himself in each different situation. Just remember that if you feel like you might be doing something stupid, you probably are.

Chunk hard, and chunk long. Make sure at least one of your lines is stripped back continually, so it sinks deep into the water column. At least one other should be retrieved after it's 50 yards away from your boat, then re-stripped. Setting a weighted line down near the bottom is a good move, too. Remember—if they're shucking scallops on-deck the fish are apt to be relatively close to the boat, and if they're not, look for the fish to be hanging out well astern, where the cage is dragging bottom.

If you get a hookup on a bait near the surface, fill the water with chunks—there's a good chance that more than one fish is near your boat, and with liberal chunking you can often pull an entire school of tuna off a dragger and hold it.

Now—let's say you're approaching a scalloper, and he stops moving. When these commercial boats "haul back" to pull up the cage and retrieve their catch, fishing them becomes a slightly different scenario. Some scallopers haul back quickly, and drift for no more than five minutes as the dredge is dumped onto the deck. Others will sit for an hour while sorting the catch. Net draggers will drift in the same place for even longer, sifting through their fish. In either case, when the boat first hauls back the tuna often go into a feeding frenzy which lasts for several minutes. Trawler Chunking Tip: If you see a big puff of black smoke come up from a near-by trawler, head for it at top speed. That black smoke is a dead give-away that the captain just reversed the engine and is beginning the process of hauling back.

In these haul-back situations, it's possible to get a little closer to the commercial boat without causing trouble. Still, never position yourself in front of the

Both bluefin and yellowfin tuna will follow along behind scallopers in the Mid Atlantic region.

bow, and never come danger-close to it.

Upon your approach to a drifting dragger, circle around the stern of the boat once at idle speed. Keep a close eye on your fishfinder; on one side or the other, you'll see a scattering of small marks (the stuff they have tossed over the side) and hopefully, a few large ones (tuna fish). This is usually the up-wind side of the boat, but not always. When the current is pushing the boat harder than the wind is, you may locate the marks on the down-wind side. Set up and chunk a safe distance from the dragger, and keep a close eye on your drift with relation to the other boat. If you're getting closer and closer to it, set up farther away, off the dragger's stern.

Sometimes the fish will hold tight to the drifting dragger, in a competition to see who eats the culled bycatch as it's tossed overboard. When this happens, you can usually draw the tuna away—and closer to your hooks—by throwing handfuls of chunks towards the dragger. If you set up 80' behind it and throw chunks 30' or 40', for example, you're bound to pull the fish over. Similarly, some anglers like to strip out 30' or 40' of line onto the deck or onto the surface of the water, then hand-throw their bait at the dragger.

As soon as you have a take, crank down the drag and apply as much pressure as possible. You need to force that tuna away from the commercial boat so it doesn't wrap the line on a bird, or rub it against the boats' keel. In order to get the fish away from the scalloper quickly, many anglers only use 50-pound class or heavier gear in this situation.

You'll find both yellowfin and bluefin behind the scallopers. Four times out of five it will be bluefin, but when you do find a boat holding yellowfin, it's usually a much larger school of fish. Yellowfin also seem to shadow the trawlers from a greater distance than bluefin. If you locate a trawler in water deeper than 250' there's a better shot at yellowfin, but most of the time, the commercial boats will be working in 100' to 200' of water. One final tidbit of info: when you spot a huge cluster of dots around a potential scalloper you see on the radar, ignore it. Those dots are a pack of boats jockeying for position on a single scalloper, and there are lots of scallopers out there working over a huge area. During the 2003 season I abandoned this tactic anywhere near the Ham Bone (off the Ocean City, Maryland, coast) for example, because there were 20 to 30 boats working a single scalloper on a regular basis. As you might guess, it was absolute mayhem. A quick run out to the Sausages proved that there were scallopers there as well, however, and they held just as many fish.

Ultimate trawler chunking tip: You have a female angler or two aboard, and there's a trawler hauled back? If a lady is willing to allow the breeze to lift her shirt for a moment or two while yelling "Give me some scallop guts!" the guys on any trawler out there will throw buckets of the stuff into the water, riling the tuna into a feeding frenzy. Believe me, this tactic works!

Bailing

Bailing is very similar to chunking, though it's a tactic commonly used when pursuing mahi-mahi. Before you can try it, you'll have to locate an item floating on the surface which is large enough to attract the fish. Anything the size of a five-gallon bucket or larger has potential, and bigger is always better. The only reliable source of flotsam in the canyons of the Mid Atlantic region is orange poly balls, which commercial fishermen use to float their lobster pot lines. Mahi will show up under these floats once they arrive in any given area, and can be found under them until the water chills down in the fall and they depart. The general rule of thumb: the more junk floating around, the better. Double floats are better than singles, and if seaweed, line, or anything else is tangled around the float, the chances of finding fish increase.

True, most of the mahi found under lobster balls will be relatively small. Count on finding mostly 2- to 5-pound fish beneath them. Larger mahi do pop up from time to time, however, and if you can find a large board or tree floating offshore, all bets are off.

The basic bailing tactic is simple: cut butterfish into domino-sized chunks, and put them in a bucket. Rig up 12- to 20-pound class gear, spinning or conventional as you please, and tie on a 4' to 5' fluorocarbon leader of at least 30-pound test. If you want to land big mahi, up-size the leader to 40- or 50-pound test. These fish have rows of small but sharp teeth, and during an extended battle they will eventually wear through light leaders. Hook a 25-pound fish on 15-pound spinning gear and it can take as long as half an hour to land it, so you'd better be prepared.

Smaller mahi will be leader shy at times, and won't hit those heavier rigs. If this is the case go down to 30- or even 20-pound test, but keep a heavy rig sitting up in the rocket launchers. You will often spot the big bull dolphin as they attack your bait. If a really large one approaches you can quickly reel in light leader rigs, grab down a heavier rig, and toss it to the fish. It's a good idea to bait this line with a whole ballyhoo, which large mahi will usually swallow with abandon but smaller fish leave alone.

Bailing rigs should terminate with a hook in the 6/0 range for heavy rigs and the 4/0 range for light rigs. Long shank hooks give you a bit more protection from the teeth, but short shank hooks are easier to hide in the bait and may get taken more often; pick your poison. Bait up with a butterfish chunk the same size as the ones you cut for chum (the size of a domino, or about half the size of tuna chunks), unless it's the big ballyhoo rig.

Whether you're fishing a polyball or a floating log or board, approach at idle from the down-current (or down-wind, whichever is stronger) side, until the bow of your boat is 10 yards or so away. Swing the wheel around hard so the stern of the boat slides towards the floating item, and shift into neutral. Time it right and you'll have the transom facing the flotsam, just a few yards away.

Next, toss a handful of chunks right next to it. Watch them closely as they sink, and often you'll see the neon blue-green missiles dart in and go into a feeding frenzy. When you do, throw your baits into the middle of the fray. Baits should be fished with an open bail, in free-fall. Since you pulled up from the down-current side your baits will drift away from the item and you won't have to worry about snagging it—unless a feisty mahi runs back in that direction, of course.

Baits should be allowed to free-fall for several minutes even if you don't see the fish, because they will sometimes hang down deep. If one gets hooked up the rest of the school will often follow it to the boat; in this case, leave the fish in the water. Land it now, and the school will disappear. But keep it swimming right next to you, and other anglers can hook up one after another. When a second fish gets hooked the original fish can be boated, when a third one is hooked fish number two can be gaffed, and so on. You can also keep the school next to the boat by continual chunking. Be careful, though. If you drift a quarter mile from the flotsam and hold the school at your boat, then break the chunk line, the school may scatter. From that distance they usually won't go back to the floating item but will merely disappear. If you lose the school or try a drift or two at an item with no takes, it's time to move on.

Note that trigger fish will also hang under flotsam. When they're spotted cut off your leaders and go to #4 or #6 hooks, tied directly to the end of your line. Not 4/0 or 6/0; but #4 or #6—the really small ones. Triggers have tiny mouths, and it's impossible to hook them on mahi-sized gear. Bait up with similarly tiny chunks.

You should also keep a rod rigged up with something heavy and flashy, like a Wahoo Bomb, in case a wahoo suddenly appears. These fish also hang around flotsam at times, so dolphin bailers stand a fair chance of running into a wahoo every now and again. Cast the Bomb out, allow it to sink 100' or 150', and crank it back to the boat as fast as your reel will spin. More often then not you won't spot the wahoo even if there is one in the area because they will be hanging well below the mahi, so savvy captains will assign one angler in the crew to take a shot with the Bomb on the initial approach, then switch over to mahi chunks with everyone else if the gamble doesn't pan out.

Of course, any other flotsam you encounter in the deep—from cargo nets to refrigerators to dead whales—can hold schools of mahi. Use these exact same tactics, and you'll often fill the cooler.

Speaking of filling the cooler: Fishing around the lobster pot balls using these techniques can lead to absolutely outrageous catches of school-sized mahi. At times, you'll look up to discover that every angler on your boat is hooked up or shoving a fish into the cooler—which is already brimming over with fish—while a hundred or more mahi swarm around you in a feeding frenzy. Be careful! It's all too easy to over-harvest these fish. Keep a good head-count on how many go into the box, and determine how many you'll consider the maximum catch ahead of time.

CHAPTER 29
Inshore Trolling

Trolling is a great way to target several inshore species. Along the Mid Atlantic coast, most anglers on the troll will be after bluefish, Spanish mackerel, king mackerel, stripers, or flounder. Targeting each of these specific fish requires specific tactics and rigs (note that conventional gear in the 20-pound to 30-pound class does the trick for just about any inshore trolling), but without any doubt, blues are the easiest to go after. They will eat essentially anything, any time. You'll find them throughout the Mid Atlantic anywhere the water temperature is in the mid-60's or higher. They'll congregate around any form of structure or in open water when schools of baitfish are present. And luckily, it's fairly easy to spot them—such schools are usually marked by diving sea gulls and fish breaking water. A common tactic used by bluefish aficionados in many areas it to troll just outside an inlet or up and down the beach no more than a mile from the breakers, while watching for diving birds. A short run to a lump, wreck or shelf 10 or 12 miles off the beach usually produces larger fish, but many bluefish lovers feel the smaller ones taste better than the big choppers, and will take home a 1-pounder over a 10-pounder any day of the week.

To target blues, use a trolling speed of about six knots. Set both sub-surface and surface lines out, with spoons, diving plugs, or rigged ballyhoo. In all cases be sure to rig a foot or two of wire leader in-line, or you'll lose more fish than you'll catch. Remember that these are toothy fish, and if you give one the chance it'll chomp down and slice through a finger just as easily as it bites through monofilament. They'll hit other lures—bucktails, pliable plastics, pretty much whatever you pull behind the boat—but you'll go through a lot of gear pulling these items because a single fish can shred anything except for metal or the hardest plastics.

Trolling for mackerel is a little more complex than trolling for blues, but not by much. Anglers who want to stay close to home can troll along the beach for Spanish mack in all but the northernmost areas of the Mid Atlantic. Since these fish like it warm, however, they usually arrive later and leave earlier in the season than most other species you'll be targeting. To specifically go after them you'll want to bump the throttles up a bit, and troll at about eight knots. Run small spoons of 3" or 4" such as Huntington drones, Crippled Alewives, or Tony Acettas. The all-time favorite Spanish mackerel lure is probably the Clark spoon. While silver works, gold spoons usually catch more mackerel. At times red is a killer, too.

Pull your mackerel spoons on rigs weighted with 4 to 6 ounces of lead. At eight knots, if you don't use some weight the lures will come skipping out of the water. Many anglers also run these spoons on planer lines. If you see fish "grayhounding," (leaping clear of the water in an arc), stay in the area—this is a distinct trait Spanish macks display.

If you see birds working over breaking blues, remember that seasonally there will often be Spanish mackerel mixed in. Commonly the blues will out-number them five or 10 to one, but put in your time and you should be able to catch a few. Won't the blues bite off your lures? Nope—because you'll have wire leaders. Spanish mackerel are toothy critters too, so you'll need that protection for your spoons in the first place.

Trolling for king mackerel is significantly different than trolling for Spanish. These fish straddle the boarder between offshore and inshore in our region, and are commonly caught from a half-dozen miles off the beach out to 30 miles from shore. They'll be found over structure and are rarely located in open water unless there are hordes of baitfish around, especially as you move farther and farther from land.

Trolling for kings is a game of in-line planers for most anglers; these fish do and will hit surface-trolled baits, but generally speaking your deeper lines will out-catch the surface rigs. Like Spanish mackerel, kings like spoons. All finishes and colors can produce, but golds and reds are top-notch. A Clark spoon with a strip of red reflective tape should always, always be in the water.

A common spread used when trolling for kings might include two planer lines, one run off each side of the boat, a couple of weighted spoon lines, and a couple of rigged ballyhoo at the surface. Regular ballyhoo rigs don't cut it for this work, however. Instead you'll need wire line rigs with a stinger hook. Instead of attempting to swallow a baitfish by the head as most predators do, kings often cut baitfish in half. The fish then turns to eat the pieces as they fall through the water. If you don't have a stinger hook in the aft end of the bait, you'll miss half the fish that initially strike. So most dedicated kingfish rigs have a single hook forward and a treble hook aft as the stinger.

Serious kingfish lovers who don't care about catching other species as they fish will take an entirely different approach, and an even more specifically targeted method: live-bait trolling. The same two-hook wire stinger rig is used, but live ribbonfish, menhaden, or other baitfish makes the bait. Trolling speed is brought way down to one or two knots, usually with only a single motor in gear. Go any faster, and the livies can't keep up and they soon die. Many hard-core kingfishers also drag a net bag of chum (better yet, sweetened with a squirt of menhaden oil) behind the boat as they troll.

Trolling for stripers is yet another completely different game. The availability of these fish along the coast tends to vary quite a bit from month to month and location to location as they migrate to different areas, but as a general rule of thumb the northernmost portions of the Mid Atlantic enjoy the presence of good numbers of stripers in the warm months of the year, the southern portions have stripers in the cold months of the year, and the mid range sees strong migrations in spring and fall as well as fair to middling numbers year-round. Because of federal regulations trolling for stripers is limited to near-shore waters, and in some areas during certain seasons, the bulk of the fish may be beyond those limits, shutting down the fishery altogether. Of course, this could change at any time depending on the whims of the politicians.

In all of these seasons and areas, trolling speed for striped bass should be between three and six knots. Try going at the slower end of the range in cool water, and go faster in warm water.

Whether you're trolling for stripers in New York in June or in North Carolina in January, there is one cold, hard fact you'll have to face: umbrella rigs are effective. These rigs have so much water resistance that reeling them up feels like a big old boot on the end of the line. A 36" striper doesn't put up much of a fight attached to an umbrella and small fish may even go unnoticed, especially when the rig is running on wire line, sometimes a necessity in high-current areas. But no matter how miserable an umbrella might make you, the darn things catch fish. In northern areas many anglers like them rigged with surgical hose eel imitations, and throughout the range shad bodies are used for the teaser lures with parachute jigs or bucktails in the hook position.

A troller in search of stripers should plan on running at least six lines: two un-weighted umbrellas, two with 4 to 8 ounces of lead rigged in-line, and two alternate lures. Good choices for the alternate lures include bunker spoons, weighted so they run low in the water column (very popular up north), diving plugs such as a Mann's Stretch 20 (a favorite in Virginian waters), and tandem bucktail or parachute rigs (use heavy heads; 2 to 4 ounces on the long leader and 6 to 8 on the shorter leader is about right). Daisy chains and Mojos also are popular in some areas but laws regarding the number of hooks they may be rigged with vary from state to state.

Most striper trolling will take place in rips, at or around inlets, and where near shore currents collide. Color changes and nervous water formed when an outgoing tide pushes through the inlet gives you an excellent shot at these fish. Remember that stripers are very sensitive to the tide, and trolling will be much more effective in the hour before the turn of the tide and during the change. Shoals also provide an opportunity for locating stripers on the troll, particularly when you pinpoint one that has a long edge you can meander along.

If trolling for stripers is a little different than trolling for mackerel or blues, then trolling for flounder is an entirely different galaxy. This is mostly a wire-line affair, coupled with a lot of lead to get your baits deep in high-current areas. Even though you only want your boat to be moving along at one or two knots—keep it extremely slow when trolling for flounder—combined with the current there could be several knots of force against your line, conspiring to lift your bait well off the bottom.

This tactic is effective in inlets and in coastal bays just inside of the inlets, as well as on shoals both in and offshore. Offshore? You bet—40 miles out and beyond you can catch flatties—in fact, I've caught them at the canyon edge in 350' of water. Of course, this isn't normally in the game plan. But during the summer months after the spring inshore run, the largest flat fish brought to the dock usually come from some of the same bumps and shoals that hold bluefin tuna.

When trolling such areas use dropper rigs and make sure the weight is always in contact with the bottom. Baits usually consist of bucktails tipped with live bull minnow and/or squid strips. Trolling live spot or menhaden is also extremely effective, though both of these types of baitfish die quickly on the hook in these fast current, deep water conditions. With dead baits of any variety, "working" the rod by swinging it fore and aft, bouncing the weight along, is often more effective than trolling with static rods in the holders.

In shallow coastal bays throughout our region, flounder can be trolled up with monofilament rigs and much less weight during the spring and summer months. In fact, one of the most effective ways to troll for them is to move up onto shoals during a flood tide, in no more than 3' or 4' of water. During low water, stick with channel edges. Bucktails on dropper rigs or live baits are the way to go in this situation as well, but it's also possible to troll jigs such as 4" twister or paddle tails on rods rigged with extremely light but strong braids or superlines. Some purists troll a bare hook baited with a live bull minnow or minnow/squid combo, and others prefer a hook dressed with a bucktail teaser and a spinner. In all cases, when using any type of bait try to drop it back when the fish first strikes, and give it several seconds to swallow before setting the hook. When trolling artificials, don't drop back at all.

Personally I believe drifting and casting is more effective (and fun) than trolling in most flounder waters less than 15' deep. That said, there are some excellent flounder pounders out there who have more or less perfected the flatfish trolling technique, and really kick ass doing it. And, in deep water with strong currents, it may be the only possible way to target this species.

CHAPTER 30
Inshore Chumming

Chumming is very similar to chunking, except that you're attracting predators with ground fish instead of chunks of fish. This is an effective tactic to employ when targeting bluefish, spadefish, cobia, and shark. When shark are the target, chumming may take place well offshore, as well as at the inshore grounds.

One of the nice things about chumming is that it requires much less weight than many trolling techniques and there isn't constant water pressure against the lines (excepting current.) This makes it possible to hunt for relatively large fish on relatively light gear. Chumming for cobia, which can approach 100 pounds, can be effectively practiced with 20-pound spinning gear, for example. Chumming takes place mostly at anchor, with the exception of shark fishing, which may take place at anchor or on the drift.

Chum is available in tackle shops in several forms: frozen logs, frozen blocks, and frozen one-gallon plastic tubs. You can grind it fresh if you see fit, but most anglers don't take the time and effort this requires for the minimal advantage it provides. It also takes a lot more work to keep up with fresh chum while fishing, since you'll have to constantly spoon it over the side. (Whereas frozen chum is evenly distributed as it slowly melts.) And consistency is the key when chumming—the idea isn't to put a ton of fish goo into the water, it's to keep a constant, steady flow so fish that sniff out the oils and bits can follow the chum line right up to your transom. Most of this chum will be ground menhaden, although ground mackerel is often sold for sharking. In my experience, however, menhaden is unbeatable as chum for any species found along the Mid Atlantic including the almighty mako.

Frozen chum logs and blocks require the use of a mesh bag to place the chum in, and hang over the side. As the chum melts the bits and oils drift out through the mesh and (hopefully) attract your prey. Unfortunately, those mesh bags are nearly impossible to clean out and will become rancid in a matter of hours if you attempt to stow them after a day of fishing. Eliminate the mesh bag, and instead, poke a dozen or so nickel-sized holes in the sides of a plastic tub of frozen chum. Then cut a hole near the top and one through the lid itself. Run a line through these holes, cleat it off, and drop the bucket over the side. Don't neglect to put your line through the hole in the top; otherwise it could pop free and drift away, releasing the rest of your chum in a single blast. If the chum isn't coming out quickly enough cut more holes, or give the bucket a vigorous shake every now and again.

Chumming for blues in particular is really no different than chunking: pick your spot, drop the hook, drop the chum over the side, and set back baits at varying depths through the water column. Running a stripper bait is also effective in this situation. Try to set up along some form of physical structure, such as a hump, drop-off, or wreck, and remember to always rig up with a trace of wire for protection from their line-chopping teeth.

Chumming for spadefish is similar but instead of using ground fish, you'll want clams. Surf clams, quahogs, and chowder clams will all work. Of course, you can't exactly drop a bunch of clams into a grinder and go at it; instead haul them out to the fishing grounds whole. Once you anchor up—make sure you're directly over a wreck or reef, when targeting spadefish—hold a clam in each hand, lean over the side of the boat, and smash them together. Let the juices, bits, and shell fall into the water, but hold the bodies back. Slice them up into tiny bits, and cut some into spaghetti-like strips an inch or two long. Drift them back into the current on light rigs (15-pound test is plenty) and small (#4) hooks as you toss more bits over the side to attract the fish. If there's a strong current running, pinch on a split shot or two to keep the bait sinking. Remember, however, that chumming for spadefish is best during a slack or nearly slack tide. As with other forms of chumming, do your best to keep the flow of chum steady and consistent.

Chumming for cobia is effective over inshore humps, bumps and wrecks, and they can often be chummed up close to inlets or near large sea buoys. The drill is no different that chumming for blues: set the anchor, put your chum in the water, and cover the water column with baits set at different depths. For cobia you won't need wire leaders, however, and using these will significantly cut into the number of strikes you get because cobia are often somewhat wary of dead baits. In fact, you'll do much better when chumming for these fish if you have live spot or eels on your hooks. Rig up with 4' or 5' of 40- to 60-pound fluorocarbon leader, and a thick 7/0 or 8/0 live bait style hook. Remember, these fish are real bulldogs—they'll bend thin hooks straight if you give them the chance.

Chumming for shark is, naturally, a completely different experience than chumming for other inshore gamefish. The gear you use will be larger. Much larger. 30's are minimal, and 50's are appropriate. A fishing buddy of mine calls shark rigs "tow truck gear," and that description is pretty accurate: a 10/0 hook rigged to a 2' section of single-strand wire, then a swivel, then a 6' length of 49-strand cable. The single strand section provides the tooth protection. Keeping its length minimal reduces the chances of kinks and breaks, while the cable section provides chaff resistance from the shark's rough skin.

While you may find mako and thresher within a dozen miles of the beach, more often they'll be found farther offshore and at times, the canyons are the best place to find quality sharking. Judging where to shark fish is much tougher than finding a spot for other species, since they're roamers. Yes, you will usually find them near some form of structure, but often mako in particular will be encountered swimming where you least expected. Plan accordingly; if you're going to anchor up do it at or near significant structure, and if you're going to drift—which is the mode most serious sharkers operate in—choose a general vicinity that you believe shark will be in from past experience, fishing reports, and talk on the dock. If there's good structure in that area, set up for a mile or two long drift that takes you over it. And remember that you need some motion to carry the chum out and away from you. If there's no current or wind, put your chum over the side and "power chum" (putt along at a couple knots) for a while to disburse a scent trail over a large area.

There are several tricks serious sharkers use to bring the toothy critters in. Some people swear by rhythmically thumping on the hullside with an open palm. Others say spraying the washdown hose over the side draws in shark. And some anglers reduce the chum stream to a trickle every now and again, believing that the sudden reduction in oils and fish bits causes the shark to search out its source.

As mentioned earlier, some anglers like to use mackerel when chumming for shark. In my experience, menhaden draws in more fish but a chunk of mackerel does make excellent bait. The same is true of fresh bluefish, and many knowledgeable sharkers start off every trip by trolling for blues. Once a sufficient bait supply is in the box, they'll start fishing for shark. If you can catch live blues in the 1-pound range, these are prime baits and mako usually won't hesitate to chomp on them.

CHAPTER 31
Bottom and Wreck Fishing

Anglers after ground-fish both inshore and offshore are usually best served by bottom fishing. This can be an effective tactic over wrecks and reefs, areas of live bottom, and on steep drops and edges. And in at least two cases—when going after golden tilefish in the deep or winter flounder in the back-bays—you'll want to fish over mud bottom. Bottom fishing can be effective both at anchor and on the drift, and several factors should play into the decision-making process when you're deciding which way to attack the fish. First consider how large the feature or structure you're going to fish over is. If you're trying to pluck fish from a small wreck, you could spend all day just trying to anchor the boat over top of it. Small features can be drifted over much more easily, and if you make a slight error in positioning the boat you have the ability to engage the motors and correct it. There's a down-side to bottom fishing on the drift, though. Since your rigs are dragging along the bottom you're likely to snag it quite often. Expect a lot of break-offs, and if you're not getting them, you're probably not catching fish, either—fish like tautog, sea bass, and grouper hold tight to structure, and if your rigs aren't banging off the item the fish are gathering around, then your baits aren't close to the fish.

When fishing over larger wrecks, reefs or live bottom, it's easier to drop the anchor and end up in a good spot. Unfortunately, it's also possible to burn out a spot you've anchored over; if the fishing starts off hot and grows slower and slower, let out some additional anchor line or slip it over an off-center cleat if conditions allow, so the boat changes position.

Current, wind and sea conditions also play into the drift-versus-anchor decision. When it's rough out drifting can be tough since many boats will turn beam-to into the waves and rock and roll violently. Anchoring keeps the bow into the seas, and will be more comfortable when the wind's blowing. If the current is strong it will make drifting tougher, especially when the wind opposes the tide, because you'll need more weight and more line to reach and hold bottom. This problem becomes more and more acute the deeper you intend to fish.

Whether you decide to drift or to anchor, one of the most important tools you can carry for bottom fishing in 100' or less is a good marker buoy. Putt along until you see what you're looking for on the meter, drop down the buoy, then use it as a point of reference as you drift or go to set the anchor. What about GPS? Incredible as this tool is, it won't help you with pinpoint positioning as much as a visual aid like a floating marker will. Of course, in deeper waters it becomes impractical to drop a marker buoy, and in this situation, you'll have to do it all with electronics. The best way to approach electronic positioning on most recreational units is not to type in lat/long numbers and hit the "go to" button, but to place the cursor on the numbers and zoom in the screen to the maximum possible magnification. When you see what you're looking for on the fishfinder screen, punch the MOB button to establish an instant waypoint. Then drift for a few minutes to establish a track line, and follow it back to the MOB mark to start new drifts.

No matter whether you're fishing for cod off New York or grouper off North Carolina, when going after bottom fish you'll either be dropping baits or large, heavy jigs. Which is preferred is purely a matter of personal preference, as either can be effective on any given day. That said, bait fishing is probably easier, especially for novices. Get that fish chunk or squid strip down to the bottom near a fish or two, and there's a chance it'll take the bait. Put a live bait in front of the fish's nose and there's an even better chance it will get eaten. But jigging takes some finess. You'll need to be able to work the rod up and down to give the jig action, yet maintain steady tension so you'll detect a strike and set the hook accordingly. Using artificials does have one big advantage, however: you don't have to constantly bait and re-bait your hooks.

What gear should you have onboard to try bottom fishing in the ocean? Rigs will vary regionally but virtually all are some sort of variation of the standard top-and-bottom rig. Deep water drop rigs are usually kicked up a notch and carry four or five hooks plus glowing beads. Hooks should be sized according to the fish you're going after: 4/0 to 5/0 for sea bass and similar fish in the 1 to 10 pound range; 6/0 to 8/0 for cod or similar fish in the 5 to 50 pound range; and 8/0 to 10/0 for bigger fish. Also note that circle hooks are useful to bottom fishers, especially when dropping into deep water with monofilament line, which will make decent hook sets nearly impossible.

Single gear reels like the venerable Penn Senator 112H (under $100) spooled with 30-pound test on a 6'6" boat rod will give you all the beef you need to take on Mid Atlantic ground fish. Don't forget that you'll need between 3 and 10 ounces of lead to hit and hold bottom, and if you plan to bottom fish for tilefish or in water over 600', it's time to consider getting electric reels and 4-pound sash weights.

What happens if you deep-water bottom fish with conventional gear? In certainly can be done, but it will take a lot of effort. Deep-dropping in 800' of water it will take about half an hour to one hour to reel up a large fish when using 30's rigged with braid and 4 pounds of lead. With no fish on the hook, it'll still take you 15 or 20 minutes.

Bottom fishing in the coastal bays is a great way to take panfish, too. Since they usually bite readily and are often present in good numbers, it's also a good option to consider when you have kids on the boat. Fish like croaker, sea trout, spot, sea bass, blowfish, and sometimes stripers or blues, will be found from just outside the inlets to throughout the coastal bays anywhere there's sufficient depth. In these areas stick with simple spinning or conventional gear up to the 20-pound class with top-and-bottom rigs and #4 to 1/0 hooks, baited with squid strips, bloodworm chunks, or Fishbites (believe it or not, these artificial bait substitutes seem to work every bit as well as the real thing.) Drifting is usually the best bet, since bottom fish in coastal bays are more likely to be scattered along an edge or in a channel than to be in one specific spot over a piece of structure. Luckily, most of the Mid Atlantic coastal bays are shallow enough that you won't need very much weight. Usually, an ounce or two will be enough to hold bottom. Casting up to rip-rap jetties is another spot you'll catch fish like these when bottom fishing, but fishing the rip rap will also lead to a lot of snags.

CHAPTER 32
Inlet Fishing

Inlets along the Mid Atlantic coast provide a lot of action for anglers of all stripes. Bottom fishers, live-baiters and lure fishermen will all have a good shot at taking fish where the ocean meets the bays. Stripers, flounder, blues, sea trout, tautog, and sea bass all gather here, to take advantage of the colliding currents, rip-rap jetties and deep channels.

As mentioned earlier, jetties provide good action for bottom fishermen. Those in pursuit of sea bass and tautog, in particular, will do well tossing their baits near the rocks. Striper anglers can also have a ball at the inlets, so long as they keep track of the tides. Drifting eels along jetties and deep channel edges is an effective way to target these fish during the last hour of the tide and the first half hour of the next tide. Concentrate on whichever section of the particular jetty is being hit by the current, and take note of holes where the water overwashes the rocks, or spots where protruding rocks create points along the jetty.

Another way to target stripers along the rocks is to drift from one end of the jetty to the other while casting diving plugs, plastic jigs, or bucktails. Toss your lures as close as possible to the rocks, and vary your retrieve radically. Remember that when the current is roaring along you're likely to catch the most fish with quick retrieves high in the water column, and during slack or slow water, try a slower retrieve that allows you to bounce your lure along the bottom.

Night fishing at the inlet is also a great way to take stripers. You'll want to fish near light lines if any are present in the inlet you're fishing at; if there aren't any, anchor up and set out your own lights. Try to position your boat so the lights you use to illuminate the water create a light line right at or near the rocks. Drop cut bait down to the bottom, and/or cast and retrieve black, purple, and chartreuse lures to the light line.

To catch flounder in the inlets fish just as you would in the bay. The one difference? In the inlets you'll usually be in significantly deeper water and currents may be notably stronger. Accordingly, you may need to up-size your weights and consider using a drift sock (sea anchor) if it's windy and the drift is too fast to effectively fish. Also remember to concentrate on these areas during a low or falling tide, when the flatfish are more likely to be located in deep water as opposed to up on the shoals. Often the largest flounder in town will be found in or near the inlet, so this is an excellent area to try drifting live 4" to 5" spot along the bottom for big doormats. Some inlets don't have jetties at all. These inlets are excellent for flounder-pounding since they provide both shoal water and deep channels. In any case, sandy shoals that are directly adjacent to the deep water channels are excellent areas to hit during a rising or high tide.

Another inlet area that's good for flounder: channel intersections. Most inlets will have feeder channels splitting off to run behind barrier islands, to marinas, and adjacent bays. The area where these channels meet the main channel is an excellent spot to fish for flounder. Count on them being at their best when the tide's running out. Unfortunately, these intersections are often busy areas. During summer weekends in busy areas, they may be more or less un-fishable.

In a few of the southern locations in this region—particularly Virginian and North Carolinian waters—these accessory channels and their intersections with the main inlet channel are also excellent places to fish for speckled sea trout and red drum. Drift through them while casting 4" chartreuse, white, and yellow twister or paddle tail grubs or bucktails sweetened with peeler crab chunks or squid. Vary your retrieve between bouncing along the bottom and fast retrieves along the channel edges. In the Carolinas look for areas where abrupt channel edges meet shallows with grass beds to provide the hottest action.

Fishing for blues in inlets is usually a matter of luck: when you see birds working, toss spoons or bucktails into the fray and there's a good chance you'll hook up a bluefish or two. At just about every inlet along the Mid Atlantic coast, schools of blues will pop in and out of inlets while attacking schools of bait, and fishing for them runs hot and cold on a minute to minute basis, much less a day to day basis. Most found in the inlet will be little snappers of 3 pounds or less, but sometimes larger fish pop up. You'll also pick up a lot of snapper blues by accident, since these fish will hit just about any bait or lure thrown into the water in search of this species or that.

If you want to target them in the inlets, your best bet is to simply fish for other species and keep a sharp eye peeled for marauding schools of blues marked by those birds. It should also be noted that bluefish can often be found at the inlet mouths, or just outside of them, along the color changes. Usually these, too, will be marked by gulls.

Sea trout are a sporadic catch at most Mid Atlantic Inlets. Some years they set up shop along this jetty or that, others they go unseen in the same inlet yet are plentiful in another. The best thing about locating trout in the inlets? Usually these aren't 18" spikes. Much larger trout can often be found in the inlets and serious lunkers in the 5 to 10 pound range sometimes pop up. When they are around, night fishing is usually the best way to target them. Casting bucktails trimmed with chunks of peeler crab is very effective. Some anglers cast twister tail jigs with varying levels of success, and others toss out chunks of peeler or soft crab on fishfinder rigs. Many anglers walk out on the jetty rocks and cast for trout, but this is an extremely dangerous method of fishing. Weedy rocks, salt spray, jagged rocks and darkness all conspire to break legs, arms, and fishing rods. No doubt there's danger in fishing the inlet from a boat at night, too, but the danger level is lower.

Between the strong current, multiple snags, and crabs and panfish found in inlets, most people will decide that using soft crab baits set on the bottom is nearly impossible in most inlets, most of the time. Those anglers that really want to hook the mongo sea trout will save the crab for another day (or night) and instead, fish live spot on a fishfinder rig.

A great way to target the big trout from a boat is to motor up-current to the end of the inlet, and set your boat up about 50 yards from the rocks. Weight your live spot with a 1 or 2 ounce in-line cigar weight, and toss your rig half way to the edge of the jetty. Set the rod into a holder, and pick up a second line—this one rigged with a dark bucktail sweetened with a chunk of peeler crab. Cast and retrieve it, while eyeballing the first rod. When the spot line has been pulled well away from the rocks by your drifting boat, reel in and cast again. Working this system you can keep two lines in the water at all times.

Many seasons trout will also gather just outside of one inlet or another, within a mile or so of its mouth. This is another fishery that varies quite a bit from year to year. Some seasons trout will set up shop outside of an inlet for a matter of months, while the next closest inlets to the north and south have no or few trout in the area. It's impossible to predict where and when they'll show from year to year, but generally speaking when they do gather and stay just outside of an inlet the fishing will be best during an outgoing tide. Look for the fish to gather along the color changes, where the dirtier bay water collides with cleaner ocean water. In this situation, drifting while fishing heavy jigs or jigging spoons is the way to go. Braid spoons (try the green and blue patterns), Yo-Zuri jigging spoons, diamond jigs and Hopkins (get the ones with the yellow bucktail hair teaser on the hook) are all good choices. Three-ounce lures are usually the smallest you can get away with using outside the inlet, and 4 or 5 ounces is often necessary to keep the lure in the strike zone.

Bottom fishermen using bait will also catch fish in this situation, for sure. Dropping squid strips on Trout Scouts or top and bottom rigs is a good way to go. But the trout will often suspend at a particular depth and jigging allows you to keep your offering in the strike zone at all times. Anchoring is no good, because the fish and the color change will shift as the tides and currents change. In these conditions, by drifting with the jigging spoons described above, you'll out-fish the bait guys just about every time.

When targeting tog and bass, it's usually more effective to anchor within casting distance of the jetty and fish bottom rigs. Drifting will allow you to cover more territory, for sure, but these fish will be located tight to the rocks and if you drift with your baits in the zone, you'll end up losing a ton of rigs.

A lot of caution must be used when anchoring this close to the rocks. Remember that at any time, your anchor could pull free and your boat could be trashed in a matter of moments. Strong currents and rapid changes in their direction can free a set anchor, and large boat wakes—ever present in all of the inlets up and down the coast—can yank it out of the sand. Conversely, if your anchor gets into the rocks themselves there's a good chance it will become permanently snagged and the only way to free your boat will be to cut the line. For these reasons, it's imperative that the captain keep a close eye on the boat and the conditions at every moment.

There's one advantage you may gain from fishing for tautog and sea bass at anchor, too. Most inlets have a rock or two that rolled out of place, and protrudes from the inlet here or there. Most of these are underwater, and out of sight. But if you can locate them, they can be gold mines. In fact, at some times casting to the spot where that one oddball boulder rests can make or break a fishing trip. Fish often stack up where such an obstruction breaks the current or creates an eddy.

Finding rocks like these takes experience (and check out the charts and hotspots in the first section of this book—you'll find some of these types of hotspots are listed). But you can also find them on the spot, by reading the water. Look for standing ripples or small waves that hold their position 5' to 15' off the edge of the jetty. Also look for visible notches along the jetty where it appears that a rock or two is missing, and probe the water immediately surrounding them. Whirlpools can indicate sub-surface structure as well, if you can spot one that remains stationary. But when the current is cranking through a rip-rap lined inlet, there can be so many little whirlpools forming here and there that it's next to impossible to isolate the ones that count with the naked eye. Of course, anything that stands out and is distinctly different than the rest of the inlet should always be checked out.

All of the species mentioned as fish to target in the inlets can be found in such spots. Stripers, particularly, will often ball up in them. But when bottom fishing for sea bass and tog in the inlets it's imperative to find a hotspot like this. Sometimes long stretches of the inlet will produce little or no fish, while baits placed in the vicinity of a notch or eddy will get immediate strikes. Since prospecting for bites by drift fishing leads to so many break-offs (and makes it hard to stick in one spot and work it, when you find a good one) it's imperative to know where hotspots like these are before you chose where to drop your anchor.

Note that specific rocks which are hot on one tide can become ice cold on a different tide. Also note that often you'll discover that either the ocean side or bay side of an inlet jetty is best during one specific tide, and that the same can be true for the northern versus southern side of any particular inlet. Even wind-driven current can change which area of an inlet will be best at any given tide. It's good to be on the side of the rocks which are hit by wind-driven waves and/or current, because these conditions will drive bait up against the rocks and force it to accumulate there. When the wind and waves grow strong enough to churn the water, however, you may need to move to the protected side to find water clean enough for the fish to actively feed in.

One more note about fishing the inlets: although you won't often find them inside the inlets themselves until you get pretty far south into the Mid Atlantic, you will locate cobia just outside of them quite often from Indian River Inlet south during the summer and early fall months. Whenever you're targeting any species of fish in these areas during this time frame, toss a couple live eels or spot into the livewell before you pull off the dock. Keep a 20- to 30-pound class outfit at the ready, and if you spot a cobia on the prowl you'll be prepared to take a shot at it.

CHAPTER 33
Surf Fishing

You'll notice that there are relatively few surf spots specified in the first section of this book. That's because each and every season, with even each and every powerful storm or tidal surge, the appearance of the beach can change radically. Sloughs, bars, and holes that you find on one fishing trip may be gone the next week when you return. This makes "reading" the beach the most important aspect of surf fishing.

If you had an unlimited budget, the best way to read the beach would be from the air. Flying along the coast, (assuming decent water quality) you can easily see where the bars and breaks are. Of course, this isn't an option for most of use. But a really hard-core surf angler might be crafty enough to find the local air strip where the banner-dragging advertisement planes take off and land. The pilots of these planes fly up and down the beach all day, and might be willing to share some information with you if you offered up a cold case of beer, or a few crisp bills.

Beach access plays a large role in the spot you'll be choosing. If you're in an area which allows driving on the beach, you have the ability to do some scouting. If not, you'll have to choose an access point close to the area you hope to fish, and hoof it. In either case, there are several visual clues that will tell you what spot is a good spot.

Structure such as jetties, pilings, and beach wrecks all will, naturally, hold fish. The corner formed where an inlet jetty meets the beach is also an extremely productive area to target. But most beaches are long, vast stretches with no overt fish-attracting structure. Fishing these areas, you'll need to keep your eyes open for features that aren't so obvious.

Bars running parallel to the beach are a good find, especially if they're close enough that you can cast to the deep water on their back side. You'll be able to locate them by looking for a spot where the waves break off of the beach, then roll, then break again. You can also spot bars by looking for places where swimmers are able to suddenly stand up. Often, a small crowd of beach-bathers will gather and "mark" the spot for you. Obviously, you'll have to return later, but on many Mid Atlantic beaches you can't surf fish during the major beach-going hours, anyway.

Another feature to look for is sloughs. These are spots where the water and waves cut into the shore line a bit, wash around, then flow back down into the breakers. These washes carry tidbits of food back into the surf and fish often gather around them. If they're significant enough to create color changes just off the beach, or small whirlpools and rips where the water flows back into the ocean, you have a winning spot picked out.

Holes are another good bet. You'll usually find them in relatively clear, calm water (because you won't be able to spot them when the water's riled up) by spotting a dark area just off the beach. Flounder, in particular, love to swim up into holes like these and wait to ambush baitfish.

The final visible feature you may find is a cliff. On extremely high tides, in some areas the waves will eat away a chunk of the beach, leaving a small cliff. When the water washes up to the base of this cliff it swirls around, then rushes back into the ocean in a way similar to sloughs, creating small color changes and whirlpools. You'll find cliffs like these often in areas where the beach has been artificially replenished, such as the Delaware beaches from Fenwick Island to Bethany.

What type of bait should you use in the surf? This will vary from season to season and spot to spot, but we can make a few blanket statements: Stick with bloodworms, Fishbites artificial bloodworms, shrimp bits, and squid strips when fishing for surf panfish. Cut fish such as mullet or spot is appropriate for larger predators, but stay away from soft baitfish like menhaden, because it falls apart too easily to use in the surf unless it's unusually calm.

In some northern areas savvy anglers like to use clam when fishing for stripers, and in southern areas, peeler crab or whole shrimp are favored for drum and/or sea trout. Just about anything of any size found in the surf will always eat squid strips, but this bait doesn't always draw as many strikes as some of the others if the fish are focused on a particular type of food.

The biggest mistake most surf anglers make is overcasting. Yup—overcasting, not under-casting. The majority of the fish you catch in the surf are feeding near or in the breakers, not 30 yards beyond them. There are exceptions, of course: bluefish usually cruise outside the breakers, as do larger stripers and drum. If you want to selectively target these fish, cast away. But if you want constant action and variety in the cooler, cover both of your bases.

Hit the surf with a 6'6" or 7' spinning rod, rigged with 15-pound test, a small doodlebug or top-and-bottom rig, and bloodworms, squid strips, or shrimp bits for bait. Also come equipped with an 8' or 9' long surf rod, rigged with 20-pound test and a large bucktail-dressed doodlebug with a 4/0 or 5/0 hook and cut fish for bait. Choose a Shimano Baitrunner, Penn Liveliner, conventional gear, or similar freespool-equipped reel to go with this rig. When you arrive at your spot, cast the big rig as far as possible, and sit it in a sand spike. Put the reel into freespool and dial up the tension just high enough that the surf doesn't strip out line.

Now bait up and cast your small rig, but instead of giving it a Hail Mary throw, flip it just beyond the breakers. Stand with the light rig in your hand so you can react to light bites, facing your big rig, so you can keep your eyes on the rod tip as you wait for the big bites. Using this tactic you can effectively target both panfish and larger predators, without missing any strikes.

In all cases, there are a few more surf fishing laws you should live by. First off, never let your reel touch the sand. That'll trash it instantly, because sand grains will work their way into the gears. Always set your sand spike far enough up the beach that waves don't wash around it, because if they do, it'll usually fall over—sending your reel into the sand. And remember to focus your efforts during changes in the tide, at sunrise, and sunset.

CHAPTER 34
Knots, Rigs, and Rigging

Must-Know Knots

The three knots described below are the ones that are imperative to know no matter where or how you're fishing. Why not include a huge portfolio of knots here, so you can know them all? I'm a big believer in the KISS attitude. When people start tying Bimini Twists and other complex knots, they make mistakes. Knots pull, and fish are lost. The fact of the matter is that with these three simple knots, you can make every connection necessary without sacrificing more than a percentage point or two on knot strength. When a simple knot retains 94-percent of the line's strength and a complex one retains 95-percent, I say go with the simple one, every time.

Before we get into each knot, there are a couple knot-tying tips you should know. Number one: before cinching a knot down tight, lick it. The saliva lubricates the line, and helps the knot close up on itself. And number two: Replace each and every knot at the beginning of each new fishing trip. Trust week-old knots, and you will lose fish.

The Improved Clinch
Use this one for attaching a main line to a swivel, lure eye, or loop.

Step #1: Make six twists around the main line. If you're tying the knot in line heavier than 30- or 40-pound test, make only four twists. With 80-pound test use just three twists, and recognize that it'll be tough to get a good knot with line this thick.

Step #2: Take the tag end through the loop between the line and the swivel or hook eye.

Step #3: Take the tag end and pass it through the loop you created during step number two. Pull on the main line and the eye it's being tied to, to cinch the knot down tight.

The Palomar
This knot shines when you're attaching a modern braid or "superline" to a swivel or lure eye. Note: do not use it to tie braid directly to a loop in monofilament, because it will cut through the mono.

Step #1: Double your line, and push the doubled line through the eye of whatever you are attaching to.

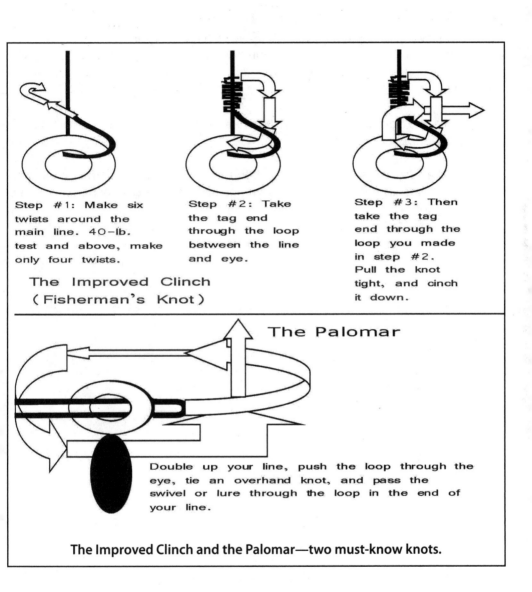

Step #1: Make six twists around the main line. 40-lb. test and above, make only four twists.

Step #2: Take the tag end through the loop between the line and eye.

Step #3: Then take the tag end through the loop you made in step #2. Pull the knot tight, and cinch it down.

The Improved Clinch (Fisherman's Knot)

The Palomar

Double up your line, push the loop through the eye, tie an overhand knot, and pass the swivel or lure through the loop in the end of your line.

The Improved Clinch and the Palomar—two must-know knots.

Step #2: Tie an overhand knot in the line.

Step #3: Slide the lure, swivel, or whatever is being tied on, through the loop at the tag end of your double line. Pull it all tight, and cut off any excess line.

Spider Hitch

This knot allows you to put a loop into the end of your main line or leader. You can also use this knot to double up your main line; doing so to the last 10' or 12' will significantly reduce the number of break-offs you have since the end of your line is where most wear takes place.

Step #1: Double your line, then form a loop in the doubled line and pinch it be tween your thumb and forefinger.

Step #2: Wrap the line around your thumb four times, then pass it through the loop you've been pinching. Pull tight, and as you pull the loops will slide off your thumb and come tight.

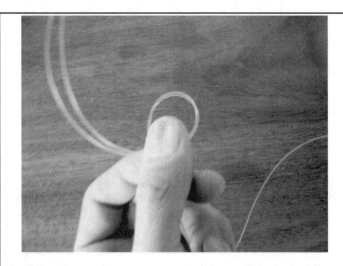

The Spider Hitch

Step 1

Step #1: Double your line, then form a loop in the doubled line and pinch it between your thumb and forefinger.

Step 2

Step #2: Wrap the line around your thumb four times, then pass it through the loop you've been pinching. Pull tight, and as you pull the loops will slide off your thumb and come tight.

Use the Spider Hitch to make a double-line, or put a loop in the end of a line or leader.

Offshore Rigs

The variations of fishing rigs are countless. Jump on one boat and you'll see it done one way, jump on another in the same marina and it will be completely different. The guys in the Carolinas favor one style, while the guys in New York favor another. Each of their methods can be applied in the other's water with great success. Those rigs included here are the basics, plus a couple of rigs that are not well known but are true killers—this is by no means a comprehensive compilation of offshore rigs. But using the included rigs you'll kill your fair share of fish and maybe a little more. Start with these, and expand as you see fit.

The Squidly

The Squidly is a unique variation of a rigged trolling squid. But unlike the kind you find in tackle shops, which can go for as much as $15 each, making a Squidly is easy, fast, and yes, fun. It's also darn effective—during one season it accounted for literally half the yellowfin tuna we caught on the Boating Magazine Project Boat. This is the only offshore trolling rig I can take credit for developing on my own and it's really just a simplified version of traditional trolling squid, but please, please, try this one. The results will knock your socks off.

Here's the scoop: Take 10' of 60-pound fluorocarbon leader and tie a 7/0 O'shaughnessy style hook onto to the end. Slide a 3/4-ounce egg sinker down the leader, so it sits against the eye of the hook. Now take a squid—not a fancy 3-pound rigging squid, but one of the sorry looking little 8"-long squid they sell for cutting into flounder bait—and using a pair of scissors, clip the tip of its mantle off. Now thread the end of the leader up along the inside of the squid's mantle and push until it pops out through the little hole you made at the top. Grab the leader, hold it vertically, and let go of the squid so it slides down the line to the hook and weight. If it settles so the end of the mantle sits right at the bend in the shank, life is good—send Squidly out and wait for him to be eaten. If it's too short or to long, pull the weight up or adjust the squid accordingly so the hook comes out right at the bottom of the mantle. Pull Squidly from the shotgun or a long rigger position, far back behind the boat.

Ballyhoo Rigs

There are zillions of ways to rig ballyhoo, and depending on who you talk to, each specific one is the only correct way to do it. Everyone's right, and no one is. Bottom line: if the ballyhoo stays in the water and swims like a real fish, then game fish will strike it. Sure, some methods are quicker than others. Some require less experience and work to learn. Some may look a tiny bit more or less natural. Try a

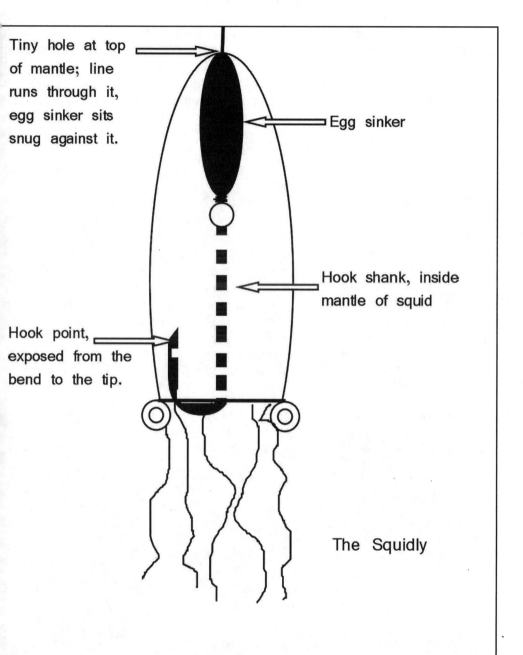

Tiny hole at top of mantle; line runs through it, egg sinker sits snug against it.

Egg sinker

Hook shank, inside mantle of squid

Hook point, exposed from the bend to the tip.

The Squidly

During one offshore season, the Squidly accounted for literally half the yellowfin we caught at the canyons.

couple of different methods, find you favorite, and so long as you produce swimmies instead of spinnies, you're good to go.

The copper wire/split bill method is the way a huge number of anglers rig their 'hoo. First, break off the bulk of the bill, leaving just a 1/2" or so. Push the edge of your thumb nail between the two parallel rigid bones, and split the last quarter-inch of the bill. Most anglers will also squeeze the stomach of the fish working from the head aft, to get out the ballyhoo's poo. (Otherwise, it often comes out during rigging and makes a mess.) Then insert the hook point under the gill flap of the ballyhoo, and run in into the fish. Bend the fish as you do so, to match the bend of the hook, so it runs easily down the body cavity without ripping the bait's skin. When the eye of the hook reaches the inside of the gill, pop the point through and allow the ballyhoo to straighten out.

If you have a chin weight—a 1/4-ounce or 1/2-ounce egg sinker on the leader—push it down so it sits between the gill flaps. Then push the end of a short length of copper wire up through the lower jaw of the fish, and through the hinge on the upper jaw of the fish. Next, grab the long wire and wrap it together with the short one. Holding the leader and chin weight flush against the bottom of the bait, bend the copper down and wrap it around the head of the fish. Work your way forward to the bill of the ballyhoo, being sure to keep the leader centered along the underside of the fish and its bill. Wrap as tightly as possible, securing the chin weight and leader to the ballyhoo. When you've wrapped down the bill all the way to the split section, pull the leader up between the two sides of the bill so it splits them. Wrap your final bits of wire on the other side of the leader, creating a small

The basic rigged ballyhoo is effective on a wide variety of pelagic predators.

Add a skirt to a rigged 'hoo for extra color and action.

shovel-like lip on the end of the bill. (This helps the bait dig into the water a bit, preventing it from skipping over the surface, and some people feel it also improves the bait's action.) Just before putting the ballyhoo over the side, bend it back and forth a few times to limber it up. Breaking the back (careful not to rip the skin and tear off scales!) will give the bait a great action, but usually damages it to some degree, encouraging its disintegration. You may get half an hour out of a ballyhoo with a broken back, or maybe as much as an hour, but rarely more than that.

Variations: The pin rig is a simple addition to the standard copper wire method that eases rigging and, for most folks, makes the process quicker. Instead of pushing the short end of the copper through the jaws of the ballyhoo, a wire pin, inserted in the crimp at the hook and secured next to the leader, takes its place. The long wire is wrapped around the pin once or twice to hold it in place, and the rest of the ballyhoo is rigged as usual. The down-side? Sometimes, especially with small ballyhoo, the stiff pin will split the upper jaw as you push it through, rendering the bait useless.

When speed is of the essence, using a pin rig along with rubber bands is a good choice. By bending a regular rubber band around the pin, the fish, and then the pin again (making extra wraps if necessary, to maintain enough tension to secure the bait in place) you can get a ballyhoo rigged and over the side in a matter of seconds.

Ballyhoo springs are another time-saving variation. Again, they require the use of a pin. Simply spin the spring around the leader and pin, and it will hold the bait in place. Like the rubber band rig this one's nearly instantaneous. Many captains feel the resulting bait swims just as well as other forms of rigging, but some feel the spring interferes with its natural look and motion.

Rigging through the eyes is another method worth considering. This requires no pin, but before rigging the bait, push out the ballyhoo's eyes with a rod or knife blade. When wrapping the copper go through the eye sockets instead of around the head. This method results in a higher success rate than regular rigging, since it gives the copper a solid bite and you can put plenty of tension on the wire when wrapping it, without worrying it may slide down the head. It's a well known fact, however, that predators like to target the eyes of a baitfish when they strike it. This being the case, it would seem important that a natural-looking bait have natural-looking eyes. Which is correct? It would be easy to find two excellent captains who will be happy to take opposing sides of the argument and argue about it until they're blue in the face; you'll just have to try the method and decide for yourself. I've gone back and forth for years without ever proving to myself one or the other is more effective.

One note of caution: you may be tempted to wrap through the eye sockets while the eyes are still in them. Sometimes this works out, if you can slide the copper between the eye and eye socket without piercing the eye itself. If, however, you do pierce the eye, there's a very good chance it'll bug out after the bait is dragged through the water for a while. Buggy ballyhoo eyes make the baits wobble and spin, and they usually don't get hit. So keep a close eye on any baits you rig this way, and expect that you may have to replace them often.

Rigging Leaders

Of course, before you rig up a ballyhoo you'll need a ballyhoo rig. You can buy these in any decent tackle shop, but the rigs you find hanging from shelves may not be the very best in the world. First off, they tend to incorporate large, thick, relatively low quality hooks which would most accurately be described as "clunky." Secondly, the leaders are usually available in 120-pound test or larger, only, and are made from regular monofilament instead of fluorocarbon. Remember that fluorocarbon is less visible in the water, and although it's not as imperative to use it when trolling as it is when chunking, it will still make a noticeable difference.

While these rigs will work, some anglers feel you'll get a lot more bites by going light. Yes, you will have more break-offs, too. But if you never get the bites you'll never have the chance to win or lose the fight. On my own personal boat, most leaders are 70- or 80-pound test. I'll only go larger when specifically targeting tuna in the 150-pound and bigger class, or blue marlin. This may be a bit on the extreme side—most Mid Atlantic captains are pulling 120-pound test leader as an absolute minimum when on the troll. Still, in my mind it's worth the extra losses to get the extra bites in the first place; you can decide for yourself if you agree or not.

Trolling leaders should be 15' to 20' long, and can be tied directly to in-line wind-on swivels if your rod eyes are large enough to accommodate them. If not, wiring will become a necessity. You can also tie a spider hitch in the end of the leader and tie it directly to the main line's doubled line. This will eliminate wiring in all circumstances. In this case, however, you risk massive line twist if a bait starts spinning, and you don't notice it immediately. The majority of the captains out there—again, remember that they're pulling 120-pound or larger test—will choose to tie the leaders to swivels with clips (which can't be reeled directly through the rod tips regardless of what type gear you're using) and will plan on wiring.

Appropriate hook sized for ballyhoo baits ranges from 7/0 on the small side to 10/0 on the large side. Long shanks make for a better hook-up ratio and a tiny bit more protection from being cut off by toothy predators, but shorter shanks make it much easier to rig the 'hoo.

Once the hook is crimped onto the end of your leader, slide a chin weight down it. Finish prepping your rig by running the copper wire through the weight, leaving one end (your short end) about 3" long. Wrap the long end of the wire around the leader several times, to hold the weight and wire in place.

Rigging Lures & Skirts

Most trolling lures can be bought pre-rigged or un-rigged. Again, the main problem with purchasing pre-rigged baits is the heavy leaders and clunky hooks they come with. Take a look at a pre-rigged Green Machine on 150-pound test as it moves through the water. It drags limply along, more or less action-free. But the same Green Machine rigged on 80- or 100-pound test dances backs and forth through the water, with a greatly enhanced motion. You may also find that the crimps on purchased rigs probably were not rigged with the same care as those you rig yourself, and as mentioned earlier, pre-rigs are made with regular monofilament, not the pricier, less visible fluorocarbon lines.

Many anglers, myself included, rig dual hooks on lures that will be run without ballyhoo. This can be accomplished in two ways: Either by running the eye of a stinger hook over the point and shank of the first hook, or by crimping both hooks to a leader in tandem. In both cases, the important thing to remember is to rig the hooks so they face in opposing directions so your chances of hooking up are improved no matter which direction the fish attacks from.

Whenever you sit down to rig up a trolling lure or skirt, look first at the area where the eye of the hook will meet it. (Each trolling lure will match up with a different size hook; no generalizations can be made here, so you'll have to take it on a case by case basis). Many lures have large openings which make it easy to rig the line through, but allow the eye of the hook to work itself too far up into the lure. In this case, slide a plastic bead or two over the line before running it through the lure to properly space it from the hook eye.

The Dancing Squid

This is a unique rig which is a heck of a lot of fun to run for tuna. Credit for it goes to John Unkart (the mate on the *Strike III,* and later the *Volcania*), who showed me this rig a few years back. Essentially, it uses the same idea as the commercial green stick: dangle a bait, and the tuna go crazy for it. Although this rig causes some tangles (some captains call it the "dangler" rig, and others call it the "tangler" rig) and requires the use of a long rigger position for a bait that will run close to the boat, it's worth running for one simple reason: the dancing squid is one heck of a crowd-pleaser. When it gets hit the tuna must literally leap out of the water to attack the bait, causing hugs boils, flying whitewater, and shouts of surprise from the cockpit.

To rig up a dancing squid you'll need a large chugger or bird—the "anchor" of the rig, which will provide lots of water resistance and tension on the line. Crimp it to 25' or 30' of 200-pound test leader, terminating in a swivel. Crimp up a second leader, this one only about 2' long, on 100- or 120-pound test. Also rig a swivel clip on one the end of this one, and on the other end, rig an 8" pearl or white plastic squid. When you're ready to deploy, clip the long leader to the end of your main line. Then, let the long leader back and clip the short leader with the squid through the swivel snap where the long leader joins your main line. Run the line through the long rigger clip, and with the squid dangling in the air, let the rig back until it's far enough away that the squid begins to splash in and out of the water. As the boat goes up and down waves, and the outriggers rock from side to side, that squid should really dance around. Remember—this is supposed to be the dancing squid, not the swimming squid. It should spend literally 50-percent of the time in the water, and no more. Interestingly, the tuna will almost always strike when the squid is in the air. Let the rig farther back or bring it closer up to the transom, until you find that sweet spot where it dances just right.

Chunk Rigs

Making a chunking rig is extremely simple: Cut a fluorocarbon leader of 5' to 6', tie a loop in one end with a Spider Hitch, and tie a hook to the other. 8/0 hooks are good for tunas, although fish over the 150-pound class require 9/0 or 10/0s. Many anglers prefer circle hooks, which are supposed to lie in the corner of the fish's mouth. I prefer Gamakatsu or Owner needle point octopus-style hooks, (tied on, not snelled, even though these hooks were designed for snelling) which will end up deep in the tuna's gut most of the time. Tuna have teeth with conical points, and a

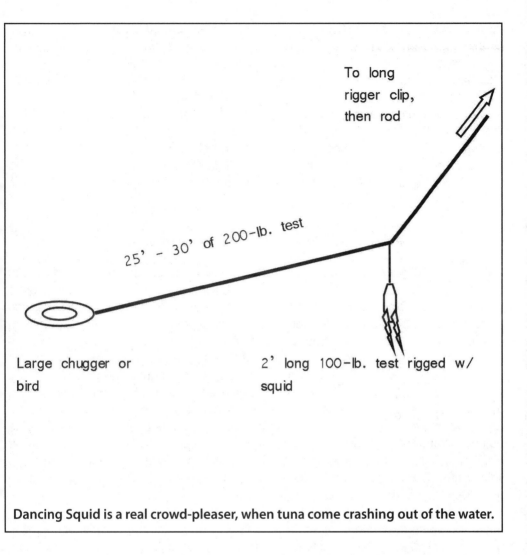

To long
rigger clip,
then rod

25' – 30' of 200-lb. test

Large chugger or
bird

2' long 100-lb. test rigged w/
squid

Dancing Squid is a real crowd-pleaser, when tuna come crashing out of the water.

thin leader will lie up between them without chaffing or being cut, for fights that go on for hours.

Shark Chumming Rigs

Naturally, chumming for shark requires a completely different rig. Most shark rigs you find in the store will be simple lengths of wire, with a 10/0 offset hook attached via a haywire twist. These work fine until a feisty mako rolls on the rig and puts twist and kinks into it. When wire kinks, break-offs are not far behind. Cable won't kink, so why not use it for shark rigs? Because a shark's teeth will eventually saw through cable. So the best rigs have a combination of both: a few feet of straight wire at the hook, attached to 5' or 6' of cable. Total rig length should be at least 10' in case a mako spins and rolls some of the leader around itself. You'll find rigs like this made up with both multi-strand wire cable, and "mono cable," which is really just another way of saying extremely heavy monofilament.

Different captains will argue over which version of the shark rig is best. I like the Custom Bill Brown rigs available from JB Tackle (www.jbtackle.com; $70 for a kit that makes six rigs). These rigs use commercial longliner mono for the upper section. Fin Strike shark rigs, which are also sold by JB and can be found in some stores (about $10) are also decent; they top the rig with 275-pound test, 49-strand cable.

Crimps, Swivels, and Hooks

All line over 80-pound test will have to be crimped, instead of knotted and tied. In fact, sometimes it's a fight to tie knots in 80-pound test, particularly an improved clinch. But, how do you know if you're crimping properly? Jon Meade, a freelance mate in Ocean City and the author of many excellent articles on offshore fishing, let me in on this learning method which will be tough to beat.

Proper crimping is as much a matter of feel as anything else. Crimp too lightly and your line will slip through the crimps; do it too hard and you'll mash the line, weakening it and causing break-offs. To get a feel for how hard you should be crimping, get a long piece of mono and a pile of crimps. Crimp a loop in the end of your line, then slip the loop over a cleat (or a fence post or any other stable object), wrap the line around a gloved hand, and lean back against it until it either breaks, or pulls. If it pulls, crimp a little harder on your next loop. If it breaks, go a little lighter. Crimp, pull, and break 50 or 60 times, and you'll start to get a really good feel for just how much pressure to apply.

Make sure you center the crimpers over the crimp and don't bend the edges down, because they can cut into the line. Note that aluminum crimps will corrode quicker, but nickel crimps tend to cut or mash the line a little more often. And note that multiple crimps will make for a net loss in overall strength, because you risk creating multiple weak points each time you add another crimp. Do it once, and do it right.

Swivels are a real pet peeve of mine, because people will spend zillions of dollars on boats, fuel, bait, and tackle, then buy cheap swivels in order to save a couple of bucks. Cheap swivels are absolutely useless. Ball bearing swivels are a must-have when you want to combat line twist. But, all ball bearings are not created equally. Those with split rings are absolutely useless—I guarantee you a 50-pound billfish or tuna has the ability to straighten out the split ring on a swivel marked 100-pound test. Instead, get ones with welded rings. And look for those with a second ring welded between the clip and the swivel itself. This extra ring prevents the swivel from amming against itself, a common problem with cheaper swivels.

Hook sizes and types have been addressed whenever applicable to a specific rig, but there's more to a hook than just the point. Most importantly, you'll need to make sure that every hook you ever lower over the side of your boat is razor sharp. Some very conscientious mates and captains are able to accomplish this by keeping a file in their belt or tackle station, and checking for sharpness every time they get out another rig. For the rest of us, I have a simple solution: when a hook begins to show any corrosion, throw it away and start over with a new one. Bottom line: today's laser sharpened and chemically sharpened hooks can never be restored to the sharpness that have when you break open the package. Sure, you can touch up hooks and make them pretty darn good. But once they've been hit with a file they will corrode twice as fast. One week in your tacklebox after a salt dunking may be all it takes to turn a good hook dull. At the first hint of crud, toss em.

Inshore Rigging

Inshore rigging is a lot easier to deal with than offshore rigging for one simple reason: you can buy most of this stuff in the store, and it'll do the job well. Those you'll need to create yourself are fairly simple, and you won't have to deal with the complexity of making dead fish swim like they were alive. Here's the low-down on the basic rigs you'll need to have on hand to cover the bases, when inshore fishing.

The Standard Top and Bottom Rig

This is one of the most widely used rigs on the Mid Atlantic coast. Wire arms hold the hooks and leaders apart to prevent tangles, and with a clip on the bottom and a swivel on the top, these rigs are easily weighted and attached to your main line. Use them drifting, at anchor, or cast them from shore when targeting sea bass, tautog, croaker, spot, weakfish, small stripers, flounder, blowfish, sea mullet, and other bottom feeders. Common baits for these rigs include squid, bloodworm, soft or peeler crab, bull minnow, and grass shrimp. When fishing with them, remember that your weight should maintain contact with the bottom at all times. Some sea bass anglers like to use similar rigs with four or five hooks attached to the main body, but note that in some state waters this may be a violation of game laws.

The Fluke Killer (AKA the Trout Scout, or Flounder Pounder)

Another popular rig is the Fluke Killer. It's most effective for weakfish and flounder. The beads and spinners forward of the hook add fish-attracting sound and vibration to your bait, while the bucktail hair skirt increases profile and contrast. A variation on this theme is the Spin-N-Glow, which replaces the spinner blade with a propeller-style spinner. Most serious anglers always carry a selection of different colors of these rigs. Start with the top producers—chartreuse or white, in dim water yellow, and in low light try purple—and experiment from there.

For weakfish, it's often best to bait up with soft or peeler crab. For flounder, most people use either squid strips, bull minnow, or a combination of both. Of course, with these baits on the hook you'll also catch stripers, sea bass, and blues on a Fluke Killer. The best way to fish it is by drifting; the advantages of the beads, spinners and hair skirt are negated when the rig sits at rest. It should be weighted sufficiently to bounce along the bottom as you drift. Maintain constant contact with the bottom for flounder, and intermittent contact when using it for sea trout.

Chumming and Live Bait Rigs

Despite its simplicity, the standard chumming rig has a million variations available from the tackle shop walls. While most inshore rigs are decent, for some reason I've yet to find a good store-bought chumming rig—you're best served by ignoring all of them. They're generally made with thick leaders and clunky, cheap hooks. Those that come with swivels usually have the cheapest swivels available. Plus, chumming rigs in the tackle store are usually far overpriced.

Making your own chumming rigs is a piece of cake: Tie a spider hitch into one end of a 4' to 5' length of leader (30- to 40-pound test fluorocarbon for stripers; 50- to 80-pound test for cobia; 30-pound test with a 1' wire trace tied to the end for bluefish) and tie your hook on the other end with an improved clinch. Use a 5/0 to 7/0 for stripers and blues, and a 7/0 to 8/0 for cobia.

Live bait rigs are essentially identical to chumming rigs. One difference: use a shorter shank hook, and make sure it's one thin enough that it doesn't kill or seriously damage the bait when you put it through the fish's jaws.

Tandem Trolling & Jigging Rigs

You can find these rigs in some in tackle shops, and there are some decent versions of it out there. But by no means will you find good tandem trolling rigs wherever you look. If you need to make your own, tie an 8' section of 50- to 80-pound leader on a triple swivel. On the end, tie the heavier of your two lures. Make the second section 14' to 16', and attach to its end the lighter of your two lures.

Tandem jigging rigs are more widely available, especially in the Carolinas where they're quite popular. Think of these as miniature tandem trolling rigs, with one important difference: the heaver lure goes on the longer leader, instead of the shorter one. Make the short leader 8" to a 1' long, and the long leader about 4'. (The commercially made rigs will have longer leaders, but you'll find the short leader reduces tangles dramatically.) Usually this rig works best with a very light

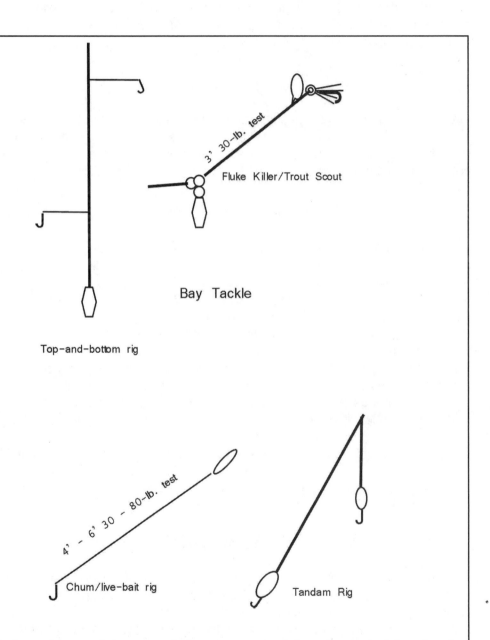

3' 30-lb. test

Fluke Killer/Trout Scout

Bay Tackle

Top-and-bottom rig

4' - 6' 30 - 80-lb. test

Chum/live-bait rig

Tandam Rig

With these rigs—and the proper bait—you can catch just about any fish swimming in a Mid Atlantic coastal bay.

lure up top—maybe a 1/4-ounce or 1/2-ounce feather jig or tube jig—and a 3- or 4-ounce jigging spoon, bucktail, or leadhead jig on the long leader. This rig is especially good when vertical jigging in deep water for trout. It's also a winner when casting and retrieving for trout or stripers, especially if you sweeten it up by adding crab chunks or squid strips to the hooks.

Surf Rigs

There are many, many types of surf rigs, but only the two basic ones are must-haves. Between them you'll be able to catch every fish that swims in the surf, and truth be told, most of the others out there are just variations on the same themes which may or may not work a hair better or worse, but surely don't make any drastic advances.

The Doodlebug-Style Rig

There are countless variations of this rig. Essentially, it consists of a short 2' to 3' leader that has a triple swivel with a clip on one end, and a hook with a float on the other. The swivel clip is where your weight gets attached, and the free eye of the triple swivel is where you attach your main line. The float keeps your offering away from bait-stealing crabs, a constant problem for surf anglers.

On most of these rigs the float rests right at the eye of the hook, and on some, the float is actually a plug of sorts with bucktail hair and a spiffy paint job. The ones painted half white/half red are killers. Some will have wire leaders (for use when targeting blues) and others have mono (for sea trout, stripers, and redfish).

Doodlebugs are usually used to target relatively large fish and have 2/0 to 4/0 hooks. Those with long-shank hooks and fluorescent foam floats can be improved by pushing the end of the shank up into the float.

For smaller fish, such as sea mullet, spot, spike trout, and croaker, top-and-bottom doodlebugs with #6 or #4 hooks are usually used. Often the floats are crimped an inch or two above the hook, with one red and one green or chartreuse float for each leader.

The Fishfinder

This rig is similar to a chumming rig set up with an egg sinker, to let the line slide freely through the weight. But a fishfinder has a swivel clip rigged with a plastic sleeve, which your line runs through. This allows you to clip on a surf weight, yet a fish can still take the bait and run without feeling the full resistance of the line. It's popular for larger gamefish, such as stripers and drum.

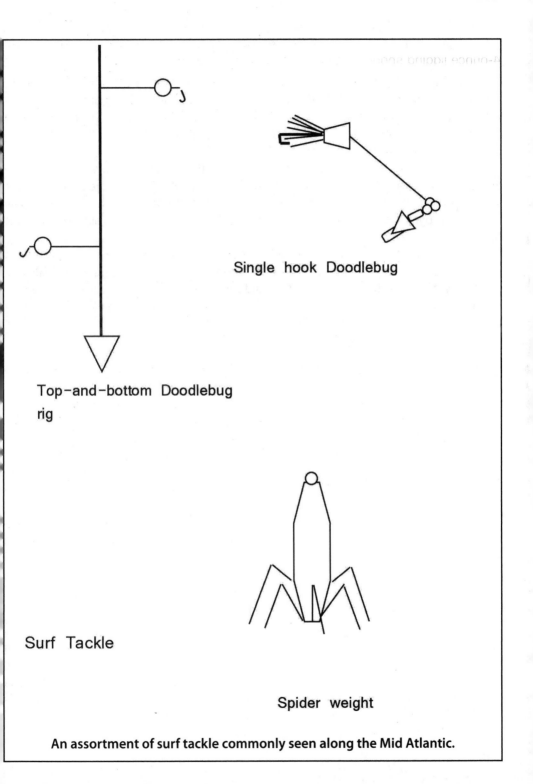

Single hook Doodlebug

Top-and-bottom Doodlebug
rig

Surf Tackle

Spider weight

An assortment of surf tackle commonly seen along the Mid Atlantic.

Surf Weights

Regular bank sinkers and eggs sinkers will be rolled around in the surf and within a few wave sets, your bait will be laying on the beach. Instead, you'll need to rig up with pyramid weights, which sink into the sand and hold position. On a calm day 2 ounces may be enough to stick, and until it gets to the point where it's too rough to fish, 4 or 5 ounces will do the job.

There are two forms of pyramid sinkers: those in the shape of a pyramid, and those that have the bottom of a pyramid with a cylindrical arm coming out the top. In rough surf, these oddly-shaped leads are much better at holding fast. Use the regular pyramids only when the conditions are calm and you are casting with relatively light gear.

The third surf weight you need to know about is the spider weight. It has wire legs (hence the name) which grab into the bottom and hold fast. These weights are extremely effective, but there's a down-side: it takes quite a bit of pressure to pop them free when a fish strikes. Accordingly, they should only be used when casting heavy gear for large fish in a big surf.

Parting Line

So there you have it—*Rudow's Guide to Fishing the Mid Atlantic.* I sincerely hope you've enjoyed this book, and that it will help you catch more bigger fish. If you have any comments, corrections, or hotspots to add for future printings, please let me know. Hard-core anglers are always welcome to e-mail me at lr@geareduppublications.com.

If you fish the Chesapeake Bay, also look for *Rudow's Guide to Fishing The Chesapeake* (published by Tidewater Publishers), which is formatted much like this book with clearly marked hotspots, sections on specific fish, and tackle and tactics. You can find it in book stores or on the web. Now go out there, and catch 'em up!